Đi·Vi·sĭ·ble

A Rememory
by
Xyola Blue

World Publishing Co.
Phoenix, Arizona

Rachel Helmkay
xyolabluecaruso@hotmail.com

First Printing: January 2013
World Publishing Co.

ISBN 978-1-300-42298-3

Chapter 1
The Amputation   11

Chapter 2
Crush   23

Chapter 3
Bad Girl   32

Chapter 4
Unwanted   39

Chapter 5
Whoppers   48

Chapter 6
Muppets   64

Chapter 7
New Car   70

Chapter 8
Long Weekend   82

Chapter 9
Grand Escape   113

Chapter 10
The Evil Beast   122

Chapter 11
Shock Therapy   139

Chapter 12
Here We Go Again   144

Chapter 13
Fuck Forgiveness   151

Chapter 14
E   162

Chapter 15
Forgotten   175

Chapter 16
Betrayed   197

Chapter 17
House of Sleeplessness   216

Chapter 18
Cracked   226

Chapter 19
Escape   239

Chapter 20
Alone   260

Chapter 21
Adopted   264

Chapter 22
The Stalker   280

I dedicate this book to my children,
Jeremy, Sarah, Seth, and Isobel.
Without them, I would have never known true love.

To my Brother, "J-Dog", whose ability to overcome
adversity with a smile gave me the power to see
that I have more in me to offer this world.

To Dr. Landrum who believed me,
not just believed that I believed.

To my Sweet Auntie Debbie,
who loves all of me without question or judgment.

To my Grandma and Grandpa Helmkay.
They don't take shit from anyone, including
me, and because of their dedication
to the family, have given me the ability to strive harder
every day that I'm alive.

To My Egg-Donor, Piece of Shit, So-Called "Mom",
Fuck You, You Cunt.

Most of all I Dedicate this book to my others,
especially "little Rachel". She suffered the most during this
process of writing. Xyolablue knew it would be hard and
held her hand, stroked her hair, and let her cry through the
whole experience.
Drunk Rachel was allowed to have her wine to heal and put
it all away for everyone. Thank you all for helping our
family. Thank you for keeping the secrets safe.

Preface

Have you ever experienced something so wonderful, so beautiful that you wanted to remember it forever? How about something really traumatic? What about the mundane bullshit that you had to do last week, last month, last year? Remembering is something that is selective, at least for most. We have the ability to remember what we want and it's what makes us hope and believe in others. It helps us trust and forgive.

If you only remembered every single little bad thing in your life, you wouldn't be so nice to others. If you only remembered every single little good thing in your life, you'd be naïve. We learn from experience, but you must remember those experiences in order to learn what to do next. Remembering is a part of every single person, even those with dementia and Alzheimer's have memories.

I have a disorder that does not allow me to forget. They call it posttraumatic stress disorder (PTSD). Usually those with PTSD have selective memories, like most people. The difference is the memories are attached to reality. The reality of smells, tastes, sounds, everything. Those with PTSD experience the memory as a reality. For them, me, it is like being transported in time to the moment of that exact instance and living through it all over again. They don't have the choice to change the memory or put it away when it pops up. It is persistent and cruel.

Triggers such as sounds, smells, a word phrase, a song will throw a person with PTSD into a memory experience and they have no choice to escape it. How many times in a day do you think to yourself of something like "I remember this song. It came out when I was in the eighth grade." A person, such as myself, not only remembers that that song came out when I was in the eighth grade, but also that it was played at the Valentine's Dance that happened on February 12th, a Friday night, that started at 7 p.m. and ended at 9:30 p.m., and the song before it was blah blah and the song after it was blah blah, and I wore a pretty blue dress that my grandpa helped me pick out at Miller's Outpost in the mall off of cross streets so and so, but my mom wouldn't let me wear the heels because they were too grown up for a girl, and the boy I liked was dancing with my nemesis, and Mrs. Hemachek was nice to me and gave me an extra cookie because she knew I was poor and didn't have enough money to buy it and so on and so forth. I could tell you the color of the gym, the words that were uttered, the songs I did and didn't dance to, how I got home, how my mom reacted, and on and on. My memories are solid and true and engrained in me. Triggers are everywhere and I live with them daily. My experiences with memories are strong and I cope with them 10-20 times a day.

I've lived with this all my life and wasn't even aware that it was something to be named until after a traumatic experience to top all traumatic experiences happened and I was forced into counseling.

After months of seeing my doctor and many tests and questions had been answered, I had been diagnosed. It's not really anything that you can take a medication for and it is certainly not curable. You need to learn how to recognize it and cope with it as it is happening. Unbeknownst to me I had already come up with my own coping mechanism, albeit not the best one, but still, it worked for me.

Living through a bunch of traumatic experiences one right after the other throughout my toddlerhood, childhood, teenage years, and young adulthood, I had learned that I didn't necessarily have to deal with any of them. So I split into different Rachel's to handle different situations.

I'm not sure exactly how many I have, but my therapist thinks at least 3. I do know that I can recognize when I've switched now. This is my second diagnosis: Dissociative Identity Disorder (DID). It was formerly known as Multiple Personality Disorder. You may remember the movie Cybil. She had it. Mine isn't as severe or as telling, but they are my coping mechanisms to get through whatever may pop up. And only those closest to me can recognize when I've changed.

Each of the Rachels possess a skill. They can paint beautiful pictures, bellydance, sew anything just by looking at a picture, draw blueprints, play instruments, compose music, ride a bike 50 miles without a second thought, cook anything from scratch, garden like nobody's business, and the list goes on and on. They have found learning an essential part of being in this world and lucky me, since I have a memory disorder that allows me to remember practically everything, we have a skill list that just keeps growing. Insatiable, they are.

It turns out that children who have an extremely traumatic experience often create others within themselves to handle it for them. And when those traumatic experiences continue they have another step in so that afterwards they can go back to life. Now what if there are numerous different traumatic situations, experiences that don't relate to one another? I believe that is when there are many different "others" that are created, and that's how I got mine.

There are moments in time when life just gets so overwhelming and I cry my eyes out and think about doing bad stuff, then Bam! All of a sudden everything's okay and I can think clearly and have sorted it all out into neat little piles and feel confident in working hard to make things better. This Rachel is my protector. She knows when to come out and just, well, take over and calm things down. But the one who freaks out all the time, she has an anxiety disorder that makes her heart race and she cannot stand confrontation. She is a child and has no idea what is going on in the here and now. And then there is the Rachel who is a flirt and a drunk. She used to be around a lot. She has had lots of boyfriends and had no regard for their feelings. If they weren't up to snuff, she got rid of them. It is her world and those who want to join it may, but they must play by her rules. Recently I, the protector, have been infiltrating the drunk Rachel. I sit back and watch as she flirts, but the second I see her getting too ridiculous with her actions, I step in. It's hard because I am also inebriated so the words come out all slurry and stupid, but the words are mean and the complete opposite of what she wanted to say. I rescue her from situations she has no idea she is getting into. I realized that she needed a timeout, so lately I have been restricting alcohol intake to make sure that she doesn't try to get out and get into situations that we all don't truly want.

After the life-changing traumatic experience 5 years ago and after I had started seeing a therapist, I really started "tapping" into my memories, purposefully triggering myself and riding out the experience. It's kind of like what I would expect an LSD hallucination is like. I've never done hallucinogens, quite frankly it would probably really fuck me up, but what I have seen through friends who have done it and being their "buddy" to make sure that they were okay while tripping out, well they were here, but not. It was like two worlds together, one make-believe and one reality mashed together.

My own experience with my triggers was thrilling. I learned that I didn't have to just go into the "bad" stuff, I could tap into the great stuff too. I got addicted to tapping and would make it a regular daily habit. I could put on a song and go back to when I was happiest. I have dedicated triggers for most of my good memories, usually music, sometimes a word phrase, but also certain smells. And if I combined them all, then I can really trip out for hours. I can go into my own mind and have my whole world to myself with only good memories playing over and over again. It's like cueing up your favorite scene in a movie and putting it on repeat in my mind, but also getting to experience the physical reality of it. I got so hooked on it that the first 3-1/2 years after my trauma I spent most of my time in my world, not here. I got so good at it that I was on autopilot and most people, except my kids, didn't see me.

After perfecting my taps, I craved them. I needed a fix and I would try and make sure that I would make time for them. It was great when the kids would go to their dad's for the weekend because I could spend an entire weekend in bed with my triggers and just be "gone" from here and be somewhere that would make me happy. Then I discovered that I could multitask.

I work from home doing a mundane little job of transcribing medical documents. I would listen to doctors talk and all I had to do was type out what they were saying verbatim. I have done this now for 15 years and have gotten quite good at it, to the point that I can put a movie on and watch it while doing my job. I also love to listen to music at the same time because the beat keeps my momentum up. I am a master multitasker, always have been, and I figured since I have to sit here all day anyway, why not put myself in a place that was happier. So I started tapping while working. It wasn't as powerful as if I wasn't working, because I literally had to do two things at once and when I was working I did have to be somewhat here. But, when I tapped, my workdays seem to fly by. I could work 10, 12, 15, 18 hours in a day and be okay with it. Of course, I was exhausted all the time, but I was happy. I was getting my fix and I was making money at the same time. I was essentially doing auto-writing. Have you heard of it? It is what most mediums do in order to contact the dead. They let go of the physical part of writing and just let it flow out of them trusting what they were writing to be part of the afterlife. That was what I was doing, except instead of writing what the spirit wants me to write, I was writing what the doctor was saying in my ear, reading what I wrote as he spoke, editing mistakes, and correcting grammatically spoken errors all the while being in my world. I loved that I could be two people in two separate places at the same time and being in control of it all.

While writing this book though, I had to go back to the bad places and times. I wanted so badly to get my story out, to bring to light the damage that PTSD can do to a person, and that I needed to show how it can develop. Hopefully, by writing this all down in some way I can let it be settled and I won't have to think about how these things happened to me as often. Of course I will always have triggers that I can't escape, but maybe, just maybe I can move forward outside of the triggers. Don't get me wrong, I still hate every person who I have been wronged by. I hate them with a passion so deep that I wish I could just get amnesia and live the rest of my life without any memory at all, even the good ones.

Forgiveness doesn't play a role in my life because I cannot forget. I am not allowed to forget. I am regularly reminded of these events that you will read and I go through these experiences over and over again regularly.

If you had been pushed down a flight of stairs and suffered a broken leg that just wouldn't heal and you got gangrene and ended up having your leg cut off, would you ever look at a staircase the same again? Nope. Would you buy a house with a staircase? Nope. And I bet every time you washed your stump, you would curse the fucker that pushed you down the stairs in the first place. Now imagine yourself with a thousand, no a million messed up memories, things that were continuously happening around you and the triggers were everywhere you looked and you were transported back to that moment in time to live through it all over again, would you forgive those that have wronged you? Nope. So I don't forgive and I don't trust.

I tried trust, giving the benefit of the doubt to those around me, but for some reason it just always seems to backfire. So I gave up on trust, and a part of me let that happen so easily. I question everything and everyone and every intention and if the bad outweighs the good, which is always the case, I don't trust. It's really quite remarkable how I have developed this skill and it is a huge part of my DID. I can just turn my feelings on and off like a switch. If I don't trust, well then I don't feel and the wall stays intact and I am secure within.

So you will read in this book my bad experiences as they happened through triggering and tapping into the memory on purpose. Everything in this book is as it happened and though the names have been changed, the details are correct. This book was excruciatingly painful to write and I am glad I never have to put myself through these again, at least not on purpose. But I wanted to grab the reader and put them in my place and feel with me and in order to do that I put myself back there and traumatized myself over and over again to bring this book to the public. I was very lucky that the career I have been working for so long has given me the ability to do automatic writing and therefore the book was able to be written as my mind and emotions went wild.

There were times while tapping heavily into my memory to write this book, I had lost sight of this world altogether. I was so deep into it that when my children would call after me in the here and now, I couldn't hear them. They would "wake" me up and it would literally take me minutes to realize that this teenaged girl standing in front of me, asking me a simple question was, my daughter. She was my daughter, I had created her and there are other kids too that I apparently had. How did I get here? Where is my mom? I can't be a mom. I was so deep, so god damned deep that I had pushed everything out and was only in the past and my future had yet to be created. I cried the first time that happened. I was so scared while writing this book that I might lose myself altogether and be stuck in the past, experiencing over and over the fucked up shit I had gone through. So I decided to set a timer. It would go off every 30 minutes and I would get up from my desk and walk outside and do a mantra of who I was, how old I was, my children's names, where I was. Once I felt grounded, I went back to writing, making sure that the timer was set again.

I also wrote this book is because I want those that have PTSD or DID to know that we do exist and we matter and that those who do not have these maladies can somehow see and try to understand us. We are everywhere and we are not invisible. We are functioning adults, parents, coworkers, and family members. I'm not in need of sympathy. I just want others to understand what it is that has made me like me and others like me the way they are. We were traumatized, we are not the same as people who can forget and forgive. We live every day on guard, waiting for that moment we have to cope. We can't "just get over it", we have to live through it repeatedly against our own will.

Chapter 1

We lived in this cute little duplex, patio home. You know the kind. They have a garage and a tiny little backyard, but the house is a normal-sized house.

Our home was conveniently next door to the community's parking lot for large vehicles, like recreational vehicles and boats. It was nice because me and my little brother were just learning to ride our bikes and on the weekends the lot was mostly empty and the perfect spot to try balancing without training wheels.

I loved that home. It was the first one that I had ever felt like we were going to stay somewhere permanently. I was only 5 years old, but I remember how awesome the blue shag carpets were and the atriums that were all over the place. The biggest atrium conjoined the living and dining rooms. It was like a secret see-through passage. There was nothing in it but small river rocks and a few aloe plants and the space couldn't have been more than a 10 foot by 10 foot space. But still, as a 5-year-old, it was the most exotic thing I had ever witnessed. And it was almost magical with the emerald glow that came from it and lit up the rooms from corrugated green plastic sheathing that covered the top to keep the pigeons out. On rainy nights, when the monsoons loomed overhead, the flashes of green lightening made everything even more enchanting.

I really loved that house. My littlest brother, Damien, was born in that house. I was just barely 6 years old the day he was born. I instantly fell in love with him. He was this amazing little creature who came and made mom happy. My younger brother, Jason, and I talked about things we were going to teach him and we would sing songs to him while my "daddy Steve" played the guitar. He wasn't our real dad, but he was our best dad. And as far as me and Jason were concerned, Damien was our real brother. We all came from Mom, so we all belonged together.

Once Damien was home, Mom and daddy Steve changed the house around. It was weird. I remember mostly everything about that house, but I don't remember the day we changed the furniture around.

You see, before Damien, I had my own room and Jason, his. But now Damien was here, and I don't know where they got the crazy idea that all three kids should have to share a room, but that's what ended up happening. Two small twin sized beds and a crib were all crammed into one room together. All of our clothes in the closet together. We were all together, which was fine because me and Jason were, well, the very best of friends and now we had Damien, only days old, but it was like our little tribe grew 10 fold with his arrival and the arrival of new possibilities of fun things to do with him. We could finally play hide and go seek properly.

So we all slept in the same room, and the other room, well that turned into our own private little play room. We had every toy, every game, every book, crayon, coloring book, Barbie, truck, seriously it was all put in that room like a dumping area.

Once a week we had to clean it up, like any other chore little kids do. That room was the best! Me and Jason spent hours in that room playing, bonding and getting closer and closer. It was me and him against the grownups.

One day Jason, me, and a couple of kids from down the street were playing in the parking lot next door. Those kids were, well, brats. But I'm biased because of what happened.

The oldest of the kids decided that we are going to play house. He was only 9 or 10, but when you are a kid, that's old. He was a real bossy pants and I only put up with him because his little brother was nice to me and was in my class at school. He decided that we needed to cook dinner because that's what families do. Not literally, of course, just play pretend. I was in charge of getting "eggs". Why we were having eggs for dinner is beyond me, but hey, I was only 6, so it was what it was.

So I went to go get the "eggs" from our front yard. They were really egg-shaped river rocks of the correct size that I was supposed pick out from the millions that created our landscape.

I was squatted down picking through the rocks when my brother runs up.

"Rach, I hurt my finger." he says.

I turn and take a quick glance. That right there, glancing, will haunt me for the rest of my days.

I tell him, "Go wash it off in the hose."

He runs around the corner and I hear the water turn on. A few minutes later, one of the other kids runs up asking for Jason. Then it dawned on me that he had been over at the hose for a while. I yelled for him,

"Hey! Jason! What are you doing?!"

He comes back over to me and tells me it won't stop bleeding. I take a look at it. It was his pointer finger and it had what looked like a nick in it. I asked him if it hurt and he said no. I honestly thought it was no big deal and I could see that he didn't think it was anything serious. He wasn't even crying.

So I told him to lie. Lie to our mom. She didn't like us playing in the parking lot without adult supervision. But she was rarely around to supervise us, so we were left to our own devices on a very regular basis, which meant, well, we could go play in the parking lot, just as long as she didn't find out. Now here he was with a hurt, bleeding finger and we were going to get in big trouble and possibly beat if she found out we were in the parking lot. So I told him to lie.

"Go show it to mom" I said.

He appropriately replied, "She's gonna get mad."

I told him, "Tell her you cut it on a stick or something. Just tell her it won't stop bleeding."

He reluctantly agreed. It was a sorry excuse, really inadequate, but I wanted to get back to playing and I knew he would just be back out in a few minutes anyway with a Band-Aid.

He went into the house and I went back to the pile-o-eggs per se. I got my load in my makeshift basket from a dead palm leaf and headed next door. There were the kids, way back in the corner behind an old fishing boat. They had all kinds of stuff from different yards: Sticks, grass, rocks, and a big-ass fishing knife.

Now, I kinda got scared at this moment. I already wasn't supposed to be in the parking lot, and especially now because mom might come outside to get me because Jason got hurt, but now, here is this gigantic knife; an item I was taught never to play with. I wasn't playing with it, Oh No, but I was in the presence of such an item without a grownup and therefore by association I was going to get in trouble if anyone found out. Then I saw the blood.

They had been using a parking block as a table, sort of, more like a chopping block. And on the parking stone there was a pile of leaves and grass that looked half chopped up. And on the side of the chopped up stuff there was blood; not a bunch, but nonetheless when you see blood at age 6, its gross.

I looked at the knife, the blood, and asked "What happened?"

The older kid tells me that Jason was holding the pile of leaves still while he chopped them up with the knife for "stew" and that's when his finger got cut. My blood ran cold. If mom found out we would definitely get spanked.

I dropped off the "eggs" and ran back to the house.

I came in the door and walked past the living room. After being outside for most of the day, it was really dark in the house and the only light there was came from the atrium in the middle of the living room.

I got to the hallway and noticed the door to the bathroom half-open. I could see my mom's back as she was standing over Jason. She was moving back and forth trying to wash his hands in the sink. I can still hear the sound of the water from the faucet. It was eerily quiet, except for that damn sound of the water running. So very quiet, no baby sounds, no daddy Steve sounds, just the fucking water running at full force. Jason wasn't speaking and my mom was silent. More water. I walked closer and closer down the hallway. I felt like I was in trouble and I was walking into an ambush of spankings.

I was only about 3 feet from the door when my mom screamed at the top of her lungs, almost to the point of raspiness:

"JASON ADAM! WHERE THE FUCK IS YOUR FINGER!!!!?????!!!!"

He started screaming. She started screaming. I started screaming.

I lost all feeling in my arms and legs and the tunnel vision set in. I almost fainted. I turned and bolted for the door.

I ran up to the big kid who was still playing with the big-ass knife in the back of the parking lot and screamed at him.

"You cut off my brother's finger!!!!"

Then I punched him in the face, twice. He immediately started crying and ran away.

So here I was, in the parking lot, crying my eyes out, just punched a big kid, my brother's finger is missing; I was for sure going to get a spanking.

It's funny the things that go through your head when you are traumatized.

Daddy Steve came tearing out of the house, yelling for me. I went 'a runnin' for him. The frantic mad sound in his voice scared me to death. It was as though he was about to tell me my brother was dying. My bestest friend in the whole wide world is dying. He was bleeding to death and I won't have him to play Mouse Trap or checkers or watch the Muppet Show with anymore. I was frantic!

I came around the corner and there was my daddy Steve, big wide brown eyes with tears in them. You should never see your daddy Steve cry. It's a scary sight. I wouldn't recommend it to anyone.

He was saying something to me, but I was really trying hard NOT to hear it. He shook me a couple of times. I think I was momentarily involuntarily catatonic. (Yeah, like there is a voluntary catatonic state.)

All of a sudden there is mom in the front yard with Jason in her arms. They are crying and mom has her hand squeezing Jason's finger. But it wasn't just his finger, it was, but it wasn't.

His finger had been wrapped up in a bright red washcloth, but we didn't have any washcloths of that color. We had the standard olive green, harvest cold of the late 70's early 80's color palate for towels and washcloths.

We were all standing there for just a minute, trying to get situated to go, when the big kid's dad ran up yelling at me/us.

"You're kid hit my kid!" he was all about protecting his kid, totally understandable. But right at that moment I really wanted to punch this guy in the face, twice.

I started screaming, "TOMMY (made up name, cause I forgot that insignificant little twerp's name) CUT JASON'S FINGER OFF!!!" I kept repeating it, even as daddy Steve grabbed me and literally drags me into the car. I kept screaming it as we drove down the street. I kept screaming until I got the slap in the face in the backseat of the car from my mom who was in the front seat holding Jason in her arms. She was a real multitasker, I'll tell you what. (I bet you read those last four words with Hank Hill's voice.)

Daddy Steve drove real fast to the hospital. I don't remember Damien being there, but he had to have been. He was a baby after all and couldn't just stay at home by himself. I remember hiding my eyes when we were in the waiting room. I hid in daddy Steve's armpit until a doctor came in. He asked for mom to take the washrag off and I averted my eyes again. Everyone was quiet.

Daddy Steve and I were in the waiting room for a long time and then it was morning.

I rolled over and saw Jason sleeping in the next bed over. For a moment, only for just one moment, it was just Jason, my bestest friend in the whole wide world. Then all at once it hit me. The events from the previous afternoon hit me like an atom bomb. The racing thoughts, the panic, the mortification, all of it came rushing in a hot flow of blood straight to my brain.

I remember yelping and stifling all at once. I turned away from him and laid there silently for a few minutes.

I got up trying to be quiet, slipping out of bed, not looking at all in his direction. He scared me. He was limbless for all I knew. He was deformed. And I definitely did not want to see him/it.

I went into the kitchen and there was mom, doing mom stuff. I made a bowl of cereal and sat down. I was surprised that she didn't act angry or upset with me in any way. I was waiting for it. I deserved it. I deserved every last little thing she wanted to dish out to me, I knew it, I accepted it, but I just wanted to have some Pac-Man cereal before she laid in on me.

Then all of a sudden Jason walked in. I can see it now, even now, as an adult, I can see him walk past the peninsula that separated the dining room and the kitchen. Walked past the gawd awful faux marble Harvest Gold counter top and over to the olive green fridge. I stared at him the whole way. I'm sure if my eyes were any wider they would've fallen out of their sockets. It was all so surreal. Like I was a fly on a wall that no one even considered killing because I hadn't buzzed their ear yet. It was a quiet, slow moment in time for me. I loved Jason more than life itself. But here I was, terrified at the sight of him.

I'm sure there was a conversation about what happened, but what that was I was never privy to. I'm sure the details between parents' stories was corroborated and confirmed, but nothing was ever said to me. And I never questioned it. All I cared about was that I didn't have to see it. I would've taken a thousand beatings as long as they didn't make me look at his owie.

I managed to escape him several dozen times. He would walk into a room and I would leave. He would follow me around the house and I would slam doors in his face. I made him cry. And I would cry every time they made me sleep in the bed next to his bed. I did NOT want to be a part of his deformity. He was a monster. He had the "cooties" and I didn't want any part of it. He scared me with his big bandage and splint. I wanted nothing to do with him and his partial finger. I wouldn't even speak to him. I ignored his inquiries and invites to friendly games of checkers. If he even tried to laugh at what I was saying, I would scowl at him. I had basically excommunicated him from my life because of his lack of appendages.

Then one day he grabbed a cup or something right in front of me. I may have been 6 years old, but I knew when he was reaching for an item to make sure to avoid "the hand" with the "missing finger".

Well, he grabbed for it and the splint and massive bandages were not there. It was a normal pink little finger staring me straight in the face. Sure, it lacked a fingernail and didn't have the tip that belonged to a fingernail, but it was normal otherwise. I don't know how I could have ever been so cruel to my bestest friend in the whole wide world.

It was only after seeing it with my own eyes that I let him be emotionally attached to me again. Only this time the bond was even stronger. We started playing games together again and basically spending all our time with each other. It only took four weeks for his finger to heal, but damn! That was a long four weeks, especially to a 6-year-old.

Chapter 2

Mom and daddy Steve had been fighting a lot and most nights one of the parents wouldn't come home.

We were living in our precious little patio home in Glendale and I was a big girl walking to school every day with Jason, my "little brother", in tow. It was awesome though because mom and daddy Steve left so early in the morning that me and Jason had the whole house to ourselves.

Mom tried to put us on a schedule, but without parental supervision, well, kids will be kids.

It was supposed to go like this: (Yes, I actually remember this shit. I have no choice with my disorder) My Sesame Street alarm clock would go off at 6:30 am and I was to wake up Jason and get ready for school. I was in charge of using the "butter knife" to make the lunches of PB&J and pick a fruit of the week. She always left us an extra 50 cents to buy a snack at the school. You know, like a cookie or whatever they had made that day. If we were really lucky, like on a payday or something, she would leave us actual lunch money. The school lunches, I thought anyway, were always way better than a PB&J. And it was a bonus because I didn't have to make it.

Anyway, I get up, get him up, and we get to watch TV until 7:30 when it was time to leave. It was perfect timing. The Ladmo and Wallace Show ended right then, so we were always on time. And if you lived in Phoenix in the 80's you knew that show. It was the best morning show for kids ever! It had cartoons and giveaways, and all kinds of skits. If you were lucky, your parents could take you down there early in the morning and be able to participate in the live audience. I never was on the Wallace and Ladmo Show, but I had friends who got on there and got their coveted Ladmo bags. Ladmo Bags: The precious little brown paper lunch bags that were filled with candy, a Coke, and various coupons to get into Legend City (our city's lame version of a Disneyland).

Well, it never ever took us a whole hour to get ready. We never brushed our teeth like we were supposed to. I barely ever brushed my hair. Our clothes were already laid out, but it didn't matter because we wore what we wanted to anyway. No parental supervision to guide us. They were already at work. It was all on me with the occasional input from my sidekick, Jason.

So we figured, heck, we could go to school anytime we wanted. There was a whole playground to play on, instead of hanging around the house waiting to go, we had the "go signal" anytime we wanted. And we wanted to go play.

Most days we would get to school way before the gates were opened, so we would go back to the big tree.

There was a humongous eucalyptus tree that had low limbs that you could climb on and swing. The tree was so big, you couldn't see the top of it and it was a popular hangout spot for kids on the way to school; located in what would be considered an alley, but was really a blocked off unfinished street at the end of a cul-de-sac. It was commonly used as the shortcut because it butted up against the schoolyard.

Well, one day I was playing on the tree, way before school started, and we all got carried away having way too much fun climbing and pretending to be Tarzan. (I truly believe playing make believe is a lost art nowadays.) All of a sudden the bell rings, we all started running. If we were late, we would have to explain why, and then a phone call would be made and mom would have been mad. So we ran.

I had my "Miss Piggy" lunch box in my hand the whole way. But I was running so hard and fast that I hadn't noticed the onslaught of ants that had infiltrated it while it was lying on the ground under the big tree.

It wasn't until after they started attacking my arm that I realized they had swarmed my arm and were making mincemeat out of it. I screamed and dropped it. Teachers came a runnin'. I had to go to the nurse. No escaping the phone call today. I was gonna get spanked. Without question, I was gonna get it. And I did.

Mom got smart, after finding out exactly what we were doing, leaving too early and messing around. I think she really believed in the "stranger danger" in a black van scenario.

Well, she devised a plan. She would call us with her "secret ring" to tell us when we could leave the house to go to school.

See, back in the early 1980's answering machines were new-fangled, and our family certainly didn't own one. There was no such thing as caller ID. We had to come up with a "code" for when to answer the phone. Mom was a bit of a genius when it came to that. She would let it ring twice, hang up, and then call back and that's when we were "allowed" to answer the phone. And if it just rang and rang then you were not allowed to answer it, no matter what. Because that could be the police and if they found out we were home alone then they would come and take us away to live with evil foster people that would never feed us and make us sleep in cars, at least that's what she made me believe.

And every single time after that, on the first ring, me and Jason would go running to the only phone in the house, in the living room, get on our knees, hovering a hand over the receiver waiting for the hang up and re-ring. It was so depressing and anxiety provoking when the pause didn't come. When the phone rang 3 times in a row, my hand withdrew immediately, like it was getting slapped. I would sit there and wonder who it was calling, because it wasn't mom. I would always imagine it was my Grandma and she just wanted to come over for a visit and take us to

McDonald's or somewhere fun, like church. I would just imagine Grandma on the other line listening to that ring and wondering about us and how we were doing. It would make me so sad thinking that we had missed an opportunity to be with her.

Nonetheless, no more fun times were had at the big tree. But it didn't matter, because mom still managed to let us get to school before the bell rang so we had time to play on the playground. I wish she hadn't though.

It was a frosty morning. It had to be late December or early January, because in Arizona that's the only time you get frost. We have a freeze period of about 35 days here. Anyway, we made it to school before the bell rang and Jason ran over to his friends and I automatically went to the jungle gym.

To those of you who are too young to remember, a jungle gym is some brilliant idea someone had to have bars welded together in geometrical patterns stretching up as high as 10 feet for small children to climb on and develop, what I like to call, their falling skills.

I loved the jungle gym, almost to death.

It was picture day. I was in the first grade, age 6. It was frosty, but when you are a kid running around you just don't feel it. Well, I, of course, was wearing my sweet little "picture day" dress with the patent leather shoes that matched and I didn't think twice about climbing to the top of that monstrous thing. I got to nearly the top when I obviously didn't have the correct footing or the frost on the bars was too slippery for my "fancy shoes" when my feet decided to just go in opposite directions.

Man, oh man, I wish I could have just fallen off that day and hit my head on the ground. Even being paralyzed would have been better than what I suffered through.

My feet did the opposite direction thingy and I came down, full body force onto my vagina right onto a bar. Then, I fell off to the ground. I don't remember landing on the ground. I just remember the wind getting knocked out of me and literally seeing stars.

Some time passed, because I remember walking down the corridor with a warm wet feeling on my legs, but don't remember how I got there.

There was a teacher, not my teacher, just some random older lady, mostly holding me up as we hurried to the nurse's office. Yes, the same nurse who took care of my ant bites and got me in big trouble just weeks before. And yes, this time there was going to be another phone call and I didn't care. I was frantically dazed with waves of pain from a spot no little girl should ever, ever, ever have to experience.

I remember most from that day, but it's in pieces, which is a strange thing because my disorder allows me to "tap" into memories. Not just visualize, but smell, hear, and feel moments in time, my time, my history. I can recall almost everything if given the right stimuli, such as music, or the way the sun is shining at certain times of the year and the shadows it gives off. But this particular day, most of it is not there, probably because I was unconscious for a lot of it.

My mom and daddy Steve came to the school and were very upset, not mad, just scared. I was carried to our car where daddy Steve drove like a bat out of Hell to the hospital. I was rushed to a room with lots and lots of lights, very bright lights and I basically woke up. The pain was searing. Someone/something was cauterizing my vagina. Not literally, but that was the pain sensation.

A nurse walked in with a hose, a tiny little clear straw looking hose thing, and my mom started in on the woman, screaming and ripping it out of her hands.

"NO Fucking Way are you going to use that on my daughter! You must have something smaller, find something!" She was mad, I know that mad voice and she was using it at another grown-up that wasn't related to us, so I knew right then and there that something was really wrong and I got scared.

Hospitals, nurses, doctors they all take care of people. They are good people. They only help, not hurt. Well, Fuck that. My mom went behind the curtain with a nurse, like that was somehow going to diffuse the yelling and arguing.   The pain was building into a tide of heartbeats.

I wasn't sure what was going on, but the next thing that happened was a sad occurrence.

A man (doctor) pulled up my gown and I immediately was scared. Nobody is supposed to see my "privates", yet here was this man putting his hands on my private area and my mom was standing right there holding my shoulders to the bed. Then I realized daddy Steve had my hand, but not in that loving "I got your back" way, more like "you're not getting away" way.

Then the nurse said, "Rachel, this is going to hurt a little bit, maybe even burn some, but it will be over real quick if you stay still."

I was six. My life was forever changed.

The catheter they used was a standard size for a woman. There was nothing they could use otherwise and it had to be done. It didn't go in smoothly. It took a few tries and I fought, which was probably part of the problem, but still, give me a break…It Really Hurt BAD!

Again, I was six.

Years and years later, as I grew up I found out through my mom that I had crushed my outer vagina and that it was so swollen that my urethra had been swollen shut and if I didn't get the catheter it would have been really bad for me. And it was until I was in my 20's before I realized that I was supposed to have a clitoris and that it was supposed to feel all weird and tingly when it was touched. You see, that day on the playground when I landed on the bar I had crushed my clitoris and had never known the joys of having one. So sex was basically ruined for me and my marriage suffered greatly from it. But that's a whole other story.

Chapter 3

Living in Arizona is heaven on Earth. We don't have natural disasters that we see on the television. Heck, we rarely even feel aftershocks from earthquakes in California.

We are centrally located to all the "cool" spots. You go 3-1/2 hours north of Phoenix and you are at one of the most "Grand" places on Earth. 5 hours south and you can party your ass off in Rocky Point. 6 hours west on I-8 and you are in San Diego. 6 hours west on I-10 and you are in L.A. And by God, We have the most beautiful mountains in the world varying in every color. I love this state with all my heart. I can't imagine living anywhere else.

Even the heat; yes, indeed it does get hot here. In fact, we hit the one-teens 4 months out of the year. But I say, "Hey! That's better than being buried in snow for 4 months out of the year!" Really most people just work around the heat and now that cars come equipped with air conditioning as a standard and not an option and houses with their air conditioners instead of swamp coolers, well it makes life just that much more enjoyable here in the desert.

Growing up in Arizona was fun. We would go camping, dirt bike riding, tubing down the river, staying out late in the evening with your friends playing "ditch-em" in the corn fields, and inventing games like dirt clot war, which is exactly how it sounds.

We would go out to a freshly tilled field with a ton of kids, pick sides, build a fort across from the other team and then go crazy with the dirt clots until someone started bleeding and had to go home. Or rather, we would stop when the farmer would chase us off with buckshot. Good times.

All the houses back in the late 70's and 80's basically looked the same. John F. Long perfected the "ranch style home" and because it was so cost efficient and came in an erector set, well they were everywhere. Seas of neighborhoods with the same houses next door to each other. He was definitely the inventor of the "cookie-cutter style" home and because of the mass volumes of same style homes, people were always trying to spruce up the landscape in the front yard.

I realize that we live in a desert and we are short on water and it just doesn't seem reasonable to have grass yards, especially when we, as a community, are in a perpetual drought. But back in the day everybody had yards. Bright green grassy yards and dads would go out and water them every day and kids would play tag on them. It's like everyone was trying to make it look like we didn't live in a desert.

Well, one day my dad, my real dad, the one who spared a sperm for me, decided that he wanted to build a faux river bed in front of our house. What it was was strategically placed river rock in the front yard about 4 feet wide and would wind around from one side to the other to make it seem like there was a river bed in the yard. It was really kind of neat when it was finished. In fact, I remember the neighbors doing the very same thing a few weeks after we did it. And as an adult I can say that was the only time in my life we were the proverbial Jones'.

Now we were not a rich family, not even close. We depended on food stamps and WIC (free money that goes strictly to cheese and milk for kids and pregnant mothers). It was rare that we went out to eat. And when we did go out to eat my mom, who is a kleptomaniac, would always end up taking the salt and pepper shakers. My point is that money was spent on important things, not landscaping. But that didn't deter my dad. He was inventive with a common sensibility about him that made him think he could do anything, build anything. I'm proud to say I got that trait. His spatial skills were astronomical. He could visualize just about anything and if he had the right tools and product he could do it in a couple of hours. It was only recently that my Aunt Deb told me how my dad and I shared this special thinking.

Well, dad wanted to build the riverbed out front, but we didn't have money for it, so he thought he would just go get some river rocks out of the riverbed outside the city, in the desert. After all, they are free rocks, just out there for the taking. Nobody would miss a couple of measly rocks and they sure didn't, but what happened that day in the desert makes me shutter every time I see landscaping that involves a riverbed. And nowadays, with everyone being all super-conscious about conserving water, the riverbeds are everywhere. You can't drive down a street without seeing 10-15 of them. If you live in Arizona, or you come here to visit, pay attention next time and remember what I'm about to tell you, because I remember every fricken time I see one.

I must have been 2 or 3 years old because Jason was just a baby and he was sleeping in the backseat of the car when we took our drive out of the city on the quest for rocks. It was really hot outside and in those days we didn't have a car with air conditioning, in fact the first air conditioned car I ever sat in was probably in 1985 when my mom got the Calais, remember those? I digress.

We were driving for what seemed to be forever, heading east. I recognized that we were going by the Zoo, and being an adult remembering this, I know it was east. And as a little kid, it was taking way too long, especially all hot in the car. Even with the windows rolled down it was like a convection oven.

We finally arrived in the desert and clambered out of the car. I was excited thinking we were going to the river. Obviously confused because I was little, we were only at the dried up riverbed and I was disappointed, but dad got me involved in sort of a game.

What I had to do was go pick up rocks and show them to him and then put them in the car. Such a simple task, but I was proud to do it because that's what mom and dad were doing and I was helping. There was a catch though; I had to remember to kick the rock over first to look for spiders. The scorpions and other desert animals love to sleep under the rocks during the day and come out at nightfall for the coolness of the evening to hunt and whatnot. So, I had to kick over the rock first, then show it to one of them, and THEN put it in the car if they said so. I was doing so well at first.

Daddy wanted more blue rocks. Sounds strange to say it and write it here, but yes we really do have blue rocks. Well, dad wanted more of them to create his masterpiece.

I started wandering off. I found what looked like the perfect rock so I kicked it over and BAM! Sure enough, there was a spider, not a scorpion, but some sort of spider-like creature frozen in the surprise of the sunlight. I leaned in for a closer look. Then I squatted down to get even closer to the "buggie". The sun was so bright and hot and the bug was in my shadow when it started to crawl away from me, not towards me, thank goodness.

I grabbed a stick nearby and started poking at the bug. It was annoyed with me as I played with its life.

My legs started to get tired from squatting down for so long and in my periphery, and just sort of a knowledge of self, I knew that there was a rock right behind me.

Mind you, I was in a very deep squat as it was and being 2 or 3 years old I was very close to the ground, so it really wasn't that far to go from squat to sit on your ass, and so I did. And as I came down onto the rock it dawned on me that rocks don't hurt like this. The pain from my asshole shot up my spine and out my ears and eyes. It was like a lightning strike. I sat down on a jumping cactus with my butt cheeks completely open because of the squatting position I was in. Therefore the cactus actually was semi inserted into my ass.

My scream was guttural and echoed through the desert. All I could do was scream and cry. My dad clumsily ran over the rocks to me and scooped me up in his arms.

The very next moment I was lying face down on the hood of the car and my parents are screaming and upset. I tried to fight to get away, not from the pain in my butt, but from the scorching hood of the car. I could feel the sizzling of my tummy and chest and just touching it with my hands to push away from it burned me severely. One of them put their forearm across my back to hold me down and I screamed and screamed until there was no noise coming from my voice box.

Then the pain in my ass got worse. They were pulling my panties off. The time spent on that hood was endless. They kept telling me to calm down and sit still, but it hurt so bad.

After all was said and done, I was naked in the back seat with my little brother again with my dad behind the wheel and my mom talking about what we were going to do for dinner. The sunset that night was beautiful; purple, pink, orange. Fire in the sky.

My butt was on fire too, but at least it wasn't bleeding anymore.

I was looking down at it. I was naked for probably the first time unsupervised, so I was looking at my parts right there in the back seat of the car. I saw little red, blood-kissed, raised bumps all over the place and it was ugly.

I was touching one of the big bumps when all of a sudden I felt my cheek (the one on my face, not my butt) cave in. I hadn't noticed my mom turn and see me with my finger on the edge of my butthole touching the owie. She smacked me a good one, left a mark, and told me not to touch myself.

"You are a bad girl, Rachel. You don't touch yourself, that's bad and you are a bad girl."

I cried. The sun went down. We were home.

Chapter 4

I'm not supposed to be here. I mean it. I wasn't ever supposed to live this life, but yet here I am.

Some say it was a miracle or just lucky, but I really don't think so. I feel in my heart of hearts that I am supposed to be someone or something else, not this mother of 4 living out my little life, trying to earn a living, and just getting through the day to do it all over again tomorrow.

My mom was a bastard. Not in the literal sense of not having a father, she had one, he was a prick, but she was a true jerk, i.e. bastard.

Growing up, being the oldest in a household of 6 kids, she was put in charge of way too many things. Her responsibility was overwhelming for her and that's why, when she found my dad, she escaped her mother's clutches as fast as she could.

My dad was exciting and cool and a master manipulator. My mom, having quit school in the ninth grade, was definitely not the sharpest tack in the box, and therefore was easily influenced. I'm sure my dad had to put forth little effort to convince her that living on the street or with friends would be a better situation than taking care of a bunch of brats and wondering if her dad was going to make one of his special trips to her bed that night. So leaving was just what she was looking for and she snatched it up.

When she was finally out on her own, she went wild. It was her time, her time to do whatever she wanted without consequences from parents. She experimented with heroin and pot, but then got hooked. My dad joined her in the ethereal haze. They lived wherever they crashed for the night and did odd jobs for money to support their habit. It was truly a sex, drugs and rock and roll lifestyle and she was free from the oppression of her responsibilities and if such a responsibility presented, well she just got high and ignored it.

Then she got pregnant.

I don't speak to my mom anymore, so I don't know all the gory details about her first pregnancy, except for the following.

She was stoned for 4 months straight when she finally realized that she had a baby growing in her tummy. She got scared, as with most women when they don't plan pregnancy. It was the early 70's and she had just gotten her independence. She knew what it was going to be like with a baby around. She knew that she didn't want that responsibility. She had already spent most of her life raising her siblings. She was only 17 and she already knew that she didn't want to have a baby, yet. But being only 17 years old and knowing exactly how her uber-religious mother would feel about her having an abortion, she snuck down to Mexico with borrowed money and got rid of the baby.

She had told me that it was a horrible situation. How it was dirty and the people didn't speak any English, and how she bled for months after the fact.

She went numb. She started shooting up to get the high effect, chasing that ultimate float. She went from here to there and back again, shooting up, staying stoned for months on end, zoning out on life.

One day she got sick, real sick. When people who use heroin say they are sick, they are talking about withdrawal. But my mom really got sick sick, like with the flu kind of sick. But it wasn't the flu. She had contracted hepatitis from sharing needles with whoever had the goods. And when she got so sick she couldn't stand up, my dad took her to her mom's house.

Grandma was shocked to see them. She immediately took my mom to the hospital and my dad, well he disappeared.

At the hospital my mom found out she was preggers, again. She was 7 months along and hadn't noticed because she had been so deeply hazed. The doctor told her that the baby was probably dead because of all the heroin and with the hepatitis and her not going for regular checkups and all.

Back then they didn't have fancy schmancy ultrasound to check on baby's progression. All they did was measure your belly size, give you vitamins, and tell you to stay off your feet as much as possible. Hell, they didn't even tell you that smoking was dangerous for the baby.

Well, to check on the baby, believe or not, they actually did an x-ray. Yes, a real true, radiation x-ray on a pregnant woman's stomach. I can't imagine that it's safe to do such a thing, but they did it. I mean, it was the 70's, and it wasn't like they had a choice.

The doctor checked to make sure that the baby wasn't just some meat mass with bones protruding everywhere. And it wasn't deformed. But, the doctor warned my mom that the baby wasn't worth keeping because it would most probably be stillborn or severely retarded and that it would need lots of care. My mom immediately said "abort it".

Grandma flipped out. Grandma, a religious nut-job, who has no idea what life outside of the "lord" is like. She actually still gives her 15% tithing even though she is on a fixed income. Yeah, like God is going to get all pissed off at you and not let you in the pearly gates because you decided food was more important than tithing. And if she didn't do tithing she would ask for forgiveness for a full year, 4 times a day, every day.

Anyway, Grandma lost it and told my mom "You made your bed, now lie in it."

From what I know, Grandma and mom had an actual argument over this subject right there in the hospital. Mom really wanted to abort a 7-month-old fetus and Grandma said that she messed up and if that child came out "wrong" that she was going to have to be responsible for it. My mom was pissed. My Grandma took her home and my dad stayed disappeared.

Two months later I was born, right on time with all my fingers and toes.

All the factors were against me. I have a theory about all of this. Think about it, if you will. When babies are being bake, it's on a cellular level. The DNA, the cells, the goop all is created right there in the uterus. What about if the DNA or cells are distorted? And the whole baking process is compromised for 7 months by a foreign substance, such as heroin? A disease is also introduced due to said substance, such as hepatitis? And then you x-ray it in utero. What the fuck does that do to a baby? And what kind of chance does the baby have to survive this? I think my cells are somehow messed up. It's not just a mental disorder brought on by PTSD. I think that I have a disease on a cellular level, something that is in me that allowed me to not only survive as long as I have, but also allow me to have my wits about me, at least for the most part.

I don't believe in miracles. They are a crock of shit. I definitely don't believe its luck because the only kind of luck I have is bad luck. So, how I got here is almost a cruel joke, almost.

See I disrupted my mom's lifestyle, well actually Grandma made her have me, and she was pissed that Grandma pulled the "mom" card on her and now she was going to have to settle down and be responsible, which was something she just escaped barely a year before that.

My mom never wanted me. I'm serious, never wanted me. She never loved me. Never Loved Me. The only time I got affection from her was when she was using me to get what she wanted from others, like a ride, food, money, whatever. I never ever felt love from her and how do I know this?

You can't miss what you never had. That's how. I never knew I was missing love, simple, pure love until I had my own children and started raising them. I instinctively knew that I wasn't going to be like my own mom. Of course, when I had my children I instantly fell in love with each and every one of them individually. But as they get older, I fall even more in love with each of their characteristics as time moves on. I love them whole-heartedly. I know what love for your child is and I never had that with my own mom. Not ever. She never, ever loved me.

Can you imagine that? Living your whole life with a mom, only to find out that you were nothing but an expensive inconvenience that is in the way of her choices in life. Yeah. You probably can't because you can't imagine something that you've never had, i.e. never NOT having had love from your parent.

One of my earliest memories was a testament to my mom's disregard for me and my little brother Jason. I woke up in a strange car, don't remember getting into it, but remember looking out the window at a string of one-story apartments. I was only 2 years old and didn't recognize the place at all. Jason was sleeping on the seat next to me, but mom was nowhere in sight. I got scared.

I stared out the window for a long time at the doors of the apartments, wondering, wishing I knew where she was. There were about 10 apartments right there in front of me, but only 3 or 4 of them had lights on. I kept thinking over and over that she would come out any minute, but the minutes passed and she still wasn't there. I had to pee and I was real hungry, so I debated and decided to leave my brother asleep and go knock on the doors with lights on. I can remember clearly reaching for the car door handle and pulling up with all my might to get it to unlatch, but to no avail. I just wanted my mommy. So I grabbed the handle to the window and it gave much easier than the door latch. I pushed it round and round until the window sat down inside the door. It was chilly outside and I didn't have any shoes when I dropped to the asphalt with my feet first then to my butt and back.

Jason made a noise from inside the car, but I was too little to see up inside of it. I tried the handle from the outside to get him to come with me, but the button to push was really hard and I just didn't have the strength. He was sort of whining inside the car, not really crying, but awake and annoyed. I needed to find mom. Jason needed her and I was scared because I couldn't take back getting out of the car window.

I went over to the first door with a porch light on, which just so happened to be the door the car was parked right in front of, and I listened. There was laughing inside and I could hear my mommy talking and giggling. I knocked on the door, but they didn't hear me over the music. After knocking a few times, the door opened up and nearly knocked me down in the process. There was a very tall man standing there with a beard and long hair. He could've been mistaken for Jesus Christ if he didn't have a cigarette hanging out of his mouth.

"Sharon! I think she's yours, right?" he yelled at her in the other room.

Mom came over and scooped me up in her arms. She had a look of terror in her eyes as she questioned me. "How did you get out of the car? Where's your brother?"

She carried me to the car with the open window, and from the view up in her arms, Jason was laying on the floorboard now. I left him on the seat, but he must have rolled over to the floor in my escape. She got him out of the car and carried us inside. There were a lot of people and a lot of smoke in the air. We hung out for a while listening to music and dancing.

As an adult, I know what they were doing now, but back then it was just fun.

She wanted to get high and me and Jason were just in the way and a bummer to her. She left us in the car, in the fucking car, by ourselves. So, I'm an orphan with a mom.

It took 24 years before I knew what love really was. I am supposed to be a vegetable, retard or dead. Except for my children, I don't understand why I'm this survivor. So I will just go ahead and live this little life, raise my kids the best way I know how, and wait for tomorrow.

Chapter 5

We had what most people would consider a normal life. (Yes, I know, no one is normal.) But on the surface everything was rainbows and unicorns. There was a mom, a dad, 3 kids, nice car, nice home in a sweet little neighborhood. The family thought my mom had finally pulled it together.

We would all go to church on Sundays and spend time with the grandparents, participate in prayer circles that would last into the night, for hours on end. Mom would put on appearances for Grandma, but at home it was a totally different story.

Mom and daddy Steve would get high every day, disappear for days in their room, and fight until someone got hurt, and even beyond that. Daddy Steve was violent and there were a few times that we went to Grandma's so that mom could get a break. It wasn't long though before we would all go back home to daddy Steve.

It was during this tumultuous time that mom clung to me. It was like every time they had a wedge between them, she would pull me in close. She would tell me secrets that I was supposed to keep, and I did. It was like I was allowed something extra special and I wasn't going to disappoint. The affection was wonderful. She held me closer, told me special things, praised me. But then she and daddy Steve would make up and I was the kid again.

I would go to give her hugs and they weren't as tight or as long anymore. She would get mad at me faster and I felt like I was just insignificant again.

Then late one evening, after all us kids were put to bed and were fast asleep, mom came in and whisper-woke me.

"Rachel, wake up. Rachel, come on wake up." I can still hear it deep in my ear.

I opened my eyes and realized it was her. I was so sleepy confused. I was only 6 at the time and I knew that it was late at night, but mom was waking me up.

Her tone was very sweet and seductive. She only talked like this to me when she was in a fight with daddy Steve.

"Mom?" I said.

"Come in the living room. Be quiet, don't wake up your brothers. Hurry up, come on." She whispered excitedly, like we were about to go to Disneyland. It was like she had some big fancy surprise she just couldn't wait until morning to give me.

I got up and followed her into the living room. The house was dark with the only illumination coming from the

TV bouncing light off the deep dark blue shag carpeting. As my eyes adjusted, I could see the atrium glowing green with its sad little aloe plant dying from lack of attention.

"Mom?" I asked wondering why in the world I was up this late.

"You want to watch TV with me?" she asked.

"Sure!"

"Shhhhh. You can stay up and watch TV with me, but only if you be quiet and don't wake your brothers."

"Okay" and I copped a squat on the floor.

She had all kinds of goodies spread out across the floor, like a picnic on a shaggy sea. There was popcorn, pop, and a big carton of Whoppers. I always loved the Whoppers. They came in what looked exactly like a milk carton, but instead of bland old milk inside, you get little round chocolaty crunchy goodness. And there was a whole carton, unopened, sitting right there.

Mom sat down across from me and asked me if I wanted a pop. This was a rare occurrence. Pop for kids really wasn't allowed, not because she thought it would rot our teeth out, oh no. It was because she didn't want to share her pop regularly with us kids. She was selfish like that.

"Really? All for me?" I was so happy because I wasn't going to have to share with Jason.

She popped it open for me and I downed almost half of it without taking a breath. Mom reached up and pulled it down and said, "Don't drink it all right now. Save some for the movie."

Okay all you youngsters out there reading this, there used to be old movies that they would show at midnight on the regular local TV channel. They played the most God-awful movies, usually in black and white so as to lull people to sleep. It was before Lunesta and Tylenol PM, when people needed to be bored to sleep. This was way back in the day when there was no Tivo, DVRs, instant cue, hell even VCRs weren't invented yet.

The movie started, it was black and white and had an old person in it. It wasn't anything remotely interesting to a 6-year-old, but that didn't matter, not at all. My mom woke me up, I am up way past my bedtime, didn't have to share with Jason, and I'm getting a pop and possibly a few of those Whoppers.

I went to reach for the popcorn and she pulled my hand away. I was really confused now. There was a large bowl of popcorn sitting right in front of me, teasing me with its buttery goodness, just waiting for a hand to dip into it and pull out a mouthful, but she pulled my hand back.

She said, "Wait a little while."

I started watching the movie and hadn't even noticed that she pulled her bong out. It must have been behind the couch or something because she didn't leave the living room to get it, in fact she didn't really shift in her spot at all. I looked over at her and she was messing with a bag.

I had seen this happen a million times. I knew she gets the green crunchy stuff from the bag and puts it on a little drink tray thing that had a Coca-Cola advertisement on it of two young kids sharing a single coke with two straws. She then would take it all apart and talk about how much seeds were in it and complain about how they shouldn't have to pay for seeds since seeds are just thrown away anyway. After complaining while separating, she would take small pinches of the crunchy stuff and smash it into a silver thingy that she sets on fire.

I was watching the TV and anticipating the "go" signal for the popcorn when she asked me something for the very first time ever.

I looked over at her and I must have had that look of confusion because she asked me again.

"You want to try it?" She was smiling at me. She was happy with me. I recognized right then and there that she was my friend again. The nice mom had returned and was sharing with me. Everything else didn't matter; the popcorn, the pop, the staying up late, the movie, it just didn't matter.

"I don't know how." I said with a sound of promise that I would be willing if only I knew how.

I had seen my mom and daddy Steve and about a dozen of their friends smoke pot so many times, but as a young child it eluded me on how they "smoked" it.

My Grandpa was a smoker of tobacco cigarettes. I had seen him chain smoke countless times and he would show me how he could make it come out his noise like a dragon. He even knew how to make smoke circles that I would chase after and try to catch. I understood the "cigarette" approach, for the most part. It was the bong concept that was so confusing.

The bong itself is a contraption so elaborate it belongs in a Dr. Seuss book. And watching the orchestration of fingers and mouth makes me think of playing an oboe filled with water. Right hand holds the match, left hand holds that weird hole in the back and your lips are enveloped by the shaft mouth, then the lungs inhale and the ears hear the boiling water sounds. The eyes see the smoke fill the cylinder and when there's a lung-full, the left thumb lets go of that weird hole and the smoke fills your head. As a 6-year-old it was complicated to say the least.

I may have witnessed it a million times and knew how it would make people happy almost instantly, I still didn't know what to do to get "happy".

Mom moved across the floor and sat crisscross-applesauce right next to me.

She said, "Watch me". So I did like I've done before.

She struck the match and held it to the silver bowl full of marijuana. She made a circular pattern around the grass, lighting it up as she sucked in and made the water bubble. The fire from the match disappeared down into the leaves and the leaves turned into bright embers.

The water was violently bubbling and sifting smoke through to the cylinder and just as it got too thick to see through anymore, she let her thumb off the hole and Fwueeeep, the smoke was in her lungs and she was waving out the match.

I watched her face intently as she scrunched it up and tightened her lips to the point of white.

Strange short little snorts were escaping her nose like she was trying to hold back a sneeze. I watched.

After what was an eternity of her holding her breath, she let go a sigh. Big and long. The strangest part was that there was barely any smoke that came out. Not even half of what she took in came back out. It was like a magic trick. And to a 6-year-old, all grownups knew magic.

She sat there for a minute gagging and coughing like she always does. Then it was my turn.

She reached over for the drink tray with the goods all separated out on it. She pulled out the silver bowl and dumped it over onto the tray: tap, tap, tap. She started explaining to me all the steps. But the most important one was that when I breathed in, not to cough.

"Rachel, whatever you do, don't cough. When you breathe it in you need to hold your breath until I count to 30. Don't let it out. Just hold your breath."

After the step by step she moved to sit behind me. She put her arms around me and pulled me back into her. The bong was in front of me with her hands on it. She was holding me in her lap on the floor and we were sharing a secret, just me and her.

She reached over and struck the match. The fire went to the bowl. The mouth of the shaft swallowed my mouth and I sucked.

"Suck harder Rachel! Keep going, keep sucking." She was encouraging me like I was making a goal in a soccer game. She was routing me on in this twisted bonding moment.

I couldn't see the smoke filling up, but I sure did feel it when she let go of the hole and the fire went down my throat into my lungs.

I wanted to cough, but I heard her start to count: "one one-thousand, two one-thousand, three one-thousand, four one-thousand…"

It was like I had taken a drink the wrong way, like a bit of spittle was stuck in my throat, tickling me, taunting me to just cough and spit it out. I held it in as hard as I could.

"eleven one-thousand, twelve one-thousand…"

Really??? I thought to myself, only 12???

"Hold it in Rachel. Don't cough!" She was almost panicky-sounding this time.

I wanted to vomit. It hurt so badly in my lungs. I thought I would turn into a flame at any second. The tickle grew in the back of my throat. I started to make that sound, the one I had heard so many times from so many different people, including my mom just moments before. I was making that "almost sneezing" sound. It was coming from my nose and it was helping.

"Twenty-eight one-thousand, twenty-nine one-thousand, thirty one-thous"….

"Mom?" Jason said standing at the doorway.

I let the smoke out and gagged and coughed and almost threw up.

Mom jumped up and ran over to Jason, spilling the bong on the ground. She blocked his view and shuffled him into the other room. I don't know what she said to him because I was choking on my lungs and heart.

I grabbed my pop and drank every last drop of it, but it didn't help. The taste of the smoke coated every crevasse of my mouth and when I coughed the spit was pot-smoke flavored.

Mom came back into the living room a few minutes later with a very serious look on her face. Normally, when they smoke out it was a happy-party-time afterwards, so her looks made me feel like I had done something wrong.

She saw the spilled bong and cursed a bit as she went to get a towel.

When she returned, she dabbed up the spilled bong water and warned me about keeping this a secret.

"Don't you tell anyone, no one at all that you did this. You could get in really big trouble. You would have to go live with a foster family. You keep this secret forever. Be a good girl and keep this a secret for only me and you." She said in her firm voice.

I agreed. I felt really guilty that I did something bad. But at the same time I was closer to mom than any one of my siblings. We were doing something together and she truly loved me to share.

A few minutes later, like a light switch flipping, she was happy and smoking another bowl. After her fitful coughs she gave me the "go" signal.

I attacked the popcorn like I hadn't eaten in years. I didn't realize it until after the very first bite how hungry I really was. Insatiable.

I will always remember that popcorn as the best popcorn I had ever eaten.

You see, years ago there were no microwaves and certainly no microwave popcorn. We had things like Jiffy Pop, which is a cheap aluminum pie pan type structure with a handle jabbing out the side with an aluminum covering the top. The pan contained popcorn kernels. The object of

Jiffy Pop was to put the pan on the stovetop and constantly shake it back and forth until the contents heat up enough to pop into popcorn.

Well, we were too poor for that. So we just did it the old fashioned way with a pot from the cabinet and some kernels. It took a while, but the result was always very tasty. Mom would melt down sticks of butter and poor it all over the top of the popped corn and sprinkle salt and shake the bowl. It was good popcorn, especially good when you are stoned out of your mind in the middle of the night.

I started to feel light. Everything around me was thick and I was lighter than all of it. I laid down for a minute and my mom giggled at me. In the dark her brown eyes were just watery sockets of black. Her face was Cheshire Cat-like and I felt a panic that made me sit up and take a better look at her.

The TV went to static because back in the olden days TV channels actually went off air. The static from the TV lit up the whole room and I could see my mom's eyes again. She was just plain old mom still and I immediately calmed down.

She got up and turned off the TV. I went to get another handful of the buttery goodness, but there was nothing left. Had I eaten all of it?

Music started. Mom put on an album, yes a vinyl album, and she started to dance across the room back at me.   It was Pink Floyd.   We sat there in the green luminescence of the atrium on our blue shag sea for a long time.   Mom sang along with the words and talked to me about how hard life was and that I should be thankful for being a kid.   She spoke, but most of the time I couldn't really hear or understand what she was saying.   As I think back on it, I was wasted.

She gave me another chance to do the bong and I accepted.   This time I coughed.   This time she got mad at me.

"You just wasted that!   Rachel, you can't cough, don't cough.   Shit, you just wasted that!"

I felt bad, but I also felt numb, more numb than bad.

Mom laid down on a big couch cushion she pulled onto the floor.   She fell asleep talking to me about life.   The record ended and I sat there in the dark, alone, six years old and stoned.

The Whoppers were still unopened.   I was hungry.   I quietly picked up the Whoppers and they shifted in the carton.   I froze.   She rolled over to see what I was doing.

"Can I have just one?"

"I forgot all about those. You can have 5. No more though. Just 5." She said sympathetically.

I couldn't get it open. It was harder than the milk cartons at school. She got up and opened it, counted out 5, handed them to me, and closed it back up. She set the carton by her pillow, got up, started the album over again and laid back down. Her slumber came immediately. Snoring gently, almost in time to the music.

I slowly ate my Whoppers, one by one, making sure to take 3 bites out of each one, you know, to make them last.

After they were gone, I laid down next to her and in her sleep she put her arm over me. I laid there for a long time, a very long time. I was not sleepy at all so I just played a game of matching her breathing. When she would breathe in, so would I, and when she exhaled, so did I.

A while later, I devised a plan of eating more Whoppers. I mean, how was she to know how many were left in that carton? She didn't count them or anything. So I could have just a few more.

I carefully escaped her embrace and sat up. The album had been over for a long time and it was really quiet in the house. I looked over and contemplated how to open the Whoppers without making noise. I reached for them and very gently lifted them up being sure not to let them shift as before. Mom didn't move, except for her chest breathing steadily in and out. I opened the carton and leaned it over. There was that shifting noise again, I froze.

Mom didn't move. She didn't hear me. I poured out a handful and left the carton on its side on the ground. I gobbled my handful in no time at all, fearing every bite, every crunchy sound was going to wake her up at any second. I kept thinking just two more, as I would fish them out of the carton one by one with my pointer finger making sure not to make any noise. After fishing 3-4 times I quit. I was afraid she would see that they were all gone.

I went into the other room where Jason and Damien were sleeping. I tried to wake up Jason to play with me. I was bored and not tired. Jason wouldn't wake up. So I returned to the living room and flipped on the TV.

I turned the channels very slowly, keeping with my quiet theme. All of a sudden Kermit appeared on the screen. All bright and green, he was bouncing around with his arms flailing everywhere. Instant happiness was in my heart.

I had stumbled upon Sesame Street for the very first time that morning. I was mesmerized. There was my favorite character on the Muppet Show on in the morning. And who was this big yellow bird, or that green ratty thing, I just didn't know. It wasn't until 5 or 10 minutes later that it dawned on me that Jason would love to see this.

I ran into our room and shook him.

"Get up! Muppets are on! Muppets are on!"

He stirred for a minute, opened his eyes and realized what I was saying. In one swift movement, he had the blankets thrown off, feet on the ground, and was through the doorway.

In the living room I told him to be quiet as we plopped down 2 feet in front of the TV. I glanced at mom, she was still sleeping, but had turned over to her other side, away from us. I was confident that I could turn the volume up just so we could hear the magical Muppets.

We sat and watched Sesame Street all the way through. It was so funny and fun! I wondered if it was only on once a week like Duke's of Hazard or Hee Haw. I actually ran to my room and got a pencil and paper to write down the channel it was on so I could remember to watch it again.

Mom finally woke up a few hours later and we started our day like any other day, except today we didn't have to go to school. We all laid around and watched TV all day. It was nice.

Chapter 6

The fights between mom and daddy Steve were getting worse. I was really missing the nice daddy Steve. He was so great, always wanting to do fun stuff with us kids. He was the one who taught me how to ride a bike and swim underwater. I will remember that forever.

Mom met him at work, sort of. She worked for Holsum Bakery in Phoenix on the wrapping line. It kept her away most days for 12 hours minimum. And lots of times after work she would go over to the local bar, Angelo's, and hangout with her friends and that's where she met daddy Steve. He worked for Holsum too, but in a totally different area. It was at the bar that fate brought them together.

It didn't take them long and they were married. I real true wedding and it was beautiful. The whole family was there and there was even a reception with cake and champagne.

After a while mom got pregnant with Damien. It was exciting for me and Jason to watch mom's belly grow. She continued to work, but was home most nights afterwards, instead of going off drinking with her buddies.

Daddy Steve really pulled us together tight. We had Friday night pizza and would play family games together like Monopoly. He was what a real dad was supposed to be.

After Damien came and mom started back to work that's when things started to get really bad. At first mom and daddy Steve would go out together to all hours of the night leaving me in charge of my brothers; Jason, 5 and Damien, 2 months. I was only 6, but that didn't matter. All I had to do was make sure Jason didn't set the house on fire, not that he was a pyromaniac or anything; it was just a generalization of making sure he stayed out of trouble. And I was in charge of Damien, but I wasn't allowed to pick him up out of his crib if he woke up.

On several occasions, when Damien woke up screaming, I would climb into his crib with him and change his diaper. If he was still screaming, I would make him a ba-ba and lay down with him until he fell asleep. Lots of times I woke up in that crib with him.

One night I was lying in the crib with Damien late at night and mom comes in. Daddy Steve wasn't with her. They had gotten into a fight and she came home without him. It scared me to think that he was somewhere without a way to get home.

It wasn't long after that that they started going out without each other. They were both still leaving, just not with each other. Our house was in upheaval. Our family was slowly falling apart and I could see it. And then daddy Steve got real mean.

I was sitting in the living room one Thursday evening watching my coveted Muppet Show. Mom was in the shower and Jason was playing in our room. I was really into it and then daddy Steve walked in. He reached down right in front of me and turned the channel to the news. There is nothing worse to watch when you are 6 years old than the news. No kid wants to watch the news. So, being 6 years old, I protested.

"I was watching the Muppet Show!" I snapped.

"Well, now you're watching the news." He scowled.

I sat there for a minute and then it came to me to tell on him. Since the fights had gotten worse and the wedge between them had gotten huge, that launched me into the #1 spot on mom's list. She was being so nice to me and the boys, I felt safe going to her and telling on him. But I didn't just go into the bathroom and rat him out, I played it real cool-like.

I got up from my spot on the living room floor, walked into the kitchen and got a drink. I could feel daddy Steve listening to what I was doing.

I went into the bedroom where Jason was and watched him for a minute. I declined a game of whatever he wanted at the moment. I heard daddy Steve laugh in the living room, so I made my move to the bathroom where mom was.

I went through her bedroom to the doorway of the bathroom and saw her standing there nude, brushing her hair. She really was a beautiful woman, even after having a bunch of kids, she bounced back very nicely. (I got that trait from her.) Her brown hair hung down to her buttocks. I stood there for a minute and waited for her.

She looked over at me in the mirror and asked, "What's wrong?" She was annoyed.

I almost shied away with a 'nothing' response. But I was more annoyed than scared and I answered her honestly, "daddy Steve changed the channel."

"Why?" She probed.

"I don't know. I was watching Muppets and he turned it to the news." I whined.

She screamed through the house "Steve!!! Turn that back. Quit being an Asshole and let her watch her show!"

She made me jump. I wasn't expecting that. I was just kind of hoping that she would go tell him to cut it out and let me watch my Muppets. I didn't think she would call him names or anything. Geez.

I was proud, I got my way. I was way too smug though.

I pranced back into the living room and sat down in my spot on the floor right in front of the TV, making sure that I didn't make eye contact. I knew he was mad at me. I knew he was in trouble and I put him there, but honestly I really wanted to just watch the Muppet Show. That was my show and I was watching it first.

I sat quietly, patiently waiting for him. I didn't turn the channel, I didn't dare. Mom said for him to change it and so he was going to have to.

I sat facing the TV with daddy Steve sitting behind me in the big arm chair.

I could see him in the reflection of the TV, beyond the man behind the desk with the picture of the United States behind him. If I looked just right I could see daddy Steve's shadow of an outline right there on the screen. He wasn't moving. He was sitting there, quietly.

He lunged at me, punched me right in my ear, pulled me off the ground by my hair, and threw me into the corner between the big arm chair and the wall.

"You fucking little brat!" he grunted at me.

I was trapped as he leaned over me. "You fucking little brat!" again grunted, almost not heard over the blow dryer from the bathroom and the Wah Wah Wah noise in my right ear.

I was scrunched up in the corner. I could get any farther back.

He leaned over farther and lifted his right leg. It came down, stomping on me. It hit my top thigh, slid over it right into my stomach. No air to breathe with.

He said something, but I can't hear him as he brought his foot down again. His mouth was open like a rabid dog showing all of his teeth. I shut my eyes as it hit full force on my stomach again. I couldn't even cry. The wind was knocked out of me.

I looked up and he was backing off. I inhaled and there was burning pain in my chest.

"Don't you even think about telling your mom about this. I will kill you, you fucking little brat. Do you hear me?"

I could only nod yes as the tears welled up in my eyes.

He turned around, flipped the channel on the TV back to my Muppet Show and walked out of the room.

Painfully I crawled over to my spot on the shag carpet and laid down. I watched that show that day and I believe it was worth it.

Chapter 7

Before Damien was born and before the little patio home, we lived in a cute little ranch house out in Phoenix. It was perfect. Me and Jason had our own bedrooms with our own stuff. We were so happy there. Daddy Steve and mom would take us roller skating and play board games with us and family would come and visit.

Mom and daddy Steve had pulled it together enough to get a semi-new car. New to us, but used, but still newer than what we had.

They planned and researched and had enough money to buy it outright. That's just unheard of nowadays.

Well, one day they left us at home alone, which is the way things were done in the 70's. I may have only been 4, and Jason 3, but we understood to just sit and watch TV. TV: The ultimate free babysitter. And when they came home they had a new car. It was so pretty and so clean. They had chosen a Duster. The color was a sort of brown/gold color and it only had two doors. It's the kind of car they would call a muscle car today. It was bad-ass. You could feel it push you into the seat, pulling you down when the accelerator was slammed. The car would jump-lunge when you punched it and the tires would make this little chirping sound that was exciting.

We had that car for all of about 3 months before we realized the defect on it and poor Jason was the one who figured it out in the most unpleasant way.

Daddy Steve and Jason left to go to the store. I was outside playing on the carport with some of the neighbor kids. I watched them back the car out and head down the street with Jason in the front seat.

That front seat was awesome. You could fit all four of us on it. Mom, daddy Steve, Jason and me; we all fit. It was a nice long bench seat.

Only a minute had passed and Steve was running back towards the house with Jason in his arms. No car.

I screamed for mom who was inside doing mom stuff and she came a runnin'.

"He fell out of the car!" daddy Steve was frantic. It was rare that I saw a man upset, well except for mad. Men don't get scared. They are men, they are strong, and they are in control. Daddy Steve was scared.

Little Jason was in his arms crying. They had only gone a few houses down and made the left turn and somehow Jason's door wasn't closed all the way or, as a 3-year-old, was playing with the handle and he fell out. The car did NOT, repeat, did not run him over. He just fell out and hit the pavement with his head.

Mom grabbed Jason and they disappeared into the house.

Moments later, daddy Steve came outside and told me to go inside. He went to the store.

I went inside and mom was tending to Jason who was shaken up, but not all that hurt. Mom was annoyed with him. Telling him how he's not supposed to play with the handle and this is what happens when you are bad. She was saying it with a tender voice, but was condescendingly blaming him for what happened. I bet now she regrets it, if she even remembers this happening.

Every time after that incident mom and daddy Steve made sure the door was closed, slamming it twice every time we got in, which wouldn't really make all that much of a difference if you didn't wear a seat belt, which we never did.

It was the late 70's and cars were not required to have seatbelts included and even if we did have them, well, we didn't use them. We would climb over the seats back and forth while driving 55 mph down the freeway and not a person would question it. The big campaign back in those days was washing your hands so you don't get hepatitis, making sure that you don't climb into cars with strangers, and not to litter or the Indian will cry.

So, even if the car door was slammed shut, twice, it didn't really save us because we never wore seat belts.

Mom was working nights at Holsum and they started around 5 or 6 in the evening. I couldn't tell time, but I knew when she put on her white pants that she was going to go to work and we would need to go to the babysitter. She would load us up in the car right after dinner and by the time it was dark we were at the babysitter's house. We always sat in the front with mom and I always made sure I sat next to her, to feel her play with my hair or hold my hand as we drove.

I asked her once "When do we go to the babysitter?"

She replied, "When the sun goes down."

So I would watch the days for the sun going down and it would get lower and lower in the sky and start to disappear behind the mountain and I could feel the anxiety grow in my belly about having to stay with the babysitter.

Mom, in all her glory of owning a nice car, now drove us to the babysitter in style. I hated that babysitter, she was mean. As an adult I understand now why she was so rigid. She must have been watching 20 or 30 kids all day long and most of the time she would just smack us around or scream at us. If you just stayed out of her way though, you could have a pretty good day there.

The I-17 was our major freeway back in the day. It ran all the way through town north to south, and it was the fastest way to get anywhere, including to the stupid meany babysitter.

As a kid going down this freeway, it always made me think about how fancy our town was. How the road with all the lights and onramps and off ramps leading up to the city level, it was futuristically fantastic. Because the freeway level was below street level, but open to the sky, as a young kid, not being able to see over the dashboard, you could look up through the window and see the city zooming by.

It was a Friday mid morning and we were driving down the freeway. It was really hot and Jason and I had our spots on the front seat next to mom. I was really confused because we were headed towards the babysitter, but the sun was high in the sky.

"Where are we going momma?" I asked.

"I have to get my paycheck at work." She said.

"Can we go in with you?" I was excited.

Holsum Bakery had wonderful smells and the bread was so yummy and everyone there was so nice to us when we got to go inside. They would give us "samples" of stuff like miniature pecan pies. Those didn't last long in our house. We would get a whole flat of them and they would be gone the first day.

Now this is not the traditional bakery setting. It's not like some little bakery where they make donuts and cakes.

This is a major manufacturing plant of bread and buns and it had tons and tons of conveyor belts and all kinds of machines that made all kinds of noise. It was like a Willy Wonka factory for bread, not candy.

"We'll see. I have to see who is managing." She replied.

We drove down the freeway in the heat of the day. I was excited at the possibility of going in and having all the people dote on us and give us smiles.

I could smell that we were getting close. The fresh-baked bread smell filled the air and my heart skipped a beat.

Mom took the off-ramp, going up the steep incline to get up to street level. It's an amazing hill going up; within a 1/4 mile you raise up 30 feet.

I was looking at mom when I felt a rush of air hit me from my right. I looked over to see an open car door, the street zooming by, and Jason missing from the seat next to me. The anxiety took over and I screamed. "MOM!"

Slow motion took over reality, almost to a stop.

I saw her look over and the moment she realized that Jason had slipped out of the car. I witnessed the contorted scream escaping her face.

I watched as the dashboard got closer to my face and felt the impact of my chin absorbing the radio dials. The screeching sound of the brakes was even slowed down, like putting a 45 rpm record on 33 by mistake, then everything slowed down even more.

I bounced off the dash as the car came to a stop. I was twisted on the floorboard hump thing that housed the drivetrain with its worn down carpet to the point of rubber. It was hot. I couldn't get my bearings straight and fumbled to right myself again.

I couldn't do it fast enough. I was moving through an air of molasses as I fought gravity. Mom was all of a sudden gone and the door was left ajar.

I forced myself up onto the seat. I got up on my knees and looked back through the rear window.

There she was, running down the off ramp at full speed. It was like watching a Roadrunner cartoon. Her legs were a blur.

I could see Jason way down at the bottom. He was so far away. My best friend was rolling down the ramp and mom was trying to catch up to him with her blurry legs. He was tumbling down the hill like we had done so many times before in the park when we would have log races down the big grassy hills. But this was no grassy hill. This was asphalt, hot from the summer sun and he wasn't tucking like he was trying to win a race. His arms were flailing around, making him leave pavement and bounce. But the force of the fall and the speed that he left the car launched him and he couldn't stop. It was going to have to just play itself out.

Mom ran. Jason rolled. Then the HONK! happened.

The off ramps on the I-17 are narrow, very narrow. They don't have emergency lanes, in fact I don't think they even invented emergency lanes until the 90's when the other freeways went in. The particular off ramp we were on had a sheer drop off on one side, down to the freeway level, and a wall of cement on the other side; a wall that led up to street level.

HONK!

A semi-truck had left the freeway and had gotten onto the ramp and was headed towards Jason and mom, who was still chasing after him.

HONK! HONK! Duh, Duh, Duh!! (Airbrakes full force were being utilized.)

Mom slowed down for a nanosecond. I know now, as an adult, it was because she contemplated her own life at that moment.

The truck was trying to slow down, but math would put that truck, when it stopped, running over Jason, running over mom, and slamming into the back of our car, probably forcing me out the windshield cause I wasn't wearing my seatbelt, still.

All of a sudden, mom found a new energy and she turned into a blur.

I screamed and cried from the front seat, witnessing the two closest people in my life about to die. And yes, it was like a fucking train wreck and I couldn't look away.

Then it almost seemed like I was getting close to them. I could see mom clearer, Jason rolling, the stupid big rig headed our way. That's when I realized the car was rolling backwards down the off ramp, chasing after mom.

In my mom's haste to save Jason, she didn't fully engage the parking gear. She had accidentally only put it in neutral. And now here I was rolling backwards down the freeway in the middle of the front seat of a big car that could easily crush my mom, Jason, and smash into that stupid truck that won't stop honking.

I flipped around and grabbed the gear shifter that stuck out of the column. I had seen her mess with this thing a hundred times, watched her feet as they danced across the pedals every time we drove anywhere. From my vantage point, it was really all I could see, well, except for the city zooming by when we were on the freeway.

I grabbed hold of that shifter and yanked on it. I didn't know that you were supposed to pull it forward before shifting, so I just forced it up and down, up and down, up and down, up and down. I screamed and cried the whole time, but the car was gaining speed. I could see the ground outside the open door starting to go by faster and faster. I was so scared.

The car was backing down the off ramp, mom was still running after Jason, Jason was still rolling, and the big ass rig was going to hit us all and pulverize us. Slow motion to a stop. I felt my heart stop and in that moment I saw my life change forever without them in it. Then I feared for my own life.

All of sudden everything turned into real time. Mom magically appeared at the door. She shoved Jason in at me, forcing me to sit by the open door that lost Jason in the first place. She slammed her door shut and we were going again. She was frantic. Jason was crying and I was screaming because I didn't want to sit next to the still open door. I didn't want to fall out. I screamed long and hard as she took off up the off ramp. The door closed part way when she gassed it, but it wasn't long before she slowed down for a stop sign and the door flew open again. I screamed.

"Rachel! Calm Down!" She yelled at me.

I scooched over and shared Jason's seat, holding, hugging him with all my might. We finally made it up to street level and she pulled over into a parking lot. I was crying and holding onto Jason as he was crying when mom got out of the car and went into a phone booth. We just sat there crying as we watched mom bawl her eyes out to Grandma on the phone. We could hear her screaming about how we almost just died.

A few minutes later she came back to the car, but on the passenger side this time. She pulled me over to the seat closest to the door and put my seatbelt on me. I was scared to death and I didn't want to sit there, but she made me and I obeyed. She slammed the door twice and reached through the window to lock it.

She walked around to the driver's side and climbed in. Reaching over to Jason she put him in his seatbelt, making sure to tighten it up. Then she reached over and shut her door and locked it before securing her own seatbelt. She started the car and we took off down the freeway, again.

"Where are we going, Mommy?" I asked.

"To Grandma's. Now just be quiet and sit there." She answered blankly.

I was scared and upset and Jason was hurt and scared and mom, well she was blank for a while. But it really didn't matter because going to Grandma's house was sure going to be a lot more fun than going to mom's work and I was okay with that.

Chapter 8

My brother Jason has always been my best friend. It was always me and him against the world. Everything we did together bonded us deeply. While growing up we had friends to play with and our own little individualities, but when it came down to it, I lived with my very best friend. We talked about everything and did everything with each other in mind.

I had a permanent live-in play buddy who liked everything I liked. As long as I had Jason, I always had something fun to do. Never a boring moment with him and our imaginations seemed to be in sync at all times. We always had fun. I feel sorry for only kids, they don't know the joy of having a built-in best friend to have adventures with and to even get into trouble with, which me and Jason did a lot of getting into trouble, but in the end we were the best of pals.

Mom had a standing rule of if one gets into trouble, we both get into trouble. It was really her way of getting us to tattle on each other, so that we would stay out of trouble, but it sort of backfired. We ended up being even closer to each other, kind of like a "I got your back" type of bond. And so when we did stuff that we knew would be bad, well, we just kind of knew that we would not tell on each other, because if I told that Jason, let's just say for instance, ate all the cheese in the fridge, which he actually did once, well I would get in trouble for not stopping him.

But there was one major drawback to this stupid little rule; Jason would hold stuff over my head and I would do the same to him, which in turn made us even closer. It was truly me and him against the world, the world of grownups. I would taunt him with stuff that he did from a year ago and he would counter-taunt with something I did, and then I would rebut with something else that he was ashamed of and he would come back with another, each time getting more and more extreme with the tattles. We would even start adding stuff that we didn't actually do just so that the consequence would make our blood run cold. It would get so bad that we knew if we ever did tell mom all that stuff, we would not only get beat, but we would never see the light of day again. So they were just taunts, trying to get control of each other, which is not uncommon between siblings, especially close ones like us.

When me and Jason would fight and taunt each other, we tried our hardest to keep it quiet from mom. We would whisper fight, but it would eventually get loud because the inflammatory lies we were threatening to tell and when mom would intervene on our fights they were ridiculous consequences, and what she didn't realize was that she was only pushing us closer together.

One day Jason and I were fighting about something and I guess we had been getting on each other's nerves quite a bit over some time because we erupted into punching each other. Mom caught wind of it and snatched us up and brought us into the dining room.

We didn't have a conventional dining room. It was occupied by an ugly little loveseat couch and little else. She got in our faces and yelled at us to hold hands. Then, while I was facing Jason, mom reached around to the back of our heads and bonked our foreheads together. Stars were seen. She went off on some tangent about how we should love each other and not fight and whatever mom's say when kids get to fighting with each other. Oh, and we had to continue to hold hands and not rub our owies. We were crying and staring at each other still holding hands. I watched the goose egg build in purple brilliance on his forehead and felt mine filling with blood.

When mom would finally stop lecturing us she would make us sit on that little couch in silence, holding hands. We would have to sit there for hours sometimes until we giggled or were friendly with each other and when she would witness that, then she would ask us if we were going to be nice to each other and of course we would say yes. Then we would have to kiss and hug, apologize, and make up. We would be friends again, until the next spat when it would start all over again.

When we moved into the patio home in Glendale with its fancy atriums and beautiful blue shag carpeting, me and Jason got even closer. And once Damien was born, our little family was complete. Mom and daddy Steve were going out more often and I became the big kid of the family, the responsible one. I was deemed babysitter and was put in charge of Jason and Damien. It didn't go over too well with Jason, but I really was kind of a brat with the control factor of being the one in charge. I would boss him around and he would resist, but for the most part it was fun being home alone with my brothers, even if Damien was just a baby in a crib and I wasn't allowed to take him out.

It was a regular thing for mom and daddy Steve to take off on Friday and Saturday nights and stay out to the wee hours of the morning and in the mornings, I was still in charge of making breakfast for me and Jason and bottles for Damien. Me and Jason would sit around and watch TV while mom and daddy Steve slept off the night before. There was really no difference in the mornings after nights out and when they were not truly in the house, except when they were physically home I was allowed to answer the phone. I wouldn't have to wait for the "secret ring".

Usually on Sunday mornings Grandma would call. She would ask me if we wanted to go to church and I would always say "Yes!" because church, when you're a kid, was fun. You had recess, snack time, singing, and you would always get to color or glitter something. I always wanted to go to church and was so happy when Grandma would ask us. The trick though was getting mom and daddy Steve to take us. That would require a lot of courage to go into the room and wake them up.

Grandma always told me, "It's okay Rachel, just go wake them up and tell them that Grandma said so." She would pep-talk me up to do it. She would tell me that she was my mom's mom and she was the boss and that mom wouldn't get mad. I believed her. The hierarchy in the family was strong. Everyone always did what Grandma said.

So one Sunday morning when she called and asked, I put phone down and walked into the dark room where mom and daddy Steve slept nude. I stood next to mom and watched her passed out on the bed, contemplating if I really wanted to do this. Grandma's words echoed through my head as I watched mom lying there on her stomach with her head turned to the side. She had a kind, gentle look that gave me the umph to go ahead and wake her up. I laid my hand on her shoulder and gave a gentle shove, "Mom?" whispering.

"Mom? Are you awake?" This is always a stupid question. When you can clearly see someone sleeping, why ask if they are awake? I don't know why people do this, even now, as an adult, I experience this in my own life when I'm being awakened. It's silly.

"Mom? Grandma's on the phone." I said a little bit louder, trying not to wake daddy Steve.

She opened her eyes immediately when she heard me say Grandma. It was like a shot of adrenaline.

"What? Grandma? Phone? Now?" she said.

"Grandma's on the phone, mom. She wants to know if we are going to church today?"

Her face changed from the peaceful dreamy state to the scared, in-trouble look of a child.

"Grandma's on the phone right now?"

"Yes, she wants to know if we are going to church."

She hopped up out of bed and stumbled out of the room, down the hallway, into the living room with me following her every step of the way.

In the living room she plopped down on the floor, gave a great big cough and picked up the receiver. While talking to Grandma I was getting daggers thrown at me. My blood ran cold. She was mad. I knew I was going to get it, but I really didn't care because we were going to church today. I would get hugs today. I would get to see Grandma today! I was excited, but scared at the same time.

When she finally hung up the phone, she started screaming and running around trying to get everyone ready. We were going to be late. You don't want to be late for church, at least as a grownup. I can't imagine being that one person who walks in after the sermon has started, when everyone is quiet and then the big doors open and you have to walk down to where Grandma has saved you a seat right up in the first few pews, in front of everyone.

As a kid it was easy. It was like being dropped off at daycare. You walk in, they hand you some crayons and a tambourine and you just jump in with everyone else.

But as a grownup, that must have been humiliating, hence the screaming and running around in the house to get ready and get going STAT. The anxiety was thick and it affected all of us. You couldn't escape it and if you didn't have the same level of anxiety and start rushing as hard and as fast as mom, well then you were going to get smacked. It just made her angry. So you fill up with fear and anxiety with either going to be late or with getting smacked for not hurrying enough. As an adult, I do this, sans the smacking. I get angry if I'm in a hurry and everyone around me is lackadaisical or lollygagging, as my Grandma would say. I hate that I have this trait.

Back to the nights out – Mom and daddy Steve started going out with their friends independently of each other and would stay out until the wee early morning hours. There were several times I would wake up because Damien was crying and half-sleepy walk down the hallway into the kitchen to make him a bottle and when passing mom's room I would peek in and see no one in bed, knowing automatically they were still out.

One morning I woke to Damien screaming his little head off. I opened my eyes, but didn't shift in bed to make eye contact with him. See, if you made eye contact or any sort of connection he would scream harder until he got what he wanted. So I laid there motionless, eyes open, realizing the sun had popped up and no one was coming to get him. Not a sound in the whole house, except Damien crying, the "I'm hungry, feed me now" cry. Usually, if I laid there long enough, mom would eventually make her way in and give him a bottle and I could sneak out of the room to go watch some TV, but there was no sound coming from the kitchen; she wasn't making him a bottle.

I got scared. I rolled over, he saw me look at him, and he screamed harder. I got up and went down the hall and peeked in their room. The waterbed was empty, not of water, but of parents. I glanced in the living room, no one there and the kitchen was void of parents too. I got real scared. It was morning and we had no parents at all. No mom. No daddy Steve. I was only 6, but I knew that they didn't have to go to work, it was Saturday. So they weren't at work and they weren't at home. The phone started ringing.

I ran past our bedroom where Damien was still crying his hungry cry and dashed into the living room. I stopped short of banging my knees into the coffee table, positioned my hand over the telephone receiver, waiting, holding my breath for the signal, the "secret ring" to happen so I can answer it and find out where my mom was. One ring, two rings, three rings…Dang it! Not the secret ring. I pulled my hand back like it was on fire. I wasn't allowed to answer it. There were no parents home. But what if it was Grandma? Nope. No parents, no answering the phone or door at all, unless I wanted a spanking, and I really didn't want a spanking.

The phone finally stopped ringing and I walked back into the kitchen and put the pot to boil some water for his bottle. Jason came in and asked "Where's mom? Where's daddy Steve?"

"I don't know." I replied dropping the bottle in the bubbly water being careful not to splash it. I did that once, only once, splashed boiling water when I dropped it in and I was so scared that I would get in trouble for messing up and getting hurt that I hid the blisters from mom until they went away.

Jason made his cereal and sat down to eat. I tested the bottle and it was perfect. I went back to our room and climbed into the crib with Damien to feed him. Just in case mom came home, I figured we would just follow the standard operating procedure of making sure Damien is taken care of and Jason didn't burn the house down. Like I said before, he wouldn't actually burn the house down, but he would do something stupid like cut his finger off, so I was in charge of that.

I fed Damien, changed his diaper right there in the crib, because I wasn't allowed to take him out. I was lying down with him in the crib when the phone started to ring again. I jumped out and ran down the hall. Jason beat me to the phone. His hand was hovering over the receiver when I got to the living room.

"Move!" I yelled at him.

"No!" he yelled back.

I pushed him out of the way and he shoved me back. It didn't matter though because the phone was still ringing. It wasn't the "secret ring", so we both backed off. It kept ringing. Damien started crying, again.

I ran into the bedroom and he was laying there bawling. I crawled into the crib again with him and held him close. He quieted down the second he was in my arms. I could hear the TV in the living room switch on after the phone stopped ringing and I knew Jason was watching our cartoons. I could hear him giggling off and on as I sat there holding my baby brother. I wished and wished for him to just go to sleep so I could go watch cartoons. Then my mind went wandering, wondering where mom and daddy Steve were.

After a while Damien finally settled into a slumber and I laid him down carefully, trying hard not to jostle him awake. I slowly, stealthily, climbed out of the crib and just as my feet hit the ground the stupid phone started ringing again. I jumped and ran, knocking into the crib with my knee, bumping it enough to hit it against the wall. I never looked back. I needed to get to the phone.

I rounded the corner, knowing that Jason had already beaten me to the phone and there he was on the second ring with his hand again hovering over the receiver. Then the third ring happened and he pulled his hand away and before the fourth ring could start he was on the floor watching cartoons.

I snuck back into the room and peeked at Damien, fast asleep, whew! Relief.

I flopped down on the carpet next to Jason, 3 feet from the big console TV that was blaring Saturday morning cartoons. Surely mom had to be home soon. They had never left us alone all night long before and they just had to come home soon.

The morning came and went. On Saturday mornings you knew it was time to go play outside when Pets on Parade came on the TV. It meant that errands and chores were done and kids were gathering outside to play and the knocks on the door would happen soon. "Can Jason come out to play? Can Rachel come out to play?" were common at our front door.

When Pets on Parade's theme music started, I got scared. Mom and daddy Steve still hadn't come home. Damien was hungry again and crying his little 6-month-old head off. So I went to the kitchen and made him a bottle. I realized I was starving and then Jason came into the kitchen looking for something to eat. Jason wasn't allowed to handle the butter knife to make lunch. I was the one in charge and I was the only one allowed to touch the knife to make PB&J for us. Even at the tender age of 6, I can remember it clearly, I was a multitasker. Not quite the master I am now, but I sure as hell knew what steps to take to be the most efficient at what I was doing way back then. As the bottle was heating up, I rushed and made us some sandwiches with Damien screaming from his crib the whole time. My heart raced (is racing now) at the tasks at hand. It was like I couldn't move fast enough to get everything done, but I did it.

I took my pathetic 6-year-old-made PB&J that had entirely too much PB and not enough J and Damien's little bottle and climbed into his crib. I set my sandwich down and picked him up to cradle him as he ate. He smelled so horrible, he pooped and it was squishy in my arms: A blowout, poop all up his back.

I had handled poopy diapers before; it was really not that bad, just the smell gagged me. This time though, it would require tons and tons of clean up. Back in those days there were no wipes. Nope, no wipes, or alternatively, if there where wipes, well, we just didn't have them. We had washrags, wet, warm washrags. I screamed for Jason. He came running in and I told him to get me a rag, he complied running out of the room.

I laid Damien down and undid his little onesy to find the poop had squished out of his leg holes too. This is the moment, this moment right here, that makes me lay down a towel or a sheet or any item, Fuck a tee shirt even, when I change diapers now. Well, the poop got on the sheets as I pulled off his onesy. And as I pulled it up over his head, shit got in his hair. It was on my hands and arms as I clumsily manipulated him without breaking his neck. It was all over his legs, ass, back, back of neck, and smeared into his hair. I held out the onesy as Jason came back into the room with the single little washrag. He did not want to take it out of my hand, but I was in charge and I yelled at him to take it and get me another rag. He reluctantly complied.

I wiped Damien, trying to get it all, but the rag was just smearing it. What he really needed was a bath and I couldn't do that. It was against the rules. I was only allowed to get in the crib with Damien, not bring him out of the crib under any circumstances; well, if the house caught fire, I would have, but otherwise he was supposed to stay in the crib unless a grownup got him out. I was in charge, but I wasn't in charge. It was a conundrum.

Jason came back into the room with another rag and after a little debate, we traded rags. I asked for another one. He left the room. I went back to wipe/smearing the poop. I really should have just given him the bath, but who knew when the parents would be back and if they caught me giving him a bath I would have been murdered. Okay, not murdered, but to a 6-year-old when you are getting a spanking with a belt, well, you feel like you are being murdered.

I wiped and smeared, wiped and smeared, exchanged rags with Jason 5 more times before the mess was finally managed. Damien cried the whole time. He was just hungry, but I had to take care of the shit first. And once that was clean, Damien diapered, and dressed in a new onesy, I realized what a huge mess I made out of the sheet.

The sheets were a horrible mess by the end of it. They had to be changed, but I couldn't take Damien out of the crib. So, yes, I climbed out of the crib and found where the sheets were and picked one out. I climbed back in and had Jason hold the clean sheet and my sandwich. I moved Damien over to a clean end of the crib and pulled the sheet up from the dirty end. Then I struggled, wrestled, fought with all my might to lift the mattress up just enough to squish my hand down and fit the corner of the clean sheet on, then the other corner on the de-sheeted side of the bed. I pulled that sheet over as I scooched the dirty sheet down towards the end where Damien was laying. I moved him over on top of the new clean sheet and turned and tackled the rest.

Finally, after all that I sat down and fed my baby brother in my arms. I was starving, and I was dirty. I sat there feeding him realizing that I had poop on my fingers. I couldn't put him down now. Poor little guy just wanted to eat and be clean...well, so did I, but he was helpless and I was in charge.

After settling Damien down, washing up myself, I had lost my appetite. I was worried. It was getting into the afternoon and the phone was ringing off and on, but we couldn't answer it.

I sat down on the couch under the big front window. The sun was past its apex and was on its way down now, still high in the sky, but on its end of the day journey. Every car that passed shined a glimmer of light through the curtains across the ceiling and would get lost in the atrium across the room from me. The sparkle would shine a little spark of hope that it was mom coming home, pulling into the driveway. I would jump up and peek out the crack of the curtains only to be dashed when I saw a car drive by. No mom. No daddy Steve. We watched TV for hours. We talked about what could be happening. Then the phone would ring again and we would jump up and hover over it, hoping it would be them with the "secret ring" and each time that whole day it wasn't them. They never called. They didn't come home.

The sun went down and my heart raced. I debated if I should call Grandma. Mom would be super pissed at me if I did. Grandma wasn't supposed to know that we were at home alone. No one was supposed to know that we were at home alone. We were threatened that we would have to go live with witches and evil people if we told any single soul that we were ever at home alone, so I struggled with the decision to call. Grandma would feed us dinner and hug us and find mom, but as soon as I was alone again with mom, well I would be, in a sense, murdered. I didn't call, but I stared at the little card with the phone numbers for emergencies on for a very long time. It was a little card that sat in a little plastic case that was attached to the bottom of the phone. It could slide in and out, like a magical little hiding place, a secret compartment. It had numbers for police, fire department, poison control, and a little spot at the bottom that was designated for personal numbers, like for Grandma. I would slide it out and stare at it and Jason would egg me on to call her and I would dismiss him and slide it back into its hiding place only to slide it back out again a few minutes later to stare at it.

It was Saturday night and no mom and no daddy Steve. Damien was sad and Jason was hungry. I made some more PB&J's and climbed into the crib with Damien. I could hear the TV in the next room. After a whole day of worrying and wondering and watching really bad Saturday movie TV, I was ready to sit down and watch Dukes of Hazard, my favorite show at the time. I laid down with Damien and played with his hands and hair, realizing I still needed to wash him more. We both fell asleep.

I woke up a few hours later and climbed out of the crib. It was pitch black in the room and I could see a dull glow coming from the hallway. Jason wasn't in bed. I went to the living room where Jason was passed out on the floor in front of the TV, which was now showing static. I had no idea what time it was. Then it hit me, maybe mom is home. I went to her room, she wasn't there. I was scared. It was dark and I didn't know where she and daddy Steve were.

I got Jason to bed and checked on Damien. I went back to the living room and sat on the couch, slightly opening the curtains, hoping mom wouldn't notice that I did that after she came home. I sat there and watched the street for the longest time. Every now and then a car would pass by, but never our car with our mom and our daddy Steve. I was so scared. I was so worried that they would never come home. I didn't know what to do. I looked at the phone, reached over, and pulled out the secret plastic card holder. I decided it was time to call Grandma.

Just as I reached for the receiver the phone rang. It was deafening. I never realized how loud it really was until just that moment. I yanked my hand back. One ring, two rings, three rings. Dang it! Not them.

After about 20 rings it stopped. It rang a lot longer that time. After about a minute of silence the phone rang again. One ring, two rings, three rings. Dang it! Who is trying to call? It rang and rang and it wouldn't stop. Damien woke up and started crying. The phone finally stopped again.

I went to Damien and he was still screaming. I checked his diaper and he had pooped again. No blowout this time though. In the middle of changing him the phone started to ring again. I was in the middle of changing Damien's diaper so I didn't run for it this time. It was just that person who keeps calling and they don't know the "secret ring" so I wasn't going to answer it anyway. Sure enough it rang 15 times that time. I counted.

I went to the kitchen and started the water for the bottle. The phone started to ring, again. My mind went crazy trying to figure out who could be calling that late. Grandma? No, grandmas go to sleep early. It couldn't have been mom or daddy Steve, they knew the "secret ring". Who was it? I let it ring through. 14 times this time.

I climbed in the crib with Damien and took him into my arms again and fed him. The phone rang two more times when I was feeding him; first time rang 14 times, second time rang 18 times. Somebody wouldn't stop calling.

Where was mom? Where was daddy Steve? I should call Grandma. I will call Grandma as soon as Damien is done eating. I thought this through. I had made the determination that it was officially an emergency and hopefully mom would see it through my eyes and understand why I had to call Grandma.

I got Damien settled down again, though not sleeping, he was quiet and sated. I climbed out of the crib and went to the phone in the living room. As I crossed the floor, on my way, with determination in my heart to call Grandma, the fucking phone started to ring, *again*. I stopped, waited for it, hoping as hard as I could that it would stop ringing after the second ring. I wanted it so badly for it to be the secret ring. It wasn't. I broke down and started crying. I lost count on the rings, but it didn't matter, it wasn't them. I sat right down where I had stopped and bawled. I felt so lonely and lost.

Immediately the phone started ringing again after it had stopped. Sparkle of hope came over me. Wait, I didn't count them. Crap! It was too many though. It wasn't two and then a pause. Dang it! Are they trying to call?

I ran to the phone and positioned myself over it like I had been doing all day long. It rang through, one, two, three, four, etcetera. Dang it! I must've missed it. Silence.

Immediate ring, this is some sort of code. What was going on? I picked up the receiver, brought it to my ear, and spoke, "Hello?"

A man's voice came through and it chilled me as I listened "This is officer so and so, can I speak with Sharon?" My knees went weak, my brain swelled in my skull, my vision went to tunnels and everything around me started to spin. I slammed the phone down and ran for Jason. I was in deep shit now.

I didn't even make it all the way to the bedroom when the phone started to ring. I woke up Jason and scream-cried at him the whole situation.

"Jason! The cops are on the phone! I answered the phone and it was the cops! They are calling again! Jason! Wake up! The cops are on the phone!"

Poor Jason, half-asleep Jason, didn't quite understand what I was saying as I ran from the room yelling, running to the phone again. I stood over the phone as it stopped ringing. Immediately it rang again; one ring, two rings, silence. Instinctively my muscle memory took over as my hand went into position over the receiver during the pause of the "secret ring". In an instance I knew it was a parent calling, the phone rang, I picked it up.

"Hello?" I said through stifling sniffles and tears.

"This is officer so and so, I have Steve here. I need to speak with Sharon." He said in that same tone as before. Crap! I slammed the receiver down again. Dang it! Did he say he had Steve? I didn't really hear all of it past the "officer so and so", my mind went spinning with the room.

The phone started to ring again. Two and then a pause. Should I answer it? How did the cops know our "secret ring"? Was daddy Steve in trouble? Oh my God! We were all going to jail. We weren't supposed to be home alone. After the pause it rang, I picked it up, again.

"Hello?" I was frozen with fear. My blood ran cold.

"Rachel! Don't hang up the phone!" A familiar voice yelled at me. It was daddy Steve. Warm relief ran over me.

"Daddy! I'm so sorry I answered the phone! I didn't mean to, I promise I didn't mean to. I am so sorry, I'm sorry daddy!" I pleaded for my life. He was going to find out that the cops called and I wanted to make sure I was in the clear.

His voice changed, it was the officer again, "Rachel, I have your daddy here. I need you to put your mom on the phone."

Was it a trick? I asked, "Is daddy Steve okay? Is he in jail? Am I in trouble for answering the phone?"

He must have realized I was a youngster because his tone changed right there, he was like a teacher, speaking kindly and firmly to me, "I need to speak with your mommy. Is she there?"

I wasn't supposed to be at home alone, not at all, so I immediately lied, "She's sleeping. She can't come to the phone right now." My mind was racing. I was lying to the police. I was for sure going to jail.

"Well, I need you to go and wake her up. This is very important. It is an emergency." He instructed me.

"I'm not supposed to wake her up when she is sleeping. She will get mad at me." I lied some more, digging my own grave.

"She won't get mad. Tell her the police are on the phone and that Steve needs her help." He said.

"Okay, hold on." I put the receiver down on the table and turned to see Jason standing there with the look of death on his face. He knew I was busted. He didn't even say anything to me, he just stood there. I walked past him and went to my parents' bedroom and pretended to wake her up. I only did this because I knew it would take time to do it and I wanted to make sure that if he could hear me, then he would hear me mock-waking my mom. "Mom, wake up! Mom, wake up! The police are on the phone. Mom?! Mom, please wake up!" After a few times of doing this I walked back out and picked up the receiver.

"She won't wake up. She is snoring really loud and she won't wake up." I lied some more

"Rachel, listen very carefully, You Have to Wake Her Up, Right Now." His tone changed to mean. I started to cry, again.

"She won't wake up, I promise. She is sleeping and she won't wake up." I bawled.

"You have to try again or we will send an officer over there to wake her up." He said and I just about fainted at the thought of the police showing up. In a millisecond my mind raced at thoughts of them breaking down the door to the house, flashlights and firearms pointing at us, finding us alone in the house. Them swooping us up in their arms like bags of potatoes to take us away from the only life we had ever known. I broke down and started crying really hard right then and there.   And the officer instinctively understood what was going on. Smart man.

"Your mom isn't home, is she?"   He asked sympathetically.

"No." I honestly answered, defeated.

I could hear him speak to Steve with a muffled hand over the receiver voice, then daddy got on the phone again.

"Rachel, where's mom?" familiar voice again, but he was angry.

"Daddy Steve! I don't know. She didn't come home today." I told him with crackles of sobs in my voice.

"Calm down, it's okay, just calm down." He turned his voice over to the other spectrum for me.

"I'm so sorry daddy. I'm so sorry I answered the phone. I'm sorry." It was all I could say.

"It's okay, Rachel, it's okay, I'm not mad. Did your mom call? When did you see her?" he quizzed.

"You're not mad, really?" I asked, trying to save my own ass.

"No, I'm not mad. I'm just worried. Where is your mom? Did she call? When was the last time you saw her?" He had a little quiver to his voice now.

I got worried for her now, "I saw her when you guys left last night. She didn't call us today."

"You mean, you haven't seen her since Friday night? Today is Sunday Rachel. You haven't seen mom since Friday night!?" He was bouncing all over the emotions spectrum now and it was really freaking me out.

I broke down and sobbed, coming clean like I had done something really wrong because mom didn't come home, "No daddy! She didn't come home. I didn't see her since I saw you." Unbeknownst to me it had turned into Sunday morning and my parents had been missing for two nights and one whole day.

"Shit!" he yelled on the phone. I felt like just that, shit. "Okay, well I need you to help me. I don't have much time, so I need you to help fast okay, can you do that for me, move fast and help me?" He was almost begging.

"Yes daddy, yes." I knew that if I was a good little helper it would work in my favor when I got punished for breaking the rule and answering the phone.

"Go to my dresser and on top of it is a book that has phone numbers in it. Go get it and find Aunt Janelle's phone number and call her. Tell her daddy is in jail........." *jail* that's what I heard. Blah, blah, blah, *jail*. He could have said unicorns, Disneyland, cotton candy, free money, jail, and I would have heard blah, blah, blah, blah, *jail.* I cried harder.

"You're in JAIL!?"

"Rachel! Calm down. It's going to be okay; really it's going to be okay! I need you to calm down and I really need you to call Aunt Janelle. Can you do that for me? Please Rachel, Call her for me..." then the automated woman's voice popped on and said "Please deposit 15 cents for the next 3 minutes."

Through her voice daddy Steve was screaming "Rachel Call Janelle Right Now!" click.

"Daddy!? Daddy?! Hello?!!" I was devastated.

I turned and Jason was still standing there at the threshold to the living room. I ran past him, down the hall, into their room. I grabbed the book with phone numbers in it and ran back to the phone in the living room. I opened the book and then it hit me. I didn't know how to look up numbers in alphabetical order. It wasn't hard to figure out, but I didn't know how to spell Aunt Janelle.

"How do you spell Aunt Janelle?" I asked Jason.

He came over to me and tried to take the book out of my hands, but I was still in charge, so I kept a firm hold on it and said "Just tell me how to spell it".

"I don't know." He replied.

I flipped through the pages, trying to grasp an idea of how to figure out this book with the letters running down the side. Well, I thought to myself, Aunt; a-n-t. I went for the A's. I read each one, no Aunt Janelle. Okay, Janelle; g-a-n-e-l. I went for the G's. I read them all.

The sun was up now and I could hear Damien making his little baby noises. It wasn't going to be too long before he was going to need a bottle again.

I failed at finding the number in the conventional way, but I wasn't giving up yet. Daddy Steve needed my help and I wasn't going to let him down. So I surrendered and started reading each name, starting in the A's and I kept on reading, which wasn't easy because I wasn't a strong reader.

Damien started crying. I knew he was going to need his diaper changed and a bottle or he was going to throw himself into a fit real soon. I kept on reading.

Finally, I got to the J's and after struggling to sound out her name I realized who it was. Aunt Janelle, but it wasn't in the A's or G's, what a stupid way to spell her name, I thought. Damien was in a fit now, but I ignored it and called Aunt Janelle.

It was early Sunday morning, very early and she was a lot like my parents; a partier. I let her phone ring and ring and ring, but to no avail.

Damien was flipping out. I somehow turned on my delegation skills and drowned out my own fear. I instructed Jason to start dialing, let it ring 10 times, hang up and call again and I ran to the kitchen for a bottle for Damien.

I started the water in the pot and went to the cupboard for a bottle, but there were none. Had we really gone through all the clean bottles? Yup. I had to wash out a bottle and I was running on pure adrenaline at this point. Damien needed a diaper and a bottle, Jason was calling Aunt Janelle, but didn't have a clue on what to say to her if she did pick up, and I needed to wash a bottle before I could get to Damien and back to the phone, daddy Steve was in jail and was relying on me, and mom, well mom was still lost. My anxiety took over and at the age of six I would suspect most kids would just kind of lose it and shut down, but for some reason I pushed myself harder and multitasked the fuck out of myself.

I ran to the room grabbed a dirty bottle, ran back to the kitchen and washed, prepared it, and threw it into the pot, again being careful enough not to splash that boiling hot water on myself.

I ran back to the room and changed Damien's diaper all the while yelling at Jason.

"Are you still calling?!"

"Yes, but she's still not answering!" he yelped back at me, scared.

I got the bottle and went to the room where Damien was screaming with hunger.

"Rachel!!!!   Aunt Janelle is on the phone!!!" He screamed at me.

I ran into the living room and handed off the bottle to him, took the receiver, and told him "Go feed Damien!"

"I'm not allowed in the crib, mom Says!" he argued.

I felt my feathers fluff up, "Go do it anyway!" I demanded. He complied.

"Aunt Janelle?" I started to cry all over again. "Aunt Janelle? Daddy's in trouble."

"What? Who is this? Rachel?" she was confused, still half-sleeping.

"Yes, it's me, Rachel. Daddy is in trouble and he said to call you. He needs help." I broke down at her.

"What happened? Where are you? Where is Steve?" She asked frantically, waking up and realizing what's going on.

"The cops called and I answered the phone and I wasn't supposed to and daddy is in jail and mommy hasn't been home since Friday! Please help!" I was losing it.

"WHAT?!?!? Where is your mom??? What Jail is he at? Are you okay? Where are your brothers? Tell me what happened!" She was screaming at me, mad, but not at me. Mad at the grownups, I could tell.

I recounted the last couple of days, what we ate, how I took care of Damien and Jason, how I almost called Grandma a couple of times. I told her everything up until I got her on the phone. She was pissed, but again, not at me, at the grownups. She told me that everything was going to be okay and that she would be over after she helped out daddy Steve. I was relieved; I wasn't going to be in charge anymore. I hung up the phone and went to finish up with Damien's feeding.

I told Jason everything I told Aunt Janelle and everything she told me. I could see a glimpse of relief in his eyes. I hadn't even thought up until that moment that this had at all affected him. I felt like it was all on my shoulders.

Damien was about done with his bottle when we heard the front door open and slam shut. I thought to myself, that was fast. Aunt Janelle must live close. But it wasn't Aunt Janelle, it was mom. She was home.

She came into the bedroom where we were and saw me feeding Damien.

"Where's Steve?!" she asked. She was mad.

"Mom! Daddy is in jail!" I started to bawl. I was going to be in trouble. She wasn't going to listen to the whole story, she was going to be mad the second I told her that I answered the phone and it was the cops.

Fear washed over her already hung-over pale face.

"What?!?!" She was freaking out.

I, once again, went through the story, except revising it to add the Aunt Janelle part of the story. I watched as I told what had happened over the last couple of days, the look on mom's face contorting and flushes of red coming and going out of her cheeks as she bit her tongue keeping it from lashing out in anger at me for breaking all kinds of rules while she was not here. I got through the whole story, the whole thing with minimal questions and accusations of wrongness put on me.

I climbed out of the crib and mom went for the phone. She made some calls, took a shower, and laid down on the couch with Damien and we all watched TV. I didn't get in trouble at all. She didn't yell at me, except to never, ever, ever, ever, ever answer the phone unless it is the secret code and I was never, ever, ever, ever to tell anyone that we were left alone in the house for 2 days without grownups.

Later that evening daddy Steve came home and he wasn't mad either. He reiterated everything that mom said just to make sure that we were all clear and on the same page.

To this day I leave the ringer on my phone turned off. I only listen to messages because I don't like the fear and anxiety that rushes through my blood when I hear a phone ring.

Chapter 9

Mom and daddy Steve hated each other after a while. You could feel it every day, all day long. The second they would come into the same room together the tension in the air was turbulent. I loved my mom and loved daddy Steve, it was confusing. They pretended to be nice, but the snips at each other made it really hard to figure out who was wrong. They hated each other, but they still loved us. The hugs and kisses didn't stop for us, but they stopped for them. Mom would leave without saying where she was going and then as soon as she would come home there would be harsh words and then he would leave.

I loved my little life in the patio home with my brothers and Friday night pizza and our friends down the street. I loved going to church on Sundays and camping and surprise trips to the roller-skating rink. I loved the way daddy Steve would play his guitar and have us kids gather around and sing along. I didn't want it to change.

We didn't belong to daddy Steve, mom would tell us that only Damien belonged to him and that we shouldn't forget our daddy. At that time I didn't really even remember him or know him. I had a few memories of my daddy, but not many, and definitely not a lot of fun ones. And now as an adult I remember even fewer fun ones, not because they have disappeared from my memory, more like they changed from fun or happy memories to "messed up, that's not right" memories. We realize so much as adults, things that we had experienced as children, just isn't something that we would want for our own children to experience.

When I lived with my daddy and mom and Jason, we lived in a little house in South Phoenix. It wasn't very nice, but it was ours. Mom worked at Holsum and I'm not sure where daddy worked, but he was gone a lot too. It turned out he spent a lot of time in jail. Mom worked and daddy was in jail; that was just what life was. But when he was out, he lived with us for a while; back and forth he would go to jail. When he was with us, we spent a lot of time visiting family, and it seemed like every time we left the house he would forget the house key to get back in.

There were at least a half a dozen times that mom would wake me up in the back seat of the car and get me to walk across the lawn (mostly dirt) in my bare feet to the front bedroom window, my window. There would be 2 or 3 people standing around talking and debating on how to get the window open. Then after a few minutes of standing there in the middle of the night, half asleep, my daddy would take a rock and just break the glass. Mom would tell me to watch out for the glass as my daddy would pick me up and set me inside the window and tell me to go open the front door, which I did. Now, as a child of 3 years, this was exciting to me. The grownups needed me to do something for them. They relied on me to get them into the house and to any kid, anywhere in the whole world, when a grownup you love needs you and you are able to give them what they need, it's an amazing feeling inside. I had the power in my little tiny hands to turn that knob and let them all in.

After they would all come in, I was put to bed and the door was locked, from the outside. They would stay up all hours and the music was loud. I couldn't sleep on nights like that and the nights continued like that for years to come.

As a child, this simple act of climbing through the window with bare feet, watching out for glass, maneuvering through the dark house, and finally letting the grownups in was an adventure. It was an act of love. It was important and fun. As an adult, I realize this was messed up and wrong. Why couldn't they just climb through the window themselves? Why didn't they put my shoes on? Why can't daddy just remember his stupid key? I don't know those answers, I just know now that I wouldn't put my kids through that.

When daddy would go to jail, which was frequent, and it was just the three of us, we would spend a lot of our time with "friends", guy friends.

Mom frequently dated other guys and they would stay the night a lot at our house. I was only 3, but for some reason when I saw her disappear into her room with a man I felt guilty. Like something really bad was going on and she was being mean to my daddy. Oftentimes mom would lock us in our rooms and I hated that. It wasn't fair.

She had ingeniously put a hook and loop-style lock on the door and doorframe to keep us in our rooms. I kind of understand why. Back then there were no tension-style baby gates, and if there were, she couldn't afford them anyway. It was the 70's and mom was working nights and needed to get her sleep during the day, so she put locks on the doors.

Me and Jason did get into a lot of stuff, mostly food in the pantry or fridge, like cereal, and we would eat all of it or make a huge mess all while she was sleeping, hence the locks on the doors. I hated those stupid locks so much. She used them too often.

I would wake up in the morning with a full bladder and I wasn't wearing diapers anymore. I banged and banged on my side of the door, trying to get her to wake up to let me out. I could sort of open my door, not much, just a crack. It gave me a view of Jason's door at the end of the hall, but I couldn't see mom's door across from me because of the angle of my door. The lock had some give, but not enough for even a 3-year-old's finger to squeeze through.

I remember clearly how my abdomen would ache and burn as I squished my face up to the crack. I just wanted to go to the bathroom and release. I would scream "MOM! I have to go, I have to go now! Mom!!!??" I would scream and start to cry thinking that she wasn't home, thinking that I would have to hold it all day. Banging on the door and screaming would go on and on and the panic in my brain and the anxiety in my heart and the pain in my gut would build and build until I would hear her yell from her room "Rachel! Go Back To Bed!"

"But Mom! I have to go potty! Please, Mom?! I have to pee!"

I could hear her slam her door open. She was mad. I had to pee and now she was mad at me. It was like a trigger being pulled in my belly. As soon as I heard that door slam open, the floodgates would start to open, not all at once, but just a trickle. I panicked, throwing my hand down between my legs, hoping to hold it in just a little bit longer. I could hear her fumbling with the lock, but my door was sort of open and it wasn't giving for her. The warm wetness started to filter through my panties and nightgown. She slammed my door shut cursing at it. I squeezed my legs harder together, smashing my hand as the urine started to seep down my legs. She was going to be mad at me if she saw the mess I was making.

The door was opened and I made a break for it. In the bathroom, sweet release. The force of the stream made such sweet music as I could feel the level of piss deflate my bladder. When I was done, it was back to the bedroom where she had put an old Folgers coffee can and she told me to use that from now on. I'm not supposed to wake her up. She has to get her sleep. She closed my door and locked it and went back to bed. I went to the coffee can and picked it up, examined it, and played with it until I had to pee again, then it wasn't a play thing anymore. It was gross.

The locks on our doors didn't really keep me and Jason apart. I could crack mine open and he could crack his open even more than mine and we would talk to each other through the cracks.

The way our doors were situated in the hall I couldn't see him, but he could put his fingers through and wiggle them at me. We would talk and giggle and be little kids, just with doors separating us. Then one day he got his common sense.

We were talking like usual through our cracks and I heard a noise from his room. It was a loud scraping on the wall noise. He was only 2-1/2 and very mischievous. I pushed my face harder into the crack to try and see into his room through his crack in the door. I could hear him and then I could see way up high by the lock something poking through the crack. It was a wire hanger. He was sliding it up and down, just short of hitting the lock. I told him to go higher, but he couldn't reach it. The hanger disappeared for a minute and my heart raced. It came back into view, only higher this time, just below the lock. Jason rammed the hanger up and down, up and down, but the lock wouldn't budge. We worked as a team; I had the view, he had the tool. We finally figured out that the door needed to be closed a little bit and sure enough, as soon as he did that, the hook lifted easily out of the loop without resistance.

He was free. He ran over to my door but he was too short to reach the lock from that side. He had been able to reach his lock by climbing on top of some stacked books on top of his dresser. But this was the hallway and there were no dressers in the hallway. He disappeared from sight of my cracked door and I could hear him in the kitchen. He was messing with a chair. How he got that chair down the hallway on shag carpet still eludes me, but he did it. He was still too short to reach the lock though. So we managed to figure out to get the telephone books. We knew that would work, it was how we sat at the table for meals. We didn't have the conventional high chairs, we used telephone books on chairs, and we did it again for him to reach the lock.

I shut the door, he set me free. Mom was passed out in bed, didn't wake up from all the commotion, which was amazing because we weren't trying to be quiet, we were just trying to escape, but there she was in her bed, nude, passed out snoring.

We went to the kitchen and raided the fridge and pantry. We got out the Lucky Charms and dumped the entire box onto the floor and proceeded to eat all the "charms", which would later be a big mistake.

We were too little to turn on the TV so we just played. Then out of nowhere Jason was standing on the counter on top of the telephone books next to the back door. He got it open and we had a whole new world to play in. The backyard was fun! Well, actually the hose was fun. We played in that hose most of the day, running in and out of the house muddy and wet, eating what we wanted, dragging whatever toys we wanted outside, just good old fun was had, that is until she woke up. Then it was on; we were busted. We got beat. Not just the conventional spanking, she hit us with a belt all over our bodies. We never left our rooms like that again.

After a while daddy just didn't come home anymore and I was sad. So when I saw the signs that daddy Steve was leaving a lot and not coming home as much anymore I started to really worry. I loved my daddy Steve. Mom started taking us along with her a lot more when she would leave the house. She didn't like leaving us with him anymore and I couldn't understand why. We would go to her friend's houses and stay there while they had parties. I would wake up in the morning on somebody's couch with Jason next to me and wonder where mom was.

I would wander strange homes looking for her, always finding her in some bedroom with some guy in some bed. The panic and anxiety that would swell up in me would be so overwhelming I would cry. I didn't see her doing anything wrong, just sleeping, but when you are 6, you understand that when you love someone one you "sleep" in the same bed with them and that means that you belong to each other. That was such a hard thing to see, my mom "sleeping" with somebody who was not daddy Steve. I was so afraid that he would find out what she was doing and that he would go away forever.

Then we started staying overnight at one man's house on a regular basis. He was nice to us. They are always nice at first, trying to get us to like them. It was uncomfortable though. I wanted to be at home with daddy Steve, sleeping in my own bed instead of on a strange man's couch. I wanted to go back to church and visit with Grandma. I didn't really understand what was going on around me, but mom took us with her to this man's home and he would let us watch TV and they would disappear into the back room and we were not allowed to disturb them. It was hard to really accept what I knew was happening. She was leaving daddy Steve, slowly.

One night mom screamed for me to get Damien into the car and yelled at Jason to get in there too. Mom and daddy Steve had been in the bedroom for a long time yelling at each other. I had heard them fight before, but the urgency in her voice this time didn't leave me with a second of hesitancy. I got Damien and got into the car with Jason. She was running out of the house and towards the car with daddy Steve screaming and running after her. She jumped in the car and yelled at me to lock the door, which I immediately did. Her voice, it was different, it was scared and it made me almost pee my pants with fear. Mom's window was down and I witnessed her fumble with the keys to the ignition. She was crying, trying to do too many things at once. I was sitting right next to her in the front seat and she was freaking out as daddy Steve ran for her side of the car. She got it started and the window was going up as she was trying to back out of the driveway with daddy Steve's hands around her neck. He was punching her and screaming as she was trying to fight him off with the car still going in reverse. Jason and Damien started screaming, mom was screaming, daddy Steve was calling her all kinds of names and trying to beat her up through the window. I peed.

Then daddy Steve wasn't there anymore and we were driving down the street, all of us crying. I never went back to my pretty patio home with the blue shag carpet and its magical atriums.

Chapter 10

Mom didn't know how to live on her own, especially with three little kids in tow. I can understand why she made the choices she did with the men in her life. The men that would come and go and contribute to half of the bills and kept us entertained. They were simple men without the thought that mom always truly held the cards, wore the pants. She controlled their relationship always by letting them think that they had the control. The second we moved in with a man she would relinquish all responsibility to them, including the disciplining of us kids. It was a very hard thing to go through, having to learn a new way of life every time we moved in with a man. Yes, we still had to abide by the original rules of mom, but then there was a whole new set of rules and regulations and standard operating procedures that each of these men would put down for us to learn. It was always his way that was the right way, no matter who he was. The only thing the men didn't even consider was that, even with her baggage, she was ready and willing to just get up and leave them whenever she felt like it. There was always some guy waiting in the wings for his turn up to bat with her. They always felt like they were rescuing us. It was really quite sad for them.

Mom had rented a small little house in Phoenix after we moved away from daddy Steve and we were on our own for a little while. It was hard on mom because she had to pay the bills all by herself and support us three kids. So it didn't take long before she started dating again, but it wasn't just some random guy. She started seeing daddy

Steve again. He was coming around, staying overnight sometimes, and having dinners with us. I was happy again. There was even talk about him moving in with us, but that was all it was, talk. One afternoon they got into a fight and he went away for good.

I would ask about what happened, but mom wouldn't give the details. She just said he didn't love her anymore and stop asking about him. So I complied. I always wondered why they couldn't work it out. Grandma really wanted them to get back together, she always asked me what happened, and all I could tell her was that he didn't love her anymore. It made everyone sad. Then one day Grandpa came to stay with us.

Grandpa and Grandma decided that they needed a break from each other. I couldn't understand this, well, I was 7 and didn't understand a lot of things, and I had never heard of grandparents getting divorced, so I just figured that they would get back together eventually. But for now, Grandpa needed a place to stay and mom needed help with the bills.

Mom started working nights at the bakery because the pay was better and that way someone would always be home with us. Grandpa worked at the same bakery as mom, but he worked days and he held a higher position than her, so the money was great. We always had good food to eat and we would go to the movies, which was a special treat. I had made some very good friends at school and one of my best friends actually lived right down the street, and it was awesome because we could walk to school together every day.

Grandpa was rowdy. He loved to roughhouse and play games with us kids. He was very affectionate and joked around, but he had his mean side too. And because he was mom's dad, well he made all the rules. He didn't have too many of them, but the consequences for breaking them was extreme. He spanked with his belt and he used brute force with it against our bare asses. You didn't want Grandpa to get mad for any reason because the only way he knew how to discipline was with that damn belt. So we "played nice" and walked on our egg shells.

My uncle Allen, the youngest of the bunch, came by one day and asked mom if he could stay with her, and of course he could stay. You always help out family in need. It was no skin off her nose, it was another income. So uncle Allen came to stay and took over my room and I moved into mom's room.

It was a modest little three bedroom, two bath ranch house, so it worked out that Jason and Damien shared a room, Allen got his own room, and me and mom shared a room with a big king-sized waterbed. Grandpa slept on the couch, or in mom's bed when we weren't in it. Logistically, it worked out perfectly.

Allen kept to himself for the most part. He was young and working odd jobs here and there, keeping his part of the rent paid. He was fun with us kids. He loved to play around and play jokes on us. We had a houseful of family and it was pure love. Everywhere I went there was a grownup who cared for me.

These three grownups knew how to throw a party too. Over the weekends we would have a houseful of people, friends independently of each other who all got to know each other through our household. Old guys that Grandpa had known for years and years, young people that my uncle had partied with, and friends of my mom. Not a lot of kids, practically none, nonetheless our house was party central for boozers and potheads. Most of the time we were shuffled off into the back rooms to leave the grownups to do their thing, but we would escape and make an appearance every now and again. And when I invaded the party, so many people would tell me how cute or how pretty I was and they would be nice to me. I loved those moments of ego building. At 7 every girl wants to be told how cute or how sweet they are.

My mom's schedule was weird. She worked Monday night through Friday night, leaving Saturday and Sunday nights free. Whereas Grandpa worked Monday through Friday, leaving Friday and Saturday nights free. It sort of overlapped on the weekend to where they both were home on Saturday nights and that's when the parties would happen. Uncle Allen worked odd hours, a rotating schedule at the KFC. So sometimes he would be home too on Saturday nights.

One Friday night Grandpa had his own party with his buddies. Mom and uncle Allen were at their jobs and it was just us kids and Grandpa. We got to stay up kind of late watching TV because all the old guys were just hanging around the kitchen table getting drunk and playing cards. Us kids knew that if we just behaved he wouldn't make us go to bed. But the second we started to pester him or made too many entrances into the kitchen, well that was it, off to bed with us. This one particular night I asked if I could have some cookies right in the middle of their game and he got mad and sent us off. You didn't argue, pout, or even sigh loudly when he told you to do something, unless you wanted him to pull off his belt and smack you with it. So we did as we were told and snuggled in for the night.

Jason and Damien went to their rooms and I went to mom's big bed. I loved sleeping in that waterbed. It was always warm and cuddly, encasing me in a snuggle, like being spooned all night long. And it was always reassuring that mom was right there with me when it would begin to move and the aftershock waves would lull me back to sleep. It was a snuggly cradle with satin sheets.

I was always afraid of the dark, mom made sure of that. It was really kind of a tactic on her part to keep us in bed. The carpet monster would eat your skin if you got up out of bed before morning.

He was this horrible beast that lived in the shadows of the carpet and at nighttime there is no clear spot without a shadow where the carpet monster wasn't, so you just stayed there hoping he wouldn't see or hear you.

But in this room that I shared with mom, well, there was a street lamp that would shine in through the window and it lit up the room pretty well. There were still shadows on the floor, but I could see every stick of furniture or piece of clothing shaped menacingly like a ghoulie on the floor. It was comforting to have my own night light right there all the time.

I settled in to sleep, but couldn't. They were making such a raucous out in the kitchen, cursing and slamming cards down on the table, laughing real hard, talking real loud, so I laid there in silence listening to the game.

Then I heard Grandpa's voice as he was headed down the hallway, telling the other guys he needed to take a piss. I was facing away from the door, but saw his shadow on the wall from the hall light shining in behind him. He walked in, along the end of the bed to the bathroom door. I half closed my eyes but could still see him turn the light on in the bathroom and shut the door. He wasn't inside the bathroom though. He was standing outside the bathroom door staring down at me. My heart raced and I got a pangs in my gut. He wasn't just standing there; he was looming like a vulture.

He whispered at me, "Rachel? Are you awake?" There's that goddamned question again. "Rachel?" He moved to other side of the bed. I didn't move. He wasn't my Grandpa anymore; he was a monster all of a sudden.

I stayed turned away from the doorway, watching the shadow on the wall with my half-closed eyes. The door was closing, the light from the hallway slipping away. My heart ached. I couldn't breathe. He was being weird, acting odd, not good. I could feel it, something bad was in the room with me.

The bed moved and I rose with the tide of the water, then sunk down with the ebb. The bed rocked me back and forth as he scooted in close to me, behind me. His warm hand on my hip, slipping up and over to the front of my pelvis. He had never touched me like this before, no one had, so it was very disturbing. I knew in my heart of hearts that this was not right, so I pretended to be asleep.

He ran his hand down the side of my hip, down my thigh and got hold of the bottom of my nightgown. His mouth moved in close to my ear and I could hear his breath, short and shallow.

He pulled my gown up to my waist and as he got to my hip he pulled me into him. His cock was hard as it poked my tiny little buttocks. I didn't know what it was and why he was trying so hard to push it on me.

He didn't say anything, not a word, and I just laid there wishing, hoping that he would just go away.

He slid his hand to my belly, rubbing across it a couple of times until his pinkie finger snuck its way under the elastic band of my big girl panties. He laid there breathing heavy in my ear, rocking the bed back and forth, pushing his dick into my back as his hand kept me close on him.

He laid there forever touching me, slipping his fingers into places that they shouldn't have gone, and all I could do was whimper from the pain. He knew I was awake, but he didn't care. He kept going, forcing fingers in me; one, two, three.

He finally withdrew his hand from my tiny little twat and I thought it was over. Quite the contrary, he was stretching me out for what happened next. He raped his 7-year-old granddaughter while his drunken friends were in the kitchen. He raped me. He fucking raped a 7-year-old child.

"Dale! Where did you go?" a voice from the hallway called out.

"I'm taking a shit!" He yelled back as he laid motionless on top of me with his hand firmly over my mouth.

I wouldn't look at him and kept my eyes shut as hard as they could shut, so hard I saw red from the vessels in my eyelids. I cried and the snot in my noise was dripping down the back of my throat making me cough through his hands making a little farting noise each time I tried to sniffle or catch my breath. I couldn't breathe, it hurt so bad down below. I felt like I was ripping apart. Each thrust creating such a dazzling sparkle of stars in my head and then he was gone.

I rolled over as he exited the bathroom and flipped off the light. The toilet was running like it had just been flushed and he was heading for the bedroom door, which was now open. I lost time. I don't have a recollection of the door opening or him going into the bathroom, but there he was and there it was.

A moment later he was joking and laughing with his buddies in the kitchen again. My little body ached with pain. I felt like I had peed my panties, there was wet everywhere. I laid in silence, shocked at the moment that had just been. He was telling some joke about a lady and a dog or something and then there was laughter again. I slowly got up, not making a sound.

I had peed the bed, I thought at the time. I was going to get in big trouble if mom knew I peed the bed. I would get a spanking for sure. I limped to the bathroom and for fear of getting beat I didn't turn on the light. I crept in and took a towel from the hamper. I had no fear of the carpet monster right then, nothing could ever be as bad as the monster that lived in Grandpa.

Every step I took gave me searing pain. I took each step slowly and surely, making sure not to make any noise. All I wanted to do was cry out, but I stifled it, kept it to myself.

I pulled back the top sheet and started sopping up the mess. I couldn't change the sheets, no way. They were too big and there was no way I could get them changed without him hearing me. I resolved to sleep on the cool wet spot hoping mom wouldn't notice when she came home in the morning.

I went into the bathroom and shut the door as quiet as possible, waiting to do it when they erupted into laughter. I flipped the switch, brilliant light filled my eyes, blinding me for a minute in pain. I returned the towel to the hamper, shoving it way down to the bottom. I had to pee.

I don't know why I felt like I had to pee, I just did. I was confused because I just peed in bed. I pulled up my gown and reached for my panties, but they weren't there. I didn't have any panties on. I sat down on the toilet and peed for a long time, stopping and starting and stopping again because of the pain. It burned and ached.

Finally finished, I wiped, but it didn't feel right. I looked at the toilet paper and it was covered in goopy white and red. I was bleeding! I threw the paper in the toilet and took another handful and wiped again, same feeling again. I looked, more white than red this time. I threw it in and repeated the process over and over again and again until I wasn't bleeding anymore and there was no more white stuff. It hurt so bad, it was so raw.

Knock, Knock, Knock! Someone was at the bathroom door. "Hey! Are you almost done in there?" It was a friend of Grandpa's. I froze, tunnel vision took over. Knock, knock, knock! Again at the door. He was going to tell Grandpa I was awake. He was going to tell on me. I flushed the toilet.

I didn't have any panties on and this man is going to know it. I was so very scared. I opened the door and walked out as normally as I could and he moved out of my way so I could go past. I didn't even look up at him. I was so afraid of him. He knew what had happened, he could see right through me, he knew what a bad little girl I had been.

He went in the bathroom and shut the door. I looked around the floor and found my panties and quickly put them on. I jumped into bed and pulled the covers up over my head trying to be invisible to the world.

I couldn't sleep and didn't. I stayed awake on my side waiting for mom to come home. I heard the men all night long laughing and talking about this and that, sometimes getting mad and then calming down to giggles.

I watched the black sky outside turn to a deep dull blue. The sun was coming up. Then I heard the front door open and mom was home. I listened as she went to the kitchen. Everyone greeted her in their drunken stupor with loud cheers and she shushed them out of consideration to us kids sleeping in the back part of the house. Mom was the killjoy of the party and the men dispersed figuring it was very late if she had to be coming home.

After the old guys left, Grandpa made his way to the bathroom again and my heart swelled with fear. This time though, he was on the right side of the door when he shut it.

I jumped up out of bed and ran/limped to the kitchen where mom was sitting at the table. She was immediately concerned with me not being in bed, nothing more. I couldn't tell her what happened, I just couldn't. I was a bad little girl and I didn't want to get into trouble. I sat down and without missing a beat she made me go back to bed, citing it was way too early for me to be awake. So I very slowly walked back to the room and Grandpa was coming out. He was shocked at the sight of me, scared almost, because I was coming back from mom in the kitchen.

He stopped me in the hallway and told me that I was a bad little girl and that I better keep this secret or I would go to jail. I was a nasty little girl and mommy won't love you if you tell her. She will hate you and put you in jail. He threatened me right there in the hallway, 15 feet from my mom. I believed him. He was her dad after all, he knew more than her; he was wiser than she was. He was the boss.

I laid in bed waiting for mom to come to bed. I listened as she and Grandpa had a whole conversation about some guy at work they both knew. I smelled food cooking in the kitchen and knew instantly it was eggs. Mom had a habit of burning the eggs all the time. She liked them that way, with the brown on them. I couldn't stand the smell, but when you're a kid you can't dictate how grownups, especially your own mom, do stuff like cooking and driving.

I always hated the way my mom drove, like she was doing it on purpose. She didn't have the ability to keep the car at a steady pace. She was always accelerating and letting up off the gas, lunging the car forward to reach maximum speed, and then dropping back only to speed up again. It made my stomach turn and so one time I asked her "How come you drive the car like that?"

"Like what?" she asked back.

So I explained, "You drive weird, making the car rock forward and backward."

She got mad at me and told me to shut the fuck up, I didn't know what I was talking about, and the tone in her voice made me feel small.

I was laying in the king-sized waterbed waiting and wishing that mom would just come to bed so I could sleep, finally. I had been up all night scared for my life and I just wanted my mommy.

The house got real quiet, Grandpa had settled in on the couch and mom walked into the room. Relief came over me. She went to the bathroom and took her shower and I laid there waiting, hoping that Grandpa was sleeping. When she finished the shower and the water was off I could hear him in the living room snoring. He was down for the rest of the day.

The sun was up in full force now and my internal clock was getting all screwed up. I felt tired, but I just wanted to get up and have breakfast.

Mom climbed into bed next to me, gave me kisses and I love yous, and fell fast asleep. I watched her and matched her breathing with mine. Her gentle snore, which was more like breathing heavy with your mouth wide open, lulled me into a light sleep. I laid there for a long time, half in reality and half in dream, not quite committing fully to the fall. The fall had dark demons in it now and they wanted to touch me in places that my bathing suit covered. They wanted to hurt me and degrade me and tell me how much of a bad little girl I was. The fall was hell now and I couldn't go there.

After a while I heard noises in the kitchen. I knew the boys were up and I slinked out of bed to meet them in the kitchen. Walking down the hallway my privates burned and ached. I felt like I had been split in two and all I wanted to do was sit at the table. Jason was making cinnamon toast and the smell filled the kitchen to the point of eradicating the burnt egg smell.

Grandpa was still snoring in the living room, so we tried to be quiet, trying hard not to wake him up because he would just get mad at us. It was Saturday morning and our cartoons were on, so we went to the living room after our breakfast and sat down on the floor 3 feet in front of the TV. I didn't even look at him. The beast was sleeping right there on the couch, snoring, drunk, and I avoided his appearance. I looked straight at the TV for hours with the occasional run to the bathroom to pee and wipe away more pink blood.

I was so scared that I had to go to the hospital because I was bleeding, but I was even more scared that I would go to jail. My vagina throbbed with pain, like when I had fallen off the jungle gym just a couple of years before. I definitely didn't want that tube thing to go inside me again.

The choice was debilitating, so I just pushed the pain and disgusting thoughts out of my mind and zoned out the TV.

Occasionally the beast would roll over and catch his breath or cough, but I wouldn't budge. His movement made me freeze inside. We watched that TV all morning long until the sun was high in the high in the sky. Jason wanted to play outside and so I followed him with Damien in tow. I was never going to be left alone with the beast again if I could help it.

We all came in for dinner starving for whatever was on the menu. Playing as a kid outside always made me super hungry. I ran into the house with my pains reminding me with every step what happened just hours before. Mom was cooking in the kitchen and the beast was nowhere in sight. I hugged mom and ran to go to the bathroom, almost forgetting that I was alone. But the moment the spark of knowledge of being alone hit me the bathroom door swung open and he was standing before me. I yelped. He spoke to me from way up high and I didn't dare meet his eyes. I stared at his belt buckle instead.

"I know what you did, Rachel, I know. And you are going to get in trouble when I tell your mom." He said at me, taunting me. He knew right then and there I wasn't going to tell and that my mom's love was stronger than my own safety, so he held it over me.

For weeks that turned into months after the beast had me, he attempted multiple times to get me to come to bed with him. If I was already in bed and I heard him coming down the hallway, well I would make a break for the bathroom and lock myself in.

If he was already in bed and asked me to come to him, I would get Jason to go with me, begging him to please, please, please go see what he wants and a bunch of times I would get Jason to sleep in between me and the beast. But as soon as the beast would fall asleep, Jason would go back to his bed and I would lay there listening to the sound of his snoring to the point that I would get up and go lay with Jason in his bed to get some sleep.

Every moment that I was alone with the beast he would torture me with taunts of telling on me.

"You are so dirty and nasty. You're a nasty little girl. You are going to go to jail and your mom won't love you anymore. I think maybe today I'm going to tell her. Yes, today is a good day to tell her what you've done. You are such a bad little girl, she should know that nasty stuff you did." Menacing beast.

I would cry and beg him not to tell mom. I couldn't handle the thought of her, the only consistent adult in my life, sending me to jail and not loving me anymore. I would have to get down on my hands and knees and literally beg, because if I didn't he would tell. He made me kiss his dirty feet and cry and beg for forgiveness and I would do it every time without fail. He had a power over me that I couldn't break, I was 7 and I didn't know any better.

One day the Beast moved out and the torture was over, so I thought. He moved back to Grandma's house. Allen moved out shortly after that and I got my room back. Everything went back to status quo and I filed the whole thing away in my cabinet that lives in my head.

Chapter 11

We moved around a lot when I was a kid. We always managed to live with some guy, like it was impossible to have a life without a second income. As an adult, I know that's what each of those men were, a second income, even if my mom thought that she loved them.

Love is a funny thing, it is a great way to excuse behavior that would otherwise be thought of as undesirable.

Once we landed at a house owned by a man named Don. He was a really skinny, hunched over guy with OCD. We didn't stay there very long, just long enough to learn his rules, which were sometimes ridiculous. Folding the towels was the big one for this guy. I didn't know you could fold a towel more than one way before him, but after him I knew that there were several wrong ways to fold a towel. It was asinine to ask a 9-year-old child to fold them and rotate and face them in a closet.

The one cool thing about this guy was that he had a pool. Not just any old pool, an indoor pool. It was like we were rich with our pool enclosed in an Arizona room in the backyard. It was like something we would see on Richie Rich. It was exciting to be able to go out the back door and still officially be in the house with a gigantic diving pool.

The Arizona room was basically what people in Arizona did to their porches. You would take the existing porch with a roof and enclose it with aluminum walls halfway up with windows the rest of the way up the wall to the ceiling, creating a room with a view all the way around. If you were poor, you didn't have actual windows, just the screens. But Don, well, he had the windows and a pool, so he was well off financially. It turned out that he was mom's boss at work, so she was kind of taking advantage on two different fronts.

Me and Jason spent many days in that pool. It was awesome! We played all kinds of games and had competitions and races; it was such a blast. That was where I really honed in on my swimming skills. We would drag the little AM radio that I got for my birthday out there and listen to music and sing along and come up with dances that incorporated diving or swimming with the tunes.

One day mom came out to join us, which was rare. She was always taking care of Damien or cleaning something, which is what mom's do. But this one time she came out and dove right in. As soon as she came up from her dive, she noticed all the bugs floating on the surface. I always thought they were gross, but when you're a kid all you can do is skim the top as best as you can and usually it was a quick skim because you just wanted to go swimming, you didn't want to have to work for it. I hated the bugs, always afraid they would get tangled in my long hair, so usually I would just skim off the ones that were the grossest, like the bees or wasps. I must have done a poor job, because mom jumped out of the pool and yelled at me to get the skimmer, which I did and started skimming.

She went around the pool to the door to the backyard; she wanted to run the filter. I started skimming as she was mumbling angry snips at me for not doing a good job. She walked all the way around to the other side of pool on the outside of the Arizona room. I watched her walking, half-mumbling, hot-footing it on the cement pavers that weren't sheltered and were scorching hot from the sun beating down on them. She reached the filter and flipped open the cover to the electrical panel. Jason yelled at me to watch him do some stupid jump/dive into the pool, which I did and just as he hit the water, I saw mom drop down out of the line of sight of the window. At first I didn't think anything of it and continued to skim.

Jason did another jump/dive thing, contorting his body in a weird shape as he hit the surface of the water. It had only been a minute, but mom still wasn't coming up from outside of the window line of sight. I went around to the other side of the pool and looked out to see her lying on the ground in her bikini twitching in the sunlight. Her eyes weren't all the way closed, but you couldn't see the iris anymore, it was all white, like a zombie.

I screamed for Jason, but he was swimming underwater. I kept screaming as I ran to the other end of the pool where the door to the backyard was. A million thoughts ran through my head right then; mom was dying. Who was going to take care of us? Would we have to stay with Don? Would we go back to daddy Steve? Would they let my daddy out of jail to take care of us? All sorts of thoughts ran through my head as I rounded the corner to see her laying there. She wasn't convulsing anymore, but she was lifeless, limp. I leaned down and yelled at her to wake up. Jason was at the open window just above my head screaming "What Happened!?". I yelled at mom, but she wouldn't move, wouldn't open her eyes. I was frightened, tunnel vision was coming and I couldn't stop it. Then I heard Don's voice from inside the pool room asking, I looked up and saw the fear in his face through the screen, then he was gone.

I grabbed mom's arms and dragged her a little bit across the concrete pavers, but she was too heavy. The heat was burning my feet, sizzling was happening, but I couldn't just leave her there. Don yelled from the pool room back door to the house that the ambulance was on its way. He came barreling through the back door, then the second door to the backyard and around the corner. In one full swoop I was moved and he had her in his arms yelling at me to get out of the way. He carried her into the living room and we all followed him. Mom wasn't talking, moving, but still breathing. We were all crying and carrying on like she was dying, because we really thought she was dying.

Once the ambulance arrived and the EMTs were in the house, we were shuffled into our bedrooms and told to stay there. I stood at the threshold listening to every word. Lots of things I couldn't understand, but then a glorious voice came through them all; it was mom's voice. She was alive and talking. I broke free from my invisible barrier and headed straight into the living room and into her arms. She was crying and it was scaring me even more. Don grabbed me out of her hold and told me to get away. I moved to the side and felt that if I was just quiet, though couldn't stop crying, that they would let me stay in the room, which they did. They did all kinds of things to her, checking her out, and once she was deemed okay, they left.

After the fact it was explained to me and Jason that we were never allowed to touch the filter, ever. It just so happened that the filter had a short in it and mom standing there with her wet self, making a puddle on the ground, it had electrocuted her. I almost lost my mom that day. She was the only consistent in my life, the one and only consistent that had all our lives in her hands and it was a scary thought that she could leave us.

Chapter 12

It didn't take long before mom got bored with Don, but before she got bored she made some friends through him. They were "normals", as I like to call them. Normals are other families, real families with moms and dads and kids. It was a nice change to what I had experienced before with her friends who were, on a standard, single people with no kids and wanted to just get stoned out and listen to music while me and Jason and Damien sat around quietly trying not to disturb them. The normals, on the other hand, well, they were fun. They had kids our ages and the kids had bedrooms with toys and fun stuff to do all the time.

One particular normal family we got to know very well were the Christy's. They consisted of a mom, Barb, a dad, Tom, and two girls, Jessica and Lori. Jessica was just a year older than me and had a great room with everything I could ever want. Lori was just a year younger than Jason, but was a girl, so she wasn't as much a match for Jason as Jessica was for me. But that didn't stop us from having a great time.

The Christy's had a wonderful home with a pool and a diving board. They had a freezer in the garage always packed with good stuff for kids, like freezer pops and ice cream. And for the adults, they had a full bar with a tapped keg on the porch in the backyard. It was the perfect party house for all of us and they had parties every weekend.

Saturday would come and we would all load up the car with our swimsuits and towels and drive over to the Christy's for a barbeque, knowing that it would turn into a sleepover for everybody.

As soon as we got there we split into groups of kids and grownups. Jason, Damien, and me would get enveloped with the gaggle of children excitedly yelling at us to hurry up and put our suits on. We would spend hours in and around that pool. Occasionally a mom would run up and ask us if we were hungry and tell us to go get hotdogs. Then the painstaking half-hour wait after we'd eat of sitting there watching the smart kids who staved off hunger still playing in the pool. You would watch the parents erupt into laughter, each holding a beer, with a sparkle in their eyes of pink elephants on parade. A fun time was always had at the Christy's.

As night would fall, the kids were brought inside, dried off, fed, and sent off to a bedroom, usually Jessica's. She was rich because she had a TV in her room. We would all hang out and watch TV until respective parents would get their kids and go home. My mom would usually have to wake us up because it would be so late at night, but occasionally we would just all stay the night. Jessica and I got real close, like having a sister, and it was nice because she was older, which, in turn, made her in charge of us kids and I didn't have to work so hard keeping tabs on my brothers.

Mom got bored with Don and started going out when he would go to work, leaving me and the boys home alone.

She would come home just in time to make it to work and just before Don would come home. It would drive me crazy with anxiety. I knew what she was doing, I had seen it before. She was leaving Don, slowly.

I would wait for hours by the front window wishing, hoping, waiting for her to be the first car in the driveway. I didn't want to have to lie to Don and I didn't want to tell him the truth if he asked where mom was. She would always tell me that she was going to go play racquetball with Billy, a guy she knew from work, but I had never met. But it didn't matter, because all the signs were there and I was worried that we were going to have to move again. I didn't necessarily love Don, but he was nice to us and he didn't deserve, in my mind at least, to be dumped. Mom was sneaking around with Billy and it scared me every time she left me in charge to go be with him.

One afternoon the phone rang the secret ring and I picked it up, it was Don. "Where's your mom?", the dreaded question. How was I to answer it? So I told him exactly what mom said to say "She's playing racquetball at the park."

"When did she go to the park?" He asked. I knew what he was doing, he was trying to put together a timeline. Hey, I was only 9, but I knew.

"Um, I don't know." I told him. I knew, she had been gone all day and I also knew you don't play racquetball for 6 hours.

"Okay, well I'm going to go find her. If she calls tell her I'm going to the park." He said.

Panic sat in. Tunnel vision is closing in. "Okay, I will." I replied.

As soon as I hung up I started crying. The anxiety took over, we were in trouble. Not just mom, but all of us. This was Don's house, not ours, we were going to have to leave if he sees her with Billy doing whatever they were doing. Jason asked me what was wrong and I told him and he was sad.

Back in those days there was no information number 411. It just didn't exist. When you wanted to find a phone number you looked in a phone book and if you couldn't find it there, you dialed 0 for the operator and asked her. I ran for the phone book and looked up Chicken Park, not knowing that was just a nickname for the park we went to on a regular basis. It didn't matter, I couldn't find it. So I called the operator and asked for the number. I actually argued with her about the name. That poor lady, she was just trying to do her job, but here I was so frantically worried about our living situation and the brink of being homeless if I didn't get that number that I argued with a grownup about the name of a park and I was clearly in the wrong. Sufficed to say I didn't get the number and actually hung up on the operator when she started asking personal questions like where are your parents, and if we were alone. Yeah, I wasn't supposed to be using the phone when we were alone, but it was an emergency, so I broke the rule.

After a bit of crying and being worried, I saw her car drive up. I ran outside to tell her what happened with Don, but as soon as I started, he pulled up in his car, right next to mom, so I froze. Mom was inquisitive, but Don was getting out and I was scared. She was getting annoyed with me, it was a close call, still was in my eyes. He was going to ask her where she was and I was going to witness her throwing this life away. But he asked, she answered, it wasn't full of tension, it was just matter of factly, so I just faded into the background and the whole situation sort of just went away. I was still worried, but nobody was upset. We went through the rest of our evening just as usual.

Then one night we all went to Billy's, all of us except Don. The boys and me sat on the couch as mom plopped down on the floor with him. They smoked out and listened to music and we sat quietly. It was getting later and later in the night and I was the last to fall asleep, but just as my eyes were closing in for that deep slumber, that falling feeling coming over me, as I drifted I watched as she leaned into him and kissed him. I knew then that our life with Don was over. No more pool, had to move, had to make new friends, it was another change.

We went home to Don's house the next day and he was at work. We should have gone to school but instead we grabbed what we could, loaded up the car and left. We didn't go to Billy's house, actually we drove around a lot until mom got an apartment that very same day. It was one of those first month's rent free kind of apartments. It was exciting because it had two stories, which was what rich people lived in; two story houses. Although ours wasn't a house, it was clean and nice and it was just us, mom and us kids. We had to take an actual bus to school, no walking for us, which was also a treat. Yes, we lived in Arizona so we didn't have to trek the proverbial 2 miles in the snow up to our waists uphill both ways, but we did have to endure the 110 degree heat with a full backpack and a half a mile walk. It was still miserable. It is more hot than cold here and it was treacherous for small kids with actual backpacks that didn't have wheels like backpacks now-a-days. And there were no two sets of books, one for home and one for school, so if you had homework in math, reading, and history, well, you had to bring home all those books. But now we had a free ride, on a bus with all of our new friends, every day to and from school and it was fun.

We didn't have Don, daddy Steve, or my daddy anymore, it was just us, which left us vulnerable. I didn't realize how vulnerable until one night mom came screaming through the house. She had gone out to get us some McDonald's for dinner and we were only home for a little while when she came bursting through the front door screaming for the phone. Apparently Don had seen her driving down the street and became very upset and started chasing her. She had disappeared on him, not telling him that they were breaking up or that she was moving out; she just left him.

Well, he had seen her and chased her home, trying to run her off the road; that's what she was saying to the cops on the phone. She was screaming about how he was tearing up her car outside and that he was insane and was going to kill us all. Tunnel vision, weak knees, vomit in the back of my throat. I ran upstairs. Ran to my room and threw open the curtains. Looking down to the street below where mom had haphazardly parked the car half on the sidewalk there was Don, with a big ass crowbar. He pulled it up over his head and threw it down into the tail light of mom's still running car. She hadn't even closed her door in her rush to get away. He hit the car over and over again with the crowbar, throwing sparks each time he connected with the metal of the car. He was yelling and screaming obscenities about my mom, saying all sorts of things that I just couldn't make sense of. Mom was screaming downstairs, Damien was crying, and Jason was hiding in the kitchen.

Two cop cars pulled up right behind Don, sirens blaring, lights blinding. Don dropped the crowbar and a cop slammed him face down on the trunk of mom's car. I ran down the stairs to find the door wide open and mom nowhere in sight. I inched out the door and looked towards the street. She was crying and throwing her hands everywhere explaining what happened. Jason moved in close to me. We cried. Mom finally came back inside and we tried to sit and eat, but there were no appetites. A few weeks later we moved again.

Chapter 13

Don's house was the first place we got cable, Cox Cable. I remember clearly the day the representative came to the house with the box with the all the channels on it. It was almost as long as the TV when it was perched up on top of it and it had a little plastic sliding indicator that you moved back and forth as it clicked through the channels. All us kids sat watching intently as the man was going through all the packages we could choose from. The grownups were talking money and I was listening to every word, then I heard it, the magical word, the word every kid was talking about at school. MTV. I got to watch a few times at the Christy's and was excited that we were going to get to have it at our house and I could watch it anytime I wanted to.

I excitedly yelled at mom "MTV, Mom! MTV, let's get MTV like Jessica!"

She turned to me and shot me a look of you're going to get smacked in the face if you don't shut up right now. But I didn't catch it fully, MTV was stronger than that look. "Please Mom, MTV?!" I begged.

"It's too expensive, maybe later. Be quiet or go outside." She warned me.

What I didn't realize was that they had purchased another box from a "friend" that allowed us to have every single channel and we didn't have to pay a bill every month for it. So I did get my MTV after all. And I got every single channel to choose from, to include the movie channels, which was so exciting, not having to watch commercials.

All of us were glued to the TV after we got cable. For weeks we ate all our meals in front of it and any free time was spent watching movies and music videos. Mom actually used the TV as a source of music when she was cleaning the house or cooking. Not that they had music channels like they do now, but she would let MTV play for hours while doing chores.

One afternoon after school I was alone watching Different Strokes. If you know that show you will remember Arnold, a small black kid who managed to get the setup to say "What you talkin' 'bout Willis" in every episode. Well, for some reason I really felt connected to him. He was going through the same stuff in his life, sort of, that I was. Arnold would get beat up by the Gooch and figure out ways to disarm him and I actually used those tactics against my own bully at school and it worked. He got his bike stolen at the same time my bike was stolen. It was like he was mirroring my life, or so I thought.

This one afternoon, while watching the show, Arnold and his brother made friends with a bicycle shop owner. The guy seemed innocent enough, nice, polite, giving, but something wasn't right with him. I got an unsettled feeling about the way he was interacting with the boys, but I couldn't put my finger on it. That is until he took them into the back room where he had them strip down to their underwear and gave them wine and candy. Then he put a "dirty movie" on the VCR, a porno. Now, they didn't actually show the dirty movie or even that he did anything to violate the boys physically, but the whole situation was just not right and made me really feel like I felt with the beast. It opened the file cabinet in my head and the memories flooded back in of that awful night.

I was on the edge of my seat, actually sitting on the coffee table that sat between the couch and the TV, only a few feet from the screen. I was waiting to see what magical solution he had to offer for me to fix my own demon. I watched as the boys told their "dad", some old guy who adopted them after their mother had died, about what happened. And then the police arrested the bike shop owner, but not the kids. I had been living with the knowledge that I would be carted off to jail if I told, never the thought that the beast would go to jail. A whole new set of fears settled in my head.

I watched intently waiting to see what happened next, but it was neatly tied up with hugs and love. The kids were getting on with their lives and nothing was ever mentioned again about that molester.

When the show was over Arnold came on the screen to address the TV audience. He spoke softly and slowly and oh so reassuringly. He said point blank:

"If you or someone you know has been molested or touched in the private areas you need to tell on them. Go to your closest adult that you trust and tell. You did nothing wrong. No one has the right to touch you if you don't want them to. You are not to blame. Tell your mom or your dad, a teacher, a police officer if you can. It's not your fault. The grownups should know better and it will be okay."

By the time his little public announcement was over, I realized I had been crying. The thoughts that flooded into my little head of relief overcame any paralyzing fear that had been holding back my tattling.

I walked right into the kitchen where mom was cleaning the stove. I hadn't thought about what I was going to say, so I just stood there watching her.

"What are you doing?" she asked.

"Nothing." I replied, lying to her. I knew what I was supposed to do, but I was inexperienced in starting a conversation that included rape.

I started to cry a little bit, scared about the words that were aching to escape me. She looked over at me and she got scared.

"What's wrong!?" she demanded an answer.

"Mom, something bad happened. I'm sorry. I don't want Grandpa to go to jail." I spoke to her in broken quivers.

Her eyes changed, I witnessed a darkness sweep over her face. She knew exactly what I needed to say, she knew and the way she looked at me right then and there changed and stayed changed forevermore.

"What did he do?!?! Rachel! What happened!?" Frantic.

I started to tell her about when we lived at the other house, she was at work and how he climbed into bed with me and he touched me. I got that far when she started screaming and crying "Oh NO, No, NO, No!!!"

The fear and disgust in her voice as she held me close to her gave me such shame in my heart that I couldn't tell her the rest. Just that alone, him touching me down there was enough for her to flip out on me. I just couldn't spit it out, no more details. She cried, bawled like someone had died. As an adult I understand she was mourning the death of my innocence, but as a kid, listening to her cry like that, well it scared me.

She held me close for a long time, both of us in tears. She eventually let me go and told me how much she loves me and how what he did was wrong and that it was going to be okay. She reached for the phone and called the police. She screamed and yelled at them on the phone and then she got mad. Not the screaming, going to knock your block off mad, the scarier mad. The mad where she was calmly explaining what happened with an underlying tone of I'm going to murder you in your sleep. That dark tone turned to childish bartering. The conversation was only one-sided, but I heard every word on our end and it wasn't promising. She pointed her finger at me and whipped it from me to the living room in such fury that I could hear her finger split the air with a whoosh. I knew to get my ass into the living room and wait for her.

I could still sort of hear what was said, but most of all I heard the tone, well, felt it. She wasn't angry anymore, she wasn't scared, or mad, or anything really. She got off the phone and I sat quietly waiting for her to come into the room or call for me to go to her, but it didn't happen.

She called Grandma. I didn't want Grandma to know. She would definitely make me feel shame for this. That's what Grandma did, made you feel bad about every little thing you did wrong. Grandma's favorite thing to say to us was, with a sing-song voice, "Shame, Shame, I know your Name." and she would use her pointer fingers while doing it. You know, or maybe you don't, where you point one finger and run the second pointer finger across the top of it like you are dusting it off. Well, that was Grandma's ammunition. Well, that and "God is always watching you, always, and if you do something wrong he writes it down in his great big book with your name on it and he reads it when you get to heaven." Yeah, that sucked. I hadn't even thought of God until that very moment when my mom was crying out to her mom about what her dad had done to me.

God knew what happened. God saw everything, because you know God is everywhere and you can't hide anything from him. He even knows what you are thinking. He's worse than Santa Claus.

I freaked out and started crying all over again, frozen to my spot in the living room, trying to hear what she was saying. Mom's tone was helpless and sad. I didn't want anyone to know what happened. I was ashamed.

I listened as she finished up the call. There was mostly silence with occasional breaks in the sound barrier of sniffles and coughs.

"Rachel, come in here." She ordered. She was calm. It scared me.

I went to the kitchen and she stayed an arm's length away from me as she explained. Grandma and Grandpa don't live together anymore. Grandpa moved away to California. The police can't do anything because he is not in Arizona and the laws are different there. Then she said something that I Will Never Forget.

"Me and your Aunt Debbie lived through it and we turned out okay, you will too." She said that sentence with a list in her voice like it was supposed to make me feel better. It didn't. It made me worry about my mom and my Aunt Debbie. They had this secret all along and they still loved their daddy. It confused me. She assured me that I will understand when I get older and I would like to tell you,

you the reader, right now, I call bullshit. I still don't understand, except that he is a sick fuck and deserves to die a slow and humiliating death. (Yes, he's still alive and happy, living his little life without a care in the world.)

The following days after the tattling, I was put into counseling through the school. It was a waste of time if you ask me. The counselor was a weirdo and gave me unsettled feelings too. I didn't like reliving it twice a week, going through the motions of feeling it all over again.

Then the prayer circle happened. I was going through a depression. My grades were slipping and I didn't want to do anything fun. Everyone I knew and cared about knew what happened and I was ashamed. All their eyes looked at me differently. They could see straight to my core. It didn't matter if they told me it wasn't my fault and that they still loved me, it just didn't matter because they knew the dirtiness in me. And they didn't even know all of it, just the beginning parts, the part I let them know.

One evening we went to Grandma's house for dinner. It was a normal thing for the family to get together and share a meal and afterwards sit and pray in a circle holding hands. Most of the time us kids got to go hang out in another room while they prayed, mostly because they would do it for a couple of hours. Well, us kids would just get bored and disrupt their worship, so we would be shuffled off into another room. But on this night it was different, I was brought into the circle.

I was trying to be invisible from all the uncles and my dear aunt and Grandma. I didn't want to see their eyes and I didn't want anyone to touch me. I just wanted to go play in the other room with my brothers, but I wasn't allowed to.

Mom brought me to my spot on the floor between Grandma and her and I took the position that I had seen them so many times before in. Kneeling down on the floor, Grandma began to speak, like the chief of a tribe. The beast wasn't there, so she was in charge now and everyone respected that. I glanced around at everyone there, our group of 8, and all eyes were on me. Grandma explained that we were coming together on that night to ask for forgiveness and to wash clean all demons from our souls. We all held hands, bowed our heads, and closed our eyes. Grandma's voice called out to the Lord calmly and lovingly, asking him to please wash his love over us and to protect and to this and to that. I went inside and washed her voice out. I had heard this prayer a thousand times before at meal times, in church, when she came over to destroy all of mom's albums because they were the devil's music and mom was on a God cycle. But then through the droning my ears perked up. She said my name, not just once to bless me in the prayer, but she said it 2 or 3 times.

I was fully aware now of what she was saying. "Please, oh Lord, please forgive Rachel for her demons. What *"The Beast"*(she used his name, but I refuse to) did to her was wrong and we ask you dear Lord to please wash over her with your love and forgiveness. She did not know what she was doing. She was innocent and did not deserve the demons that live inside her now." Grandma went on and on like that for hours on end, no joke, hours. Every few seconds a family member would whisper talk "yes Jesus, please oh lord forgive her". All my uncles, my mom, aunt, they all said it intermittently.

"Please Lord, don't let her be overcome with the demons. She didn't know what she was doing. She didn't understand what she was doing, Lord, oh Lord, please forgive her." The mantras were surrounding me. I was being ganged up on. Then to add insult to injury, the prayer changed to forgiving the beast.

Grandma started it all, "Lord, precious Jesus, my Lord, please forgive *"The Beast"* for what he did. He didn't know what he was doing. His heart is heavy with the devil and he has lost his way. Please Lord guide him back to your light and help him see the path to your love..." blah, blah, blah.

I couldn't believe what they were saying. I was 9, only 9, I was 9 years old for God's sake, and they were asking for forgiveness for me and him, like we were in cahoots the whole time. I understood right then and there, I understood that I was alone with this tragedy and that I probably should have kept my fucking mouth shut.

For hours upon hours they continued to pray for my soul and for the beast's soul and for the Lord to wash this and guide that.

I woke up the next morning in my bed, having fallen asleep at Grandma's. I was alone, even though mom and Aunt Debbie had been where I had been, I was alone.

As an adult, growing ever closer to my Sweet Loving Aunt Debbie, I learned that the Beast never touched her in *that* way. It was only mom he came after.

Chapter 14

Mom dated a lot and everyone in the neighborhood knew it. I was taunted on a regular basis about how my mom was a slut or a whore. It really hurt my feelings because she was my mom and no matter how bad she was acting, she was the one at the end of the day who told me she loved me. She was my one consistent in the sea of inconsistent men that would pop in and out of our lives. And having the Beast living with us she had a live-in babysitter for anytime she wanted to go out on a "date", which she did a lot of dating.

One night, sleeping in my mom's big bed on my side, I heard her come in. She wasn't being very quiet, she was drunk or high, and I could hear her dad tell her to be quiet because he was trying to sleep on the couch. She said some hateful things to him and I could hear a man's giggle, not the Beast's giggle, a different man.

After the confrontation of a grouchy beast, I heard her head down the hallway into our room. My back was turned away from the door, but I could see her shadow and another shadow move into the room. They were clumsy, kissing, ruffling clothing.

"You have to be quiet. She's asleep." She whispered to her companion. I didn't move. He didn't say anything. They continued to make sloppy wet kiss noises. I knew that sound. It was the sound that she and daddy Steve would make when they kissed.

I remember sitting in the back seat of our Duster and witnessing mom and daddy Steve have long wet kisses at stop lights, only stopping when the car behind us would beep their horn because the light had changed but they hadn't noticed.

I laid there quietly for a while and then the bed moved and I rose with the tide. They plopped down right beside me and as I sunk down with the wave ebbing I gently rolled over to see what they were doing. Mom was lying underneath a man I didn't recognize. She was topless and kissing him.

She looked over at me and saw me watching her.

"Turn over and don't look Rachel!" she whispered-yelled at me.

"Are you sure we should be doing this here?" the man asked.

"Don't worry she'll go back to sleep in a minute." She assured him. But I didn't sleep. I faced away from them, but couldn't sleep with the noise and the bed moving back and forth.

Mom reached over and touched my shoulder and gave me a little push, "Rachel? Are you awake?" There's that dumb question yet again. I ignored it and pretended to be asleep.

I could feel the bed move more violently, quicker sloshing under the sheets. The moans and deep breaths made my heart quicken. I was scared. I didn't really understand why this was happening. I knew what it was they were doing, but I just didn't know why she would do that right there with me in bed with her and him. It had always been taught to me that sex was dirty and gross and that you shouldn't have it unless you were married or you would go to hell. Now I was scared because I knew my mom was having sex and that she was going to go to hell. I didn't want her to go hell. I wanted to be able to meet her in heaven.

The not-so-quiet sex went on for hours. The sloshing, the moaning, the grunting, it just kept going and going until the man yelled out "Oh Yeah, Fuck Yeah" and then there was a big releasing sigh by the both of them. I could feel him roll off of her, over to the spot between me and her. His elbow found my back and rested there. It was very uncomfortable, but I didn't dare move for fear of them knowing I was awake the whole time.

I felt the bed sink in as mom got up and went to the bathroom. The man scooted off the bed and the water mattress sunk even more into the frame. I could hear rustling of clothing, change and keys being rattled. Mom came out of the bathroom and asked him if they were going out again next weekend and he said something about working and then he left.

After walking him out, she came back to bed and snuggled in for the night. It took a while, but I finally went to sleep.

That wasn't the only time I had witnessed her doing nasty things, just the closest instance.

Mom started dating this guy named Joe. Joe had a couple of kids around me and Jason's ages. They were cool kids, not rich, really much more poor than we were, but nonetheless, they were fun. Joe was nice to us kids, you could really tell he had kids of his own just by the way he treated us.

When mom and Joe first started out they spent a lot of time together, leaving us kids to basically fend for ourselves, not out of the normal cycle with mom and her guys, but still just a lot of alone time was had for us kids. They spent a lot of time in the bedroom doing whatever grownups do in private.

One day me and the boys were watching TV, actually it was a UHF channel because we didn't have cable. Well this channel played music videos, but not the top of the chart videos, more like the "B" videos that weren't good enough to get on MTV. Nonetheless, it was awesome to me.

Mom and Joe walked into the room and sat down together in the arm chair that was behind us kids. The glare from the window on the TV screen let you see like a mirror behind you if you looked at it just right and adjusted your eyes to only see the shadow figures in the background. I was very proficient in doing just that. I would use that to see who was walking down the hallway or who was in the kitchen because if I relaxed my eyes just right I could see into the rooms beyond the living room and across the hall. You just had to practice and I always did.

I was watching the show and then heard the kissing noises from behind me and instead of turning to look I just adjusted my eyes to see what was going on behind me. Now, you couldn't exactly see detail, just figures and I saw mom straddling Joe and her head was in the same spot as his so I could tell that they were kissing, well that and the noises they were making. Jason turned to look at them and I followed suit. There was mom on his lap, still fully clothed mind you, but still in a position that made me uncomfortable. Jason giggled, mom looked at us watching her and snapped at us to watch the TV and don't look at her.

We turned back towards the TV and I remember precisely at the moment one of my favorite songs coming on. "You dropped a bomb on me." Great song at the time.

I heard them shift and I switched to shadow eyes and saw mom on the floor. I heard the zipper. I saw her head in his lap. I didn't really know what she was doing at the time, but now realize she was giving him a blowjob right there in the living room while all three of her kids were watching a TV show.

In between slurps she would remind and instruct us not to look, to keep our eyes on the TV.

Why she just didn't go into the bedroom is beyond me. She was the adult, we were the kids, and the only thing I can think of is that she was playing with her power over us, which is fucked.

I watched with shadow eyes her head bobbing, but flipping back to my favorite video when she would half slurply say to not look at her, only to come back to the shadow eyes to see what she was doing. It seriously only took her the length of the song to get him to cum and he was back in his pants and she was on his lap again talking about what we should have for dinner.

I get it now why they would say my mom's a slut or a whore, because if she was willing to do that right in front of her own kids, who knows what she has done in front of my friend's families or the neighbors.

My friends started to turn on me and I couldn't understand why. They started saying all sorts of rude things about me and my mom and it struck my very core. The bullying wouldn't stop. Then it started happening to Jason too.

My best friend Lisa lived diagonally behind us. The corner of our fence was shared by the corner of her fence and instead of walking all the way around the block to get to her house me and Jason would just hop the fence to her yard. She had a younger brother just about Jason's age and Lisa was exactly my age, so we were all really great friends and it was nice to have them right behind us to play any time we wanted to.

Mom would get mad at us for hopping the fence, telling us it was just too dangerous and we should go around the block. We followed that rule any time she was home, but when the cat's away, us mice would hop that fence. On our side, we had a four foot chain link fence and on the other side with all four corners blocking it in there was a big green utility box. All we had to do was climb over our fence, land on the utility box and climb over Lisa's 8-foot wood fence and we were in her yard.

One day Jason went over the fence to play. We weren't supposed to leave our yard when mom wasn't home, but really semantically we didn't leave our yard, not really; okay we did, but it was Lisa's house and our fences touched. Well he was over there and I saw mom pull up in the drive way. I knew Jason was going to get busted and if he got busted, I got busted for not stopping him. I ran through the backyard and yelled at him over the fences, "Mom's Home!".

I saw his toe-head pop up over the first fence and I turned and ran into the house just in time for mom to come into the house.

"Where's Jason?" She asked.

"He's playing in the backyard." I lied.

"Go get him. Tell him I said come inside." She ordered. I complied.

I ran out to the backyard and Jason was walking towards the house, holding his arm with tears in his eyes.

"What happened?" I asked.

"I fell off the fence. My arm hurts really bad, Rachel." He confessed. I told him to go into the house and play in his room and put on a long sleeve shirt to hide the cut. He did as I told him.

Mom started dinner and went for a shower. Jason came out as soon as he heard her in the shower and showed me his arm. It was bright red, not from blood, but angry looking, and it had a bump in it. It didn't look right, it looked broken and he had tears in his eyes. My little brother was hurt, time to uncover the cover up.

When mom came out of the shower, Jason told her the whole truth after trying to lie about it, which really made her mad. She yelled and took him to the hospital. Poor little guy ended up having a fractured arm.

They came home later that evening and Jason had a cast. She was mad at us for disobeying, but we didn't really get punished. I believe she was too tired. We weren't allowed to go over to Lisa's anymore ever. If we wanted to play with her and her brother, they had to come over to our house and only when mom was home. We didn't get our standard beating, we just got grounded.

A few days later, at school, some big kid told Jason that our mom was a bitch. Jason told him to shut up, but when that didn't work and the kid kept saying it over and over again, well, Jason hauled off and hit him in the face with his casted arm. And after the kid fell to the ground, Jason proceeded to hit him a few more times with his cast.

When mom got home from work that night she got a call from the school about what happened with Jason and the bully. She was pissed. Not just because Jason got into a fight, but because she had to take him back to the hospital to reset his fracture that he fractured again from hitting the kid in the face. That kid never talked shit again about our mom, but it didn't stop the other kids.

My friends got mean. Then they weren't friends anymore. I really wanted mom to move us again to start over in a different school, but it wasn't happening any time soon. I was getting threatened every day that someone wanted to fight me and that my mom slept with this kid's dad or that kid's dad. It was really scary. I couldn't really understand it at the time and so all I could do was back up my respect for my mom. I would change the way I went home every day, switching it up, leaving later and later, hiding out in the library, or running nearly all the way home trying to outrun the haters.

I waited one afternoon so late at school that the janitor had to tell me to go home. I didn't want to because I didn't want to get beat up. This one girl Elizabeth was pissed at me and she was going to beat my ass. I didn't have a choice. I left school grounds and started walking home, by myself. Jason had left way before me and was already home by this point with Damien.

I remember clearly almost peeing my pants when I saw Elizabeth following me down the street. There was no reason for her to be at the school this late, unless she was waiting for me, which she was. She was there with one of her friends and they were yelling obscenities at me about my mom. I have no clue where the strength came from other than it was too far for flight so my fight kicked in.

"Your mom is a Whore!" She screamed at me from across the street. I ignored it.

"Your mom is such a Slut!" she yelled louder.

I said "You're a Fucking Bitch!" I wasn't looking at her, I was just sort of saying it into the air and as I said it I felt cold blood run through my veins. I knew what I was doing; I was starting a fight, or rather perpetuating a fight.

She said "What?!? What did you just call me?!?"

So I stopped, turned and faced her from across the street and said it again with a louder, meaner voice, "You Are a Fucking Bitch!".

She froze, but just for a moment, still she froze. Her face got flushed and she screamed at me, still standing on the other side of the street "Come Say that to my Face!"

And I have absolutely no idea where I got the idea to say this, but I said it like it was just second nature "I don't go to dogs. Dogs come to me!"

That set her off. She ran across the street with her little friend following every footstep, right up to my face and said "Say it to my face! What did you call me?"

Tunnel vision set in, but not to blindness. I could feel every vein in my body pulsate with fear as my mouth opened and the words slipped out again, inching my nose closer to hers I yelled in her face "You are a Fucking Bitch!"

The world slowed down, almost to a stop. I watched as her hand reared up behind her ear and her eyes shut as she brought her fist down toward my head. Her fist swung through the air of where my face had been before I moved it out of reach. My hand came up and as I was closing my fist I made contact with the side of her face with a full follow through. As her head ricocheted off my half-closed fist, my other fist caught her jaw in mid air, knocking her straight back into her friend.

Real time came back and I stood there looking at the bloody mess of a girl screaming in front of me on the ground. Her friend screaming at me that she was going to tell on me. Then there was a big kid, at least 3 years older than me screaming and running down the street right at me. She had the look of a charging bull. It was Elizabeth's sister, an 8th grader, and she was going to kill me.

I ran for my life. I was still at least 5 blocks from my house when I was running out of steam. The bull was still charging when I looked back. I rounded the corner and saw the big red "E" in the window of a house.

When I was a kid there were no cell phones and everyone was afraid of the "stranger danger". So neighborhoods would hand out placards with a big red letter "E" for emergency on them that people would put in their windows for kids and other people who needed help to know that they could receive help at this house.

Most of the time when I would use these houses it was for a drink of water in the summer heat. But this time it was a real emergency. I needed them to keep the crazy bull from beating me into the ground. I ran right up to the door and started pounding and screaming "HELP ME!! Please Help Me!" No one came to the door to rescue me.

The bull was getting closer, so I ducked down behind some shrubs in the front of the "E" house and hid. She found me and beat me up. She used both her arms and legs on me. I cried and begged for her to stop and finally she did, but only after she warned me to stay away from her sister.

I got up after she left and walked home. I was going to get in big trouble. Mom was going to be really mad at me. As I walked up to the house, mom was already in her car coming to find me. I was surprised to see her home so early from work, or was I really that late coming home from school. It didn't matter; she was mad and told me to get in the house.

She told me about the phone call she got from the school principal and from Elizabeth's parents and that I was in a lot of trouble. I listened to her yell at me and kept my tongue quiet until she finally asked me "What is wrong with you?"

"She called you a whore, mom. She kept calling you a whore and I didn't think it was right." I confessed. She heard me. She actually heard what I was saying and got it.

I went back to school after a few days and Elizabeth came back to school a couple of weeks after that. It turned out that I had hit her with an open fist and scratched her face from temple to lower lip so bad that she needed 15 stitches and I dislocated her jaw. I was left alone after that fight. I just wanted to move again, get away from all these awful kids, start anew. We ended up moving again, just far enough that it was a new neighborhood with new neighborhood kids, but we still had to go to the same school. It sucked.

Chapter 15

After the fights at school we moved into this little apartment over a mile away from the school, which made walking to and from a pain in the ass. Our "Good Grandparents", my Dad's dad and mom, got us bikes to make it easier on us. We had the best bikes in the whole school because all we had to do was tell them what kind we wanted and they got them for us. My Good Grandparents were the absolute best, not just because they owned their own pizza restaurant, which meant we get free pizza for life, and not because they were rich and gave us whatever we wanted for the most part, and definitely not because they took us to Disneyland every summer, sometimes twice, but they were the best because they were stability, a foundation. I looked at them as what I wanted to be and have when I grew up.

Damien had started kindergarten, but it was only half-day so mom had arranged it with the school that I got a half-day also. So at lunchtime I would grab whatever books I needed and get my assignments from my teacher, loaded up my backpack, and got Damien from his class.

Mom was working a lot of hours, but she was also brunting the full load of the bills by herself, so daycare just wasn't an option for her, and since I was old enough in the school's eyes to babysit, they released him to my care every afternoon to take him home and look after him. I would go to his class, load him up on my handlebars, and peddle us all the way home.

Everyone was jealous of me for getting out of school so early, but what they didn't see was that my grades were falling way behind because I didn't care about doing my "homework" and no one held me accountable. They were still taking me out of class twice a week to go to counseling, which I absolutely hated, so when I passed the 6th Grade it was purely a pity-pass. I was real lucky, I would have to admit.

The apartment we lived in was flanked by a grocery store/strip mall on one side and a gigantic corn field on the other, which made it easy for mom to send me to the store to get random things like milk, bread and other stuffs that run out too fast in a house with 3 growing kids. Even beer, yes beer, I could, at the tender age of 12, go to the grocery store with a note from mom with her phone number on it and with her driver's license and get her a 6-pack of Bud Light. It might sound strange in these days, but it was really quite the norm back then and no one thought twice about it.

The apartment kids spent a lot of time in that corn field. That was where I learned the game Ditch 'em. We could get a group of kids that numbered in the 30's and we would take over that corn field, creating paths like a maze throughout it. We even managed to pull stuff out of the dumpster, like mattresses and boards, to create club houses. We tore that field up. And the poor farmer who owned it, I feel so bad about it now, but he must have had a heart attack when he finally went to harvest and ended up throwing a ton of garbage away. At the time, it was the best place to play, even though the apartment complex had a little playground, we always found our way to the field next door.

The apartment we lived in was little, but had enough rooms for me to have my own, which was awesome. I had made a best friend, Brenda. She was so exotic, so I thought. She didn't have a mom, but lived with her Dad, uncle, and brother. She would go through a can of Aquanet hairspray every three days and always had the coolest clothes. She was a bit overweight, but she had big boobs, which were bigger than her tummy, so she still had the illusion of an hourglass figure. I loved her dearly and we spent tons of time together listening to music and walking around the complex and talking about boys. She lived in the apartment behind mine, but went to a different school, which sucked. I would have loved to be able to have the opportunity, just a chance of ending up in her class. But it just didn't work out that way and we would just meet up as soon as we got home.

One afternoon me and Brenda were walking through the playground, heading towards a boy's house that lived way in the front of the complex. He was a cute boy, a bit older, but he had shown special attention to me and I wanted to go and just hang out.

The playground was barely a playground. The swings had been abused to the point of chains hanging with no seats. There was a set of teeter-totters, but they hadn't been oiled in years, totally neglected, and the force you had to use to launch yourself up was hardly worth the ride. The sand had worn away and most of the ground was now just hard dirt and you definitely didn't want to fall on something that resembled concrete, so basically hardly anyone played there anymore.

There was a building that ran along one side of the playground, it was the pool house. It separated the pool from the playground. It was painted in the same gross rust color as the apartments, and had signs for rules and regulations for entering the pool area. It held all the pumps and filters and probably spiders.

Well, we were walking through the playground and could hear laughter coming from the other side of the pool house. There was a party going on and it sounded pretty rowdy. I walked on, talking with Brenda about the boy when a sudden pain came over me, like I had been shot in the stomach. I reached for my tummy but there was something in the way of my hand, blocking it from making full contact to my belly. I looked down and couldn't comprehend what it was I was looking at. Time slowed down.

I looked at Brenda and her face was contorted and scared. I looked back down at the foreign object, wrapped my fingers around it and pulled it out. It was a dart, not a lawn dart, just a dart. I held it in my right hand looking at it for what felt like several minutes, trying to assess my internal pain scale. My left hand covered the hole and my mind went in circles. Tunnel vision.

I looked back up at Brenda and realized she was screaming. My heart quickened and I flipped out and started screaming right along with her.

Real time kicked in and a bunch of kids came running from the other side of the pool house. One kid, just a couple of years older than me, kept repeating I'm sorry, I'm sorry. But what I heard was that he was at fault for my imminent death. I got mad at the thought of my stomach bleeding out into my body cavity because this dumb kid was careless with a dart. I thought I was going to die a slow and painful death. I really thought that. I screamed at him, Brenda screamed at him, and all he could do was look stupid and apologize.

I still had the dart in my hand, but I needed to get home to go to the hospital so they could operate on me (my panic thinking). I took that dart and threw it down as hard as I could at the ground and as I did it my blood ran cold and my skin crawled with fear. I knew right then and there what I was doing, but couldn't stop myself from doing it, he deserved it after all. I was aiming for his foot. I knew it, but I didn't know it, not really.

As the dart left my hand, time slowed again. My eyes went from his eyes, which turned in an instant from apology to fear, looking down, down, down and as soon as my eyes caught site of the dart it was inserting itself slowly into his foot. I swear I saw waves of flesh move aside to make way for the object that was now taking a place in his foot. It landed right between his first and second toes, about halfway up his foot. Real time started back up as soon as the scream left his face.

I looked back up at him to see his face twisted in pain. All I heard was "Rachel Run!". Brenda was literally pushing me to get home. So I ran, with my hand on my tummy, all the way home, screaming and crying.

I busted through the front door, stopped right inside and screamed for my mom, "Mom! I've been stabbed! MOM!!!".

"What?!" She screamed back at me, moving instantaneously from the kitchen to right in front of me, pulling my hand off my belly.

I couldn't get all the right words out. They were a mixed up soup inside my head, all there, but not put in correct order, and with the babbling bursts of hyperventilating cries, I just couldn't get it all out in order correctly to her.

"Rachel! Calm down! What happened?!" she pleaded. She dropped to her knees and pulled up my shirt. "What happened?!"

She ran her hand across my tummy, feeling it back and forth. She looked up at me with a confused face. I was flipping out on her, but there was nothing there. She got up as Brenda ran in. I was bawling and confused. I had just been stabbed by a dart, but there were no gushes of blood dripping down.

"Brenda! What happened?!" mom asked.

And just as soon as Brenda started telling the story, I found my words. She was the jumpstart I needed to get going. I spoke so fast that I couldn't catch my own breath in between sentences. I watched as I got further into the story how my mom's eyes changed from confusion to fear to angry.

Just as I was getting to the end of the story, a man appeared at the open front door. I turned and saw him standing there with a mean look, and behind him was the boy I threw the dart at, and he was crying. Mom got up and went outside to talk to them and sent me to my room and sent Brenda home. I was in trouble.

My window faced the front of the apartment. It wasn't hard to hear what they were saying. Mom was pissed and apologetic at the same time. Both of the grownups were arguing who was at fault and she didn't back down. It was decided that I wasn't allowed to go past the playground anymore and he wasn't allowed either, so our paths would never cross again, and they didn't.

It was during this time, living in this apartment, that I started to have anomalies happen in my physicality. My emotional self, my subconscious, my memories and stress from such memories started affecting my physical self.

This was when I determined I was full up, like a glass filled to the brim with water. I only had so much space to hold onto memories or feelings of memories and it was getting filled and it started to overflow into the real world.

One afternoon I was riding Damien's Big Wheel around and around the parking lot. I was bored and no one wanted to play. Jason and Damien were busy playing in their rooms and Brenda was spending the day with her dad at her brother's football game.

Out of nowhere my eyesight started to go. It wasn't the normal tunnel vision I got when in a high anxiety situation, in fact it was just the opposite. I stopped immediately and got up of the Big Wheel and looked around at the different cars parked right in front of me. It was hard to understand exactly what was happening. Like when you get a little squiggly floater in your eye and you try to look at it but it moves as you move your eyes, it was like that. I could see in my periphery, but the center of my eyes had this blind spot of visual static. It was black and white and moved sporadically within its borders. I imagined that my pupils were burned out and I was only seeing through my irises. I stood there for a long time wondering what was happening to me, then a strange pulsating pain took over my temples. I ran for mom.

"Mom! I can't see!" I screamed as the door flew open. "Mom?! I'm going blind! I can't see!"

I stood there at the door looking sideways to see her standing dumbfounded in the middle of the room.

"What do you mean blind?! What happened?!"

I couldn't really see her, just sort of knew she was there, her outline was all I could really acknowledge. Fear took over, panic set in. I was going blind. The static spot in the middle of my sight started growing. The periphery was diminishing to smaller and smaller slivers of light and shadow. I was in full panic mode. Mom screamed for the boys as she shoved me through the doorway. She gave them the "staying home alone instructions" and got me into the car. The boys were freaked out, asking all sorts of questions and mom just demanding them to shut and lock the door and stay in the house until we got home.

Mom drove like a bat out of Hell straight to the emergency room. By the time we got there, I was blind with static visuals. Mom was yelling at the doctors and nurses to find out what was wrong with me and the panic in her voice made my own heart palpitate with fear even harder.

By the time I was in the MRI machine, strapped down, my vision had changed again. Now it was static with a pinhole of the world right in the center. The noise inside the machine of the chunk-ka-chunk-ka-chunk was deafening. I could barely make out the sliding mechanism above my head. My pinhole was getting bigger and wider, bordered with an annoying static of black and white snow.

The conveyor rolled me out and I could see the nurse's face smiling down on me. I told her I could see again and she looked confused.

After explaining over and over again what happened to each person who asked, and there were a lot of them, they diagnosed me with an unexplainable seizure disorder.

It wasn't until almost a year later that I had another seizure, and boy oh boy was it a doozy. It was my first school dance and I was excited and scared. I knew how to dance, shit I danced every day in my room while listening to my music really loud. Every girl did that, but I had never danced in front of anyone and I was going to the school where practically everyone hated me. My brother was a year behind me so he wasn't going, and since my very best friend, Brenda, didn't go to my school, she wasn't going to be there either.

For weeks I had been listening to all the girls at recess and in the lunchroom talk about who they were going to the Valentine's Dance with and what they were going to wear. I was humiliated. I wasn't allowed to have any boyfriends, not even friends that were boys. And my clothes were all hand me downs from my mom. I was worried, but I really wanted to go.

Mom had arranged for my Good Grandpa to take me shopping for a dress for the dance. He was so sweet. He had no idea at all what was "in" and he really didn't care what I got, but he built me up telling me how beautiful I was and that I'm a very handsome young woman. I always thought how handsome only belonged to men and boys, not to women and girls and I thought he was sort of dumb for calling me handsome, but I understood that it was a compliment, just an old guy kind of compliment.

He took me to the mall for my outfit and that alone was a huge deal. Mom couldn't afford to buy us clothes from the mall, paying retail wasn't in her budget. But Grandpa had lots of money on credit cards and he took me to Miller's Outpost, a very popular store at the time. It was were anyone whose anybody got their clothes. And just announcing that you got your jeans at Miller's Outpost when someone complimented you on how cute they were, well, that was the best boost to an ego.

He didn't help me pick out my outfits, in fact he walked me into the store, found a young saleswoman and took her aside and talked quietly to her, just out of my earshot. His back was to me as he was talking and she looked around him at me and shot me a smile and a wink. She was so cool looking with her rubber, neon bracelets and teased-fanned hair. I wanted to look just like her.

Grandpa told me to get what I needed and that he was going to go to a different store and this young lady was going to help me with everything. Then he was off to do whatever grandpas do in the mall by themselves.

The saleslady helped me pick out stuff that I thought was cool, and before I knew it I was holding an armful of dresses, skirts, jeans, shirts, blouses, belts, accessories. She shuffled me into the dressing room and told me to try on stuff and come out and show her, which I did, and every time I came out in a different outfit she awed at me and told me how gorgeous it was and how beautiful I looked. She spoiled my little ego.

When Grandpa came back he was munching on a pretzel. He asked me which one I liked best and he made me try it on for him. It was a cute little jean skirt with a belt that was purely for design not necessity, and a deep blue blouse. I agreed that it was perfect for the dance and told me I could wear it home. The young saleswoman took my scrubby clothes and put them in a bag that was overflowing with the clothes I had tried on. I looked at the bag as she handed it to Grandpa and I gasped. He had bought me everything, everything I had tried on, it was now mine.

On our way out we stopped off at a shoe store and he bought me shoes to go with every outfit. He pulled each outfit out of the bag and laid them out so the woman could match up shoes that would go with each one, including the outfit I was wearing. He made me feel like a princess. It wasn't the money that he spent on me, let me make that perfectly clear. It was honestly the affection, the time he spent on me, just me and him. I loved him dearly for giving me his time.

Later that afternoon, when I got home and after Grandpa left, mom went through my bag of new clothes and she was pissed. She was mad that Grandpa spent all that money on me when the boys needed new stuff too.

She told me to pick out my favorite outfit for the dance because she was going to take the rest of them back to the store. I started to cry and she told me to shut up and quit being so selfish. I just wanted nice clothes to wear to school, that's all, but I did what I was told and I shut up, pushed the anger down and accepted that she was right. Why should I be the only one with nice clothes?

The night of the dance, in the car on the way, the static came back. I leaned my head back, shut my eyes, and told my mom "It's happening again. I can't see, mom."

I could feel the car slow down and make a sharp turn. She had pulled off the road. Her hands grabbed the sides of my face and she firmly told me to open my eyes, so I did.

"You're fine. Stop it." she told me staring straight into my eyes. I nodded, but was half-blinded by the squiggly static.

She dropped me off at the front of the school and told me she'd be back when it was over. I stood there staring at the back end of her car leave the parking lot. I waited in front of the school; half-watching the kids walk past me heading for the gym. I listened to the music; Adam Ant, Bon Jovi, Cyndi Lauper. Song after song played while I waited for my sight to return.

After the dance I went back out front to the spot where mom dropped me off. Cars were lined up down the street in single file, waiting their turn to pick up their respective kids from the dance. My only two friends got picked up right away, so I stood there alone in a sea of children excited from the sugar rush of the Kool-Aid punch and sugar cookies served. I watched as each car would pull up and kids would hop in and drive away, letting the next car make its pick-up.

Mom was always late, always. Never once were we the first picked up, for anything. So I knew that it wouldn't be until after all the cars were gone that I would expect her car to show up. I waited patiently.

It was almost 10:30 (according to my new watch Grandpa got me that had Minnie mouse on it) when all the cars were finally gone. One of my teachers saw me standing alone and asked me if I wanted to call my mom. I was afraid that if I left my post she would show up and be mad, so I declined and assured her that my mom would be there soon.

It wasn't long after that that I was truly alone in a dark school, just waiting on my mom. My feet hurt from standing in my new shoes, but I didn't want to sit down knowing that I would get dirt on my new clothes, so I just kept standing there in pain. I think that's when I learned that it hurts to be pretty.

11 o'clock, still no mom. I should've called.

We lived about a mile and a half from the school and I knew the route mom would take to come and get me, so I decided to just go for it and walk home, but not before taking the shoes off first.

I figured I could make it to an "E" house and call her from there, so I started the trek home.

At the first "E" house there was no one home. The second didn't have a phone. That should've disqualified them, that's what I thought anyway. It was going on 11:30 by the time I was getting to the third, which was only a couple blocks away from home. As I started to walk up to the door I heard her car coming down the street.

She beeped the horn and I ran out to the car. I opened the door and in the light from the dome, I could see she was pissed off.

"What the Fuck!?!?!? I told you I was going to pick you up!!! Why didn't you just stay there?? You could have been raped or killed, Rachel!!" She just kept up with the screaming all the way home, and I just sat there, quiet, took it.

We pulled into our spot and walked to the apartment. She opened the door and as soon as I took my first step in, she pushed me from behind so violently that I was lunged forward onto the coffee table. She slammed the door and jumped on top of me with fists flying, connecting each time with a thud. I couldn't breathe. I couldn't scream. I couldn't move.

After a while she got off me and was breathing like she had just run a marathon.

"Go to your room and think about what you've done. You are grounded until I say so." She was speaking so cool and collectively, it was scary.

Tears welled up in my eyes and I ran for my room. I shut the door very quietly, because in our house if you slammed it, you were so busted. I fell on my bed, face down, and scream-cried into my pillow. I felt betrayed and lost. I was supposed to be thinking about what I had done, but what was that exactly?

This wasn't the first time she had done this to me. Just a year before this I had to walk home from the movies with my friends because she was too "out of it" to remember to pick us up. It was humiliating.

I was so happy to be going to the movies with my friends. I was excited because mom was being an active participant. She agreed to take me and 4 of my friends to the mall so we could walk around and then we were going to go to the movies, which was right there at the mall. It was the late 80's and the mall meant everything to a young teeny-bopper like me. She dropped us off and told us she would wait for our call to come get us. I was so, just so happy.

After the movie I called and called, but she didn't answer the phone. We waited on the steps of the movie theater waiting. My friends were getting disgruntled with me. I kept calling every few minutes, waiting for her to answer, and after an hour of calling she finally did.

"Hello?"

I could hear it in her voice, she was wasted.

"Mom? Mom?"

"Rachel? Where are you? Get home right now!" she scolded.

"Mom?! You need to pick us up."

"What? You need to call Lisa's mom. I can't drive right now." At least she was honest.

"We don't have any more money to call. Can you please pick us up?" I was worried. My friends were listening to every word I was saying and I was so embarrassed.

"What's the number to Lisa's mom?" she asked.

I asked Lisa her number and relayed it to mom, but then she couldn't remember it and she had to go get a piece of paper and a pen. I heard her when she put the phone down that there were a bunch of laughs and giggles going on in the background. She was having a party and she was already past the point of no return. She was laughing and having a conversation with someone while I waited and waited. I could just see her, standing in the kitchen with the phone receiver in her hand, talking it up with some guy while I stood waiting in the lobby of the theater with all my friends' eyes on me.

When she finally came back to the phone the little voice announced "please insert 25 cents for the next 3 minutes". She told me to hurry up with the number and I handed the phone over to Lisa.

I watched the anxiety flow over Lisa's face as she recited the number. Then she said it again, and one more time, but the last time quit halfway through, pulling the receiver from her ear. She turned to me and said that the line went dead. Lisa didn't think my mom got the number, and she was right.

Me and my friends waited out in front of the theater for a couple of hours, waiting and watching for Lisa's mom's car to come. We had asked the manager at the theater if we could use their phone and he flat out refused. Something to do with if he let us use it then he would have to let all the kids use it. "Next time you should bring more money to use the phone." He told us.

I sat and listened to my friends talk shit about my mom and how horrible she was and how she didn't care about me. I let them. I was ashamed. We were stranded and it was her fault.

So, I took the reins of the situation. No one else was. They were just a bunch of bitchy betties and I wanted to go home and bury my head in the sand.

"We have to walk home." I announced.

"What?" was the collective unison question. They were flabbergasted at the thought of having to walk home.

"My mom's not coming, she said so. And Lisa, your mom didn't get the call, or she would have been here already. It's starting to get dark and I'm hungry. We have to walk home." It was what it was and I accepted that.

They whined, "We don't even know where we are. We don't know how to get home, how are we supposed to walk all the way home?"

"I know the way." I half-truth told them. I had been to this theater before, but never walked to it. Mom was always driving and since I was the oldest, I was always in the front seat and I watched how we got there. It was just over 4 miles home and we could do it, at least I knew I could do it.

We walked all the way to my house. It took us a while, but we did it. When we walked in there was my mom, stupefied. Then she got mad at me.

"Where have you been?! I've been worried!" She was actually surprised that I didn't make it home earlier.

She didn't get the whole number for Lisa's mom. She thought that Lisa would call her eventually and we would be home. But she didn't, and we had to walk.

After that day I was banished, exiled. All my friends' moms and dads hated me and my mom for making them worry so much. I lost all of them. I wanted to die.

So when I walked home from the Valentine's dance, I didn't see any problem with it, but she did. What was the difference? I had to discern what was so different about those two occurrences. And the only thing I could figure out was that it was nighttime and it was more dangerous at night to walk one mile than to walk 4-1/2 miles during the day time.

The very next day after the dance we had to go to Quartzite, Arizona for the big mineral show. It's like a Comicon for gem and mineral nerds. They all meet in the middle of the desert, set up tents and sell their wares. My mom had been recently dating a man who was involved in making jewelry and he invited all of us to go with him for the weekend.

So mom loaded us up in the car with the new boyfriend, Rob, and we all went to Quartzite. It was a swap meet looking town, overrun with trailers and RVs. Dusty, dirty roads quartered off the displays. Barbeque and cotton candy smells filled the air. It would have been the perfect place for a kid to run amok, but I was grounded, and bruised. Mom made sure that I remembered too. I wasn't allowed to leave her sight the whole time. My brothers on the other hand, well they got to run and play with the other kids that were forced to come. They got to eat big pretzels and slushies and even got toys. Not me though, I was grounded, and she made sure that she showed me what happens to bad girls. I was devastated. So I resigned to her will and just did everything she wanted me to do.

Later that evening, after all the portable shops were closed up for the night, we got to go to a party at an RV. It wasn't a cake and ice cream kind of party, not at all. It was a grownup thing. My mom left my brothers with a friend and made me go with her and Rob to this so called party.

Walking into the trailer, I spotted the carpet first thing. It was gold shag and very worn out. To my right were a small trash basket and a set of small stairs leading up to a loft bed that was above the driver and passenger seats. Immediately it hit me, like a cow prod to my gut, I felt dizzy and anxious. I wanted to run, run screaming away from there, so I did.

I ran out of the trailer and stopped a few feet away, just as the pain stopped. My mom ran up to me.

"Rachel! What is wrong with you?" she was scared.

"Mom! I can't go in there. Something is wrong. I can't be here, I can't be there, I can't be in that place. Please!? Can I just wait outside? I can't go, I can't!" I begged her.

"Why? What happened?!" she was so worried. But when I explained to her I watched her face change from concern to disbelief then to anger.

"I just can't go in there. I dreamt of that place. I know what kind of blankets they have. The man in there has a beard and it's brown. He has yellow pots and pans. I can't go in there." I pleaded with her.

"You're being ridiculous, Rachel. Stop it right now. Stop crying. How do you know what he has? Just stop it." She wasn't caring, she was just plain frustrated with me.

That was the first time ever that I had deja vu and it scared the crap out of me. I had never experienced it before, but have experienced it thousands of times since.

She allowed me to stay outside, but I had to sit on the steps to the trailer and I wasn't allowed to go anywhere, not even to the bathroom. I was fine with that. Mom and Rob went inside and I waited for a very long time.

Chapter 16

One day, out of the blue, mom came to us and said we were going to visit with our Grandpa in California. The Beast. Mom wanted him to meet her new husband, Rob. It had been only 5 years since the rape and everyone, I mean every single person in my life, decided that I should get over it and forgive him. I was alone in my hate and distaste for him.

She told me that I needed to just let it go and get on with my life. She demanded that I have a good attitude and not make him feel bad when we see him. After all, he was taking us to Disneyland and he still loves all of us. I swallowed my fear and hate because I didn't have a choice. She was taking me, us, to see the beast and I had better have a good attitude or I was going to get it.

It's kind of a long drive to California, especially when you're a kid and you don't have fancy iPods or DS or even portable DVD players. Basically you filled a bag with toys and crayons and coloring books and climbed into the car and made sure that your brother didn't lean on you when he fell asleep.

On the way there my mom reminded me a couple of times that I was being a brat every time they talked about him and that I needed to cheer up and be pleasant. I kept trying, trust me, I tried very hard to swallow it up and put it away, but my conscience, my soul kept telling me this was wrong and I was going to have to face my attacker.

When we arrived I wanted to cry and scream and run away, but I didn't. We got out of the car and mom made sure we were brushed up and nice appearing. She reminded us to be on our best behavior because we were going to be there for a few days.

What?!?!? That was the first I heard of that. She sprung it on me that we were going to be staying at his house with him for the weekend.

My blood ran cold. I was now going to have to hold all my fears and anxiety in for an entire weekend in HIS house.

I lagged behind as we walked up to his door. I made sure that I was behind everyone and he didn't have a clear sight on me when he opened it.

When he did open the door, he had loud cheers of happiness. "Hey! There's my Little Girl and all her brood!" He was so happy and so cheerful. I didn't dare look at him.

My brothers didn't know what he had done to me. They just thought he moved away to California and this was the first time he had seen us in a long time. So they rushed him and gave him big bear hugs and he hugged them back with grunts of joy. Then he went to hug my mom, who incidentally was standing in front of me. He grabbed her up in his arms and his chin rested on her shoulder and his eyes looked right down at me. He had a warped smile on his face. He won. He won. He fucking won. He was more important than my safety, my peace of mind. He won and he knew it. His daughter had forgiven him, everyone had forgiven him. He had won the right to do whatever he wanted to whomever he wanted without consequence. He won and I couldn't do a thing about it.

He hugged her and locked eyes with me over her shoulder. He knew and I knew, I was fucked.

After setting her down, she introduced her new husband, Rob. They shook hands and I watched as the beast held his hand and looked him square in the eyes and told him how happy he was to have him as part of the family. They laughed and gave a man hug to each other. Then it was my turn.

"And I know who this young woman is. There's my Rachel! How are you Honey? Give your Grandpa a big hug!" He reached down to put his arms around me. I stumbled back. He was going to touch me and I was so frightened. I wasn't protected and he knew it.

Mom grabbed my arm and pulled me to him. "Quit it Rachel! Hug your Grandpa. He loves you very much." She was annoyed with me.

He put his arms around my waste and lifted me off the ground in a hug that made me want to vomit. And my mom, my mom, she was acting like I was being a brat.

He hugged me for an uncomfortable amount of time, well in all actuality, any amount of time you have to hug your rapist is too long. But, for just a regular hug with a family member, this was just too long, and everyone felt it. They got quiet for a second, but then he spoke.

Still holding me, he said "Well! Let's go inside and get settled in." He carried me into the house. I was not holding onto him. I was removed from the situation at this point, practically dead weight.

When he set me down in the living room, I immediately flopped onto the first thing I could sit on, the big couch.

An older woman appeared. She was petit, kind of elf-like with short blonde hair and very nicely done makeup. She could have been a look-a-like for Tammy Faye with a very sweet smile and very proper. The beast announced her as his new wife, Connie. I was confused. How could someone so nice looking be with such a beast? I sat stunned in my spot on the couch.

The beast offered everyone a snack and some drinks, but I just couldn't take anything in. I was numbly on guard. I stared at my feet most of the time and kept quiet. My brothers and mom and Rob were having a gay time of it. Talking and laughing and sharing about each other and what has been going on in life. I kept my mouth shut and disengaged.

"Rachel! Answer your Grandpa!" mom demanded.

"What?" I asked. I hadn't realized the conversation had shifted to me.

He asked me all sorts of questions and I turned into a monosyllabic droid. Mom would try to elaborate for me, trying to make me seem better than I let on. I just didn't care. I wanted to leave. I could tell my mom was getting upset because I wasn't playing along in the manner she had hoped. She wanted this little fantasy family and I just didn't have it in me to be the perfect little daughter who lets her beast of a Grandpa rape her and then forgive him for it because she said I had to. I didn't let her know that I held in the hate for him, but she knew it by my dissociation with the situation.

My brothers asked if we could go outside to play and in that moment I saw my chance in that little question. The answer was not yet, but after we got all our stuff put away, we could. So us kids made a break for it, putting our stuff away as fast as we could, then out the door we went with mom screaming at us to stay close by and shut the door.

In the parking lot I finally got to breathe. My brothers wanted to play hide and go seek and I was up for that. I just didn't want to go back in that house ever again.

After playing outside for a while, mom came outside and yelled for us to go back in for dinner. My blood ran cold and the prickly hairs stood up. I lollygagged my way to the house; mom met me halfway and stopped me.

After getting down in my face she sternly, unforgivingly told me, "You are being a fucking little brat and you will cut it out right now. You go in there and be thankful that your Grandpa still loves all of us. He doesn't deserve to be treated this way, you cut it out or I will spank you!"

What could I do? I was her daughter, I was taught to obey her. I was taught to love her. She loved me right?

She followed me into the house and we all sat down for dinner at the table. I couldn't eat. I honestly just couldn't eat. My stomach was turning and churning and all I wanted to do was go home and be in my bed. I didn't care about going to the beach or even Disneyland, I just wanted to go home. But I didn't get to go home. I sat there staring at my plate and I felt mom staring at me, boring holes in the top of my head as I looked down.

New Grandma Connie took my plate after everyone was done and went to the kitchen only to return with chocolate cake. There was nothing wrong with the cake, but I just couldn't eat it. My mom was so mad at this point. I made eye contact for just a second, just long enough to see that I was going to get a big spanking when we got home. Shit, she wasn't even going to wait until we got home. She was going to yell at me for at least 100 miles and then, when we are in the middle of the desert, she is going to pull over and drag me out of the car and beat me right there next to a big saguaro cactus. The hate in her eyes in that second was more than I could bear.

I picked up my fork and took a bite of the cake. It was tasty, not poisonous at all. I looked at her again and she motioned for me to take another bite, and so I did. Looked at her again, but this time she was laughing at a joke or something and wasn't paying attention. She lost interest, got distracted, and I was off the hook. I put my fork down and went to the bathroom where I threw up yellow bile and chocolate cake.

The weekend lasted forever. Saturday we all went to Knott's Berry Farm, not Disneyland as promised, and we rode the rides and the beast bought everyone presents from the shops around there, everyone, including me. I didn't choose my present though. He kept pressing on me to pick something, but I just couldn't accept anything. If I did, then he wins over me. He may have won with my mom, with the situation, with the control, but deep down inside he knew, he knew that he hadn't won me over. And I wasn't just about to hand over the win, not ever.

Mom, once again, took me aside and yelled at me for being a "little ungrateful brat". But I didn't give in. I was stronger than her and him combined when it came to will. After refusing gift after gift, mom finally picked something out for me. It was a little stuffed snoopy dog. She made me thank him out loud and to his face, which I begrudgingly did. On our way back to the parking lot I set the snoopy on the ground next to a big planter with palm trees and beautiful pink flowers in it and walked away. It wasn't until after we got back to the beast's house that mom asked me where my gift was. I played it off like I must have left it in the car. She made me go look for it. When I returned without it she was mad, real mad. I was definitely going to get beat. She knew that I had gotten rid of it, threw it away, and that she still hadn't won. This was a war of wits, but I was a child and didn't realize that she had already won.

Sunday we all went to the beach. My brothers and I played in the surf all day long. We loved body surfing and building sand castles. My mom had gotten me a real nice turquoise bikini at the beginning of summer and I loved that suit. But wearing it there in front of the beast, I felt dirty, nasty, gross, like a "bad little girl". I wanted to wear my tee shirt, but I wasn't allowed. So I just stayed away from him and mostly in the water with Jason and Damien. We had so much fun that day when it was just me and them in the ocean. Like the real problems that laid up on the beach didn't even exist.

That night was going to be our last night staying with the beast. We were going to go home the next day at least that is what I assumed. It turns out that the beast offered for mom and Rob to go ahead on their honeymoon and he would watch us for a couple of weeks so they could have some alone time, get-to-know-you, kind of honeymoon. When she broke the news to me, well I was crushed. I wanted to go home, just to be at home away from him. I cried, she got mad at me.

"You stop that right now. Don't you dare cry. I deserve this vacation and you are going to stay here with your Grandpa! Stop crying right this second or I will give you something to cry for! Stop it! You have no reason to cry!" She demanded me to stop crying or I was going to get slapped in the face. She's done it before, simply for crying I would get an open hand slap right across my face. So I swallowed my heart and pulled back the tears. I had to stay with the beast for two weeks. (No wonder she packed so many clothes for us.)

My brothers and I slept in the extra room on the pullout couch. All of us squished together in one bed. It was a perfect fit. Damien was still little and Jason and I were a bit on the skinny side, not because we were malnutritioned or anything, more like because we bounced off the walls and stayed very active. I was thankful to know that I didn't have to share a bed with the beast, but still, I was uncomfortable knowing that when I woke up in the morning mom would be gone.

I had a fitful sleep. Nightmares invaded me every time I closed my eyes. Seeing the shadow and feeling the bed rise and fall like a rough tide. Moving up and down, shaking me awake. I opened my eyes and the bed was moving, but not because someone was climbing in with us, oh no! Actually the bed was violently bouncing up and down off the floor. It was an earthquake! It only lasted for a few seconds, but enough to scare me and I didn't sleep the rest of the night.

I only got up in the morning when the boys got up, to make sure that I was never going to be alone with him. I was on guard constantly. Clinging to my brothers every chance I got.

New Grandma Connie was being nice, but she didn't know the truth. She had a job that she had to go to everyday, and the beast, well he just had his knee replaced so he was not working, which left him at home alone with us all day. The two weeks we were there never seemed to end. We were stuck with him 24-7. He took us to the beach and out to eat and every time he was around I purposely didn't make eye contact with him. I stayed out of his way and made sure I was never alone. I was on edge. When I did accidentally see his eyes, I saw lust. Lust is not something a 12-year-old should know, but I knew it and I felt it any time he touched me or tried to give me a hug.

Mom finally came and got us and we went home. I slept hard for weeks after that, not wanting to get out of bed. I was emotionally spent, exhausted from being on guard. I hated her for making me go through that, but she made me love her again. I wasn't allowed to be mad or moody or unforgiving, so I pretended because I still had to live with her.

A few months later, after I had just gotten back into the groove of being normal again, she announced that the beast was coming for a visit to our new house. I was floored. Immediately she turned on me, instructing and demanding that I better have a better attitude. I couldn't even answer her. I was lost in a sea of fear and anxiety that swept over my whole being. I was being challenged, yet again. I wanted to die. I literally wanted to run into traffic and die. She yelled at me over and over again about how much of a little bitch I was the last time and that I was really mean to the beast, he said so when he talked to her, and how I will not, absolutely will not be a brat when he gets here. I was stunned. Why didn't she just kill me? It would've been easier.

Then she told me that he was going to sleep in my bed. My bed, my personal safe haven, he was going to invade it. My sheets, my pillows, my smells, my happy place, he was taking it over and I didn't have a chance at an argument. She made up her mind and this was what was going to happen, end of story. I cried.

"Stop it right now! This is what I'm talking about! Stop your crying right now or I will give you something to cry about! What is wrong with you?! You need to just grow up and let go of this! He is your Grandpa and he will always be a part of your life!" She was screaming at me.

I sucked it up and pushed it down, way down, because they can make me pretend, but it won't be true or real.

"Shut up right now, Rachel! Shut your fucking mouth and stop crying!" She was really pissed and annoyed now.

I tried really hard to hide it. Put it away. Put it away before you get slapped. Just don't show your hate, just put it away. Lock it up in the cabinet and open it when he gets here. You'll be safe in front of him. You will be an embarrassment, but you'll be safe.

The day he showed up at our door he was full of hugs, except this time I didn't hug him. I stayed in my room hiding, pretending to work on homework.

My room was the only one downstairs and I had my own bathroom down my own little hallway. Sure I had to share the bathroom with whoever was downstairs at the time they needed to relieve themselves and with any guest that might be visiting, but for the most part I had my own little wing, if you will.

I listened from my room to the greetings and the cheers on how big the boys were getting, turning into fine young men. Then I heard him ask.

"Where's my Rachel? I bet she's turning into a beautiful young woman." He said with a list in his voice that was incestual. I cringed, it was coming. Wait for it, wait for it –

"Rachel! Get out here and say hi to your Grandpa!" mom yelled at me like I was next door at the neighbor's house in their basement. She knew I was avoiding. I knew she knew, but I was safe, sort of.

I ignored the first call.

I heard them talking for a minute, happily connecting in the foyer. Then she screamed, this time extra mad.

"Rachel Eve! Get your ass out here RIGHT NOW!"

I felt my blood run cold. That tone was definitely a slap in the face and a groundation for a month. So I yelled back, through my closed door, and from the other side of my room,

"Just a Minute, Please." The please was to cushion the blow I was going to get later. If I used please and was polite and proper, well she couldn't be all that mad at me. Respectful responses are taken with a grain of salt in defiance.

I waited in my room, on purpose, hiding. I heard them head past my little wing of the house and onto the kitchen area, talking the whole way. I waited.

A whole 20 minutes I was safe in my room, then I heard them say my name about something. I heard mom head back to my area of the house, so I ran for my desk and pulled out a history book and hovered over it just as she busted through my door. "Rachel!" she was practically snarling.

I slowly turned my head, barely shifting in my seat. I knew I was in for a world of hurt for blatant defiance. In my sweetest (manipulating) voice I replied, "I was just finishing this last question". My periphery vision started to fade into blackness. My anxiety was at full throttle and about to take me down to the ground. I knew in every fiber of my being what I was doing was wrong, at least wrong in her eyes, but I also knew at the same time that I was saving my own life.

She rushed me and pulled me up by the shoulders. Her fingertips dug into my shirt, skin, and muscle. She was mad. Beyond mad. Eye to eye she held me and as her lips grew thin and her face took on the look of a possessed person, she scowled at me in a whispered growl, "Get out there and say hi to your Grandpa. He came all this way to see you, to see us (she corrected herself). You better be on your best behavior." All I could do was nod in acceptance. My sight narrowed further, almost to the size of a pin. I worried that I might go blind, but I worried more that I had to face the beast and his toothy smile of lust.

She whipped me around and thrust me to the door and as I stepped over the threshold I felt her strong manly hand on my upper back, right between my shoulder blades, and I knew what was next. I was shoved. Not uncommon for her to shove me, I kind of expected it, and didn't flinch when it happened, because if I had, well I would've gotten her even madder at me. So you take what you're given and push through to the next situation.

The physical pain of being beaten, the mental anguish and anxiety of what an impending unjust punishment of defiance, those things didn't matter to me. I was more upset that I had once again been betrayed by the one who was supposed to love me most. I was repeatedly pulled from her teat to be thrown to the wolves, or the beast as it were, and then demanded, when it suited her, that I latch on once again or else suffer the consequences.

I righted myself after bouncing of the wall and turned the corner to see IT sitting there at the end of the hall, in the kitchen, at our table, in my chair. My tunnel vision, actually my pencil tip vision, zeroed in on him like a sniper. All I needed at that point were the crosshairs.

He turned and his eyes burning bright caught sight of me in all my mid-puberty essence. I was never more ashamed of my body than at that point in time, at least up until that point in time. His big voice boomed through the house.

"There's MY RACHEL!!!"

That smile, those teeth, UGH. I felt the bile rise up in the back of my throat and hadn't realized that I came to a stop, a short-stop right in front of my mom's momentum. She took a step into my back, smashing into me like I was a pillar of concrete.

Its face turned sad, like a poor little puppy dog. He was hurt, not genuinely, but just enough to make her rile up and push me forward violently. "Go Over and Give Your Grandpa a Big Hug and a Kiss Hello." She tried to sound encouraging. She tried to make it sound fun. But she knew that I knew I didn't want to do this. She said it again, but this time the list had turned from encouragement to instruction.

His big smile and his open arms were waiting to take me in. I looked down and watched my feet make the steps, I saw my legs with forward momentum, I watched as I sat down on his lap and his arms folded around my body. I watched as I fell into my own cocoon within myself. I watched my eyes turn blank.

"Rachel! Hug Your Grandpa!" No encouragement this time, not even a little. It was the annoyed demand.

I weighed the options: Be beaten to within an inch of my life and grounded for all eternity to play Cinderella in her house and do all of her bidding, or, give a hug, get out of this situation and hide all day on my turf. I chose the latter.

I flatly pulled my arms up and listly, almost trying not to touch, patted him. He did not accept this. He pulled me in deep and firm and bear-hugged me. I kept my eyes closed. I watched from across the room as he leaned in to give me a kiss and I pulled my head back.

"Rachel Eve, You GIVE YOUR GRANDPA A KISS RIGHT NOW! You are hurting his feelings! He loves you very much!" she was so mad and I was still going to get beat and a groundation after this. He was winning, looking like an ass while doing it, but still winning. I embarrassed my family, my mom, him, the whole situation was awkward and everyone felt it. I wanted to die.

I didn't lean in, but I didn't pull away either (and this will always haunt me), so he took the opportunity and gave me a big wet kiss. Not a total make out session or anything like that, but more like a sucking of my lower lip with a little tongue. A "first kiss" kind of kiss. It was not what any grandpa anywhere in the whole world should give their teenaged granddaughter, not ever. I was shocked. I had never been kissed by a boy at this point, so for him to kiss me like that, it was humiliating. I felt raped all over again, yet this time my mom was standing right there in the kitchen drinking a beer. She didn't necessarily see it, but she knew what happened.

As soon as I felt the tension in his arms give I made a break for it. I wasn't allowed to go hide, I was instructed to stay and "visit". My vision had come back to full view and I saw myself sit down at the table with everyone. Lots of conversation was had about school, work, and whatnot. Beer after beer they became louder and louder and every time there was a burst of laughter my skin began to crawl. That laugh of his, it creeped me out. It was the same laugh, that same fucking laugh that I heard before he crawled into bed with me. I was tortured with it. Over and over again flashes of incest came flooding over and over again with his outbursts. All I could do was sit there and listen to it. Anxiety and fear of sitting and listening to that laugh coupled with the fear and anxiety of leaving the situation without permission was more than anyone should ever have to bear. I went into myself.

I wasn't safe in front of my own mom, brothers, stepdad, no one. He stayed with us for the whole weekend and I made sure that I stayed hidden when I was able to. My room was off limits as the beast had taken it over, so I temporarily moved in with Jason. He had a large warm waterbed and he didn't kick me in his sleep. I tried hard to stay away as much as possible. Even when the family decided to take the Beast out to dinner or to the Swapmeet, I kept to myself. I became my own best friend, the only one who really knew what was right and what was wrong. I kept my mouth shut and at the end of the line, opposite end of the table, in the next room, whatever I could, I kept him at arm's length.

At the end of the weekend, the goodbyes were subtle. Big hugs were forced on me, but this time I turned my head and got a sloppy kiss on the cheek. And when instructed to give a "proper" kiss, well I refused flatly. I had enough internalizing the whole weekend to come up with the choice of absolute defiance and the consequences thereof and controlled defeatedness. I chose my driven virtue of morality over my mother's demanding instructions to comply with a rapist who had money. I wasn't going to be bought.

I didn't stare at my feet this time. This time I looked her straight in the eye when I said "No". I felt a fire behind that no. It was strong and hot. My stomach burned with it, my gut said "No" this time. My gut was behind me and though my vision narrowed with anxiety when I said it, I still said it and meant it. Her aura of demanding hierarchy stumbled back and fell on its ass. I watched her eyes finally get it as she shifted from my gaze to the Beast's eyes. I stood there in the yard with the family who were all waving goodbye to him as he drove off down the street. I felt strong, scared and strong because I knew what was next. My consequences that I had so boldly chosen. I took them proudly without complaint. I didn't fight, try to explain, bargain, cry. I didn't give her the satisfaction. I took into my own hands what I had chosen and I wasn't going to be manipulated by it any more.

Chapter 17

Stepdaddy Rob was a pretty decent guy. We had gotten into a big beautiful house with a pool and he gave us things like an allowance, took us bowling and camping. He played the drums for a hobby and had a band that he would play with sometimes at parties. We did normal family stuff with him. So when mom and he started arguing a lot, it really worried me. We were going to have to move again. I had finally settled into this life and I loved everything about it. I had a ton of friends and really loved my new school.

One night, being the only one downstairs, I heard mom come in really late. I had assumed that she was at work or something because Rob hadn't been in a bad mood at all that evening. So it totally surprised me when the screaming and yelling started up. It was common to hear vile words spill out of grownups when they are pissed, but this night took on a whole new level of violence. My mom was actually screaming "STOP!" and "NO! PLEASE DON'T!".

The crashing and sounds of breaking glass made my hairs stand on end. I sat there in my bed motionless, frozen to the spot. I knew I was supposed to do something, but I couldn't wrap my head around it.

"ROB! NO!!! OH GOD HELP ME!!!" She was frantically screaming now.

I jumped out of bed and ran to the bottom of the stairs, froze again. What was I supposed to do? Surely Jason and Damien could hear what was going on as their rooms were right across the hallway from her's.

More breaking stuff sounds, really loud this time.

I slow-motioned my way up the stairs, waiting for the call to come and help. Each step, painstakingly slow.

I got to the top of the stairs and turned to Jason's room. I peeked in and he was lying motionless. So dark, I couldn't see his eyes.

BAM!

I whipped around and faced her door. It was moving, like lungs inflating and deflating. I moved closer still. I could hear her crying and he was grunting.

I got up to the crack, pressed my lips against it, "Mom? Mom? Are You Okay?".

"Rachel! Go Back To Bed Right Now!".

I started to cry and the crackle in my voice revealed my fear. "Mom? Are you Okay?"

"Yes! Go Back To Bed." I did as I was told.

The next day was just another day and no one even mentioned the night before, like it didn't even happen.

Over the following weeks Mom was spending a lot of time away from home. She left us on our own for the most part because Rob was rarely around too. When they did come together, there were always a lot of tears. You could feel the tension, see it, but not talk about it. I could feel it falling apart again.

We were all invited over for a party at Rob's best friend's house, Bobby, so we went. This was Rob's demise right here, and the rest of our lives would never be the same after this night.

I dreaded "parties" with parents. Usually it meant there was never as much food as there was booze, and never as many kids as parents, and I was always the oldest so I was always put in charge of the little kids. Basically, it was a long night of free babysitting a bunch of kids who were going to get bored. I wasn't looking forward to it.

Upon arriving I was surprised to see numerous kids of all ages out front. Maybe this was going to be a fun night after all.

Mom and Rob were unloading his drum kit when Bobby came out of the house. He greeted us with a big smile. He seemed genuinely joyous at our coming over to his house. He introduced us kids to his kids and some of the other grownup's kids. I immediately set my sites on one girl named Naomi who looked a year or so older than me and had really pretty hair. She was kind of standing by herself over in the driveway.

After unloading the drums from the car, each of us grabbed something, including Bobby, and started inside the house. Stepping in, I was amazed at the site of the living room. It had been completely transformed into a music room. There were all sorts of amps and instruments. The couch and chairs had been pushed out of the way and had some grownups plopped down on them. I stood there as Bobby introduced each of us properly to everyone who was in the room and each person seemed enthusiastic that Rob was there with his kit. I was so proud at that moment that he was my daddy and he was the one who was going to play the drums that all these people get to hear.

We set the stuff down and mom made us go outside to play with the other kids. I was kind of disappointed. I was a teenager and totally deserved to stay inside to watch the band, but alas I was sent out with the kids, so I begrudgingly did as I was told.

It was about an hour later when I heard those first sweet notes of a guitar tuning up. It was so loud that even though I was out by the street it startled me. I swung around and stared at the house for a moment, anticipating the next strum. It came without disappointment. A kid ran past me and then another, up toward the house. I ran after them.

I got up to the big window in front and peered in. The band was starting their first song and there was Rob playing his heart out. His smile was so big and it reminded me that he could smile that big. I hadn't seen it in quite a while and had almost completely forgotten it. I could see mom perched on a stool behind him with a beer in her hand. She was bopping her head up and down and was smiling, almost laughing. She was so happy. I had almost forgotten that look too. It swelled pride and joy inside me.

Then the guitarist went into his solo and I shifted my eyes to him. Wow! This guy was really going at it. I couldn't see his face beyond the long thick black hair. Had I met him earlier? I wondered. I crushed hard. I stood in front of that window staring hard, wondering how I could meet this Guitar God. His solo ended and he came up. His face was angelic, so cheerful and accomplished. He revealed his pride in a "Hell Yeah!" as there were whoops and hollers at his good performance. I wanted to be in that room with them all and cheer right along with them. He had real talent. He was no hack, no flake. He loved his music and it showed.

They must have played for 2-3 hours before their first break and it was only at that break when us kids were allowed back into the house. Oh sure we were allowed to run through to the bathroom, or to the kitchen to get a drink, but the rest of the time we were admonished to the front yard to "play". But for me and Naomi we just stood there at the window to watch.

At break the grownups all went back into the master bedroom. Yes, all 15 of them. I don't know how they fit in there, they just did. And us kids, well, we weren't supposed to bug them. They locked the door and turned up the music. I could only guess what they were doing, no wait, I take that back. They were getting high. You could smell it, it was undeniably strong and when they opened that door, well, anyone standing in the hallway automatically got a contact high.

They were in there for an awfully long time, but once they emerged it was back to the music and kids were back outside. This cycle went on and on through the night until finally we were told that we were going to stay the night. The girls were in one room and the boys in another. I was lucky, there were only 4 of us girls to two twin beds, but the boys on the other hand, that was tough. There were 6 of them and only one queen bed. We were told to go to sleep, but then they played music all night long, loudly. I don't know where the grownups got the reasoning out of this, it was ridiculous. The music was loud and it was in the next room, how were we supposed to sleep through that? It didn't matter, we were just supposed to. So I laid there and listened.

Every time they would break I would get the excited feeling in my tummy that we would get to go home and I would finally get to go to sleep. A parent would come into the room and escort a child out to go home and I would wait for my turn, anticipating my mom coming in for me. I would listen to the door shut to the master bedroom, the music get turned up, and the laughs, knowing that we weren't going home yet. I would settle in and just as I would drift, off the break would be over and I was wide awake listening to the same 5 songs being played again.

I watched the window, waiting for the sun to come up, my only indicator of time because the room I was in lacked a clock and there was no way I was going to piss off mom and ask what time it was and when were we going home. Finally, the sky started to change color and the music died down. I got hope that we would get to go home. I wanted my bed. I wanted sleep.

I listened intently at the voices and giggles as they walked down the hallway. I sat up in bed and waited for my cue. The voices walked past and the door shut again, but no music this time. I waited and waited.

The sun was fully up when I decided to climb out of bed. The house was silent except for the sound of the swamp cooler. I walked to the threshold of the bedroom and peeked out, down the hallway. The master bedroom door was closed. I walked out past the music/living room and into the kitchen. The clock on the microwave said 8. I went back to the master bedroom door and pressed my ear up against the crack of the frame. Snoring sounds. They were sleeping. I knew full well that I am not allowed to wake up mom, not unless it was an emergency. And going home and sleeping in my own bed was not considered an emergency.

I went into the boys' room and there were my brothers fast asleep on the floor, along with some other boys. So I went to the living room and sat patiently waiting for the grownups to emerge. I finally got the courage to turn on the TV around 11 when Jason and Damien woke up.

We were so hungry, but being in someone else's house, well you just didn't go rooting around their fridge. But listening to Damien say "I'm hungry, go wake up mom" so many times makes you reassess your priorities. I could go wake up a bear or I could break Ms. Manner's protocol and raid the fridge. After the umpteenth time of Damien's declaration of starvation, I decided to raid the fridge instead of getting yelled at.

I walked into the kitchen and opened the fridge and right then Bobby rounded the corner and startled me. I was busted for sure.

"What are you doing?" he questioned.

"Damien is really hungry." I replied sheepishly, blaming it all on poor defenseless little Damien, even though I was starving too and would've made something for all of us kids.

Then Bobby surprised me. "Oh! Okay! Well, let me make some crepes for you guys."

Okay, now this was weird. A man we hardly knew was willing to make us an exotic breakfast, (I had never heard of crepes and hoped they were yummy and not something gross like poached eggs), and he wasn't mad that I was in his kitchen going through his stuff. I was impressed. I was naïve.

We ended up staying the whole weekend. We just sort of fit ourselves in and when we were hungry someone fed us and when we were sleepy, we slept where we could, when we could. The parents would spend all their time in the bedroom together doing what they do and us kids were told to go play, so we did.

When Sunday night finally rolled around I was exhausted. Finally in my own bed, I slept hard and long, missing the alarm clock and running late to school.

We had all gone back to a normal schedule for two weeks. It seemed as though mom and Rob had made up and I had gotten back a semblance of security. Then mom made an announcement. It wasn't all official, sitting us down and talking to us type of an announcement, it was while we were driving over to Bobby's house.

"Me and Rob are getting a divorce. Things aren't working out and Bobby is going to give us a place to stay for a while." I was devastated. My mind took over and it was running wild. I lost control and started crying which sent mom into a frenzy of hissing/scowling/venomous rants of how this will be better for us. Then she said something that stopped everything.

"Rachel. He raped me." She only had to say it once. I heard her over my own streaming thoughts. Rob raped her. He was a bad man. We had to get away. So we did.

The move was relatively uneventful. We had moved so many times, it was almost easy. Except this time we were moving into a house with a man who had kids; a boy and a girl. So I had to share for the first time and I was not excited about it to say the least. She was at 10 years younger than me and she wet the bed every night so my room always smelled like urine. I hated it. I hated her. She was a brat in every sense of the word. Because it was his house and this was his daughter, I was automatically third rate and my voice didn't matter at all for any reason. She was golden and I was shit. And mom, well, she didn't stand up for me for anything because this was our last hope and she needed me/us to play nice. So I did, for the most part.

Chapter 18

Living with Bobby was hard. I was so far away from my high school that in order for me to continue there I had to make a deal with mom saying that I would get myself there and home every day by using the city bus and we would have to lie and use our cousin's address for the report cards. But I needed to keep that foundation of stability in my life, so I fought hard for that opportunity.

Mom and Bobby started spending a lot of time in the bedroom. A lot, really, like 18 hours a day were spent in the room. Mom lost her job. Bobby lost his. We got on welfare and food stamps. All sorts of people were "staying" with us. The "band" would practice at our house, but they never played any real gigs to make money. And within weeks of starting high school, Jason dropped out.

My brothers and all of their friends had gotten into a gang and were doing drugs, selling drugs, robbing places and people. Mom and bobby continued to hide in their room. Then I joined a gang.

But my gang was the exact opposite of my brothers' gang. Oh, we weren't rivals or anything like that. Just our principals of what our gangs stood for were polar opposites.

In the late 80's early 90's in Phoenix a club of sorts was created. Phoenix Area Straight Edge (PASE). I don't know exactly why I was pulled in this direction. It wasn't

226

like a teacher, friend, or family member told me that I could be so much better than what I was being brought up in. It was just some sort of an intuition. One day I heard about it and what it stood for and something inside me clicked and I knew this was something for me.

PASE changed my view on so many things in my life. It was like waking up one day and seeing that the world is 3 dimensional when all you've ever known was 2 dimensions. I always had a feeling that something wasn't right in my life, that it wasn't supposed to be the way it was, and PASE validated my internal conflict. This gang was important to me, more important than my family. Almost cult-like, but in a positive way. We believed in No Sex, No Drugs, No Alcohol, No Smoking. We took our aggression out in the mosh pits at concerts. Our raging hormones were subdued with trips to the skate park. We had each other and there was no pressure in your clean choices because we shared them. You were automatically passed over from imbibing in illicit activity when you wore that big black X on your hand. And you wore that Big Black Sharpie X on your hand with pride, knowing who you were and knowing that others automatically understood what you were about. There was no debating it, no compromise. You were straight, period.

I never had a problem being straight edge anywhere, except at home. Wearing that X on my hand drew negative attention. It was a fight with my mom and brothers. I was automatically thought of as "better than them" and they didn't like it. The fact was, I wasn't better than them, I was different from them. They chose a different path and I didn't argue their path with them, but they sure felt like they had to argue with me. I was the white sheep in a flock of black ones. I had put myself there, I'll admit it. Fine. I was putting myself out there as someone different from them and I isolated myself from them and their lifestyle. But in my defense, it fucking saved me.

My mom started doing some really hard drugs, not sure exactly what they were, but I wouldn't see her for days on end because she was sleeping. And as for Bobby, he would only emerge when they needed food. He would make late night runs to McDonald's or Jack in the Box only to return and hurry to the bedroom with bags full of food. No, he would not share with us. We were left to go hungry or eat whatever we could find. There were five kids in the house and we were getting food stamps for all 7 of us, but there was never any food, but plenty of drugs to stay fucked up on for days on end.

I was only 14, but I knew we needed more money coming into the house. So I got creative with my birth certificate. I owned a typewriter that my mom gave me years before when we were doing really well. I got it for Christmas one year because I loved to write stories and I was very good at it. (It only took me 30 years to actually write something I want to have published. Wink wink.) So, I didn't want to actually mess with my original birth certificate, instead I walked down to the drug store and made a copy of it, took it home, whited out the year I was born, walked back to the drug store, made another copy, took it home and lined it up perfectly in the typewriter and made my age 2 years older. Then I canvassed every business within two miles with applications. My Mom was pissed when she found out. Not pissed about the creative altering of my birth certificate, oh no, that would have been the legitimate disappointment. She was pissed at the fact that I was trying to get a job and earn money. Her reasoning was that if I started earning money that they wouldn't get as much in food stamps or welfare anymore and that wasn't good.

I got a call for an interview at a local pizza parlor and I got the job. She was super mad at me. The only way I was going to be allowed to have the job was if I handed all my checks over to her and she would give me an allowance. I agreed. Again, I was naïve.

I worked my ass off at that job. 25 hours a week washing dishes and cleaning bathrooms and when I would get my checks at the end of the week I had to hand them over and get my measly $30 in return. It didn't matter if I worked more hours, which I did on several occasions, I would only get my little $30. And with this allowance I was now supposed to pay my own way with food, lunches for school, and bus fare. Her reasoning at the time was that if I thought I was adult enough to have a job then I was adult enough to pay my way. So I agreed. It was infuriating, but I couldn't disagree. She made the rules.

I was spending a lot of time away from home and it opened my eyes even more. My best friend at the time let me stay at her house any time I wanted to and with that and going to school full-time and working part-time, I was rarely at home. I started to see how families are really supposed to work. The parents work, bills get paid, and children go to school every day and food is readily available at mealtimes, oh and there are mealtimes. How could I have forgotten that in such a short amount of time living with Bobby. Our whole lives had taken a 180 since we moved in with him. Our lives sucked. I started not caring about school as much as making money. I saw that if I worked hard enough I might have a chance to get away. So my grades slipped.

One day at school I broke. The silence of our family was broken, by me. The counselor called me into his office because he actually noticed that I was slipping. I just didn't care about school anymore. I had been working my ass off for a year now and I didn't see what difference it made if I stayed in school. No one was holding me accountable, except this guy, this day.

I went in with a chip on my shoulder. There was no way I was going to let him convince me that school was my answer to a better life. So a debate was had. He was giving me the good old speech about good grades equals good college equals great job equals better life. Then I rebutted with drug-addicted parents, drug-addicted siblings, living in the heart of gang-land Maryvale, coupled with no money, no food, no adult supervision worthwhile equals Rachel gets a crap job, moves out to anywhere and tries to live a full life without poverty. He was stunned. That shut him up. Score one for the little girl who sees life in a totally different way than the college grad.

I told him there was no hope. He told me there was and signed me up for counseling at the school. I told him if my mom ever found out that he would never see me again, which was the truth. My mom would have never put up with anyone knowing what was really going on in our household and she would pull me out of school and I would never see the light of day again for telling the truth. Then he called in another advisor and the vice principal. I explained what was going on at home and they cried. I was numb, no tears for me because, well this was life. My life. It was what it was, like the sky is blue and the grass is green, at least when you water it.

They told me that they were really concerned and that I needed help and I agreed. I didn't necessarily agree for myself, I had a job after all and could take care of myself. It was my brothers I was worried about. Bobby's kids, well they could go live with their mom. But me and my brothers we didn't have anyone but my mom. Our dads were way out of the picture so we had no one to help us. I had to help us. These people had to help us. I told them that it had to be completely anonymous from my end and they agreed. I believed that they were going to help. Child Protective Services were called and I had to talk to them and explain my situation. I told them the truth about everything. I answered all the questions fully without hesitation. I was scared, but I did it anyway. Anything, any fucking thing would be better than living within that situation.

I stayed afterschool that day, called in sick to work, and when the school closed I went to the mall and hung around contemplating on what had transpired. I wondered if I had done the right thing telling on her, them. I wondered what was going to happen. I worried. It took a couple of hours to sike myself up to go home knowing that I had nothing to regret. That I made the right decision.

I took the bus home like usual, just later. I walked up my street and up to the house. When I walked in my mom was waiting for me on the couch. I stopped dead in my tracks. It was weird to see her outside of the room and lucid. I could see the anger in her eyes. I frantically went through the situation in my mind, trying to anticipate how the conversation was going to go, trying to get a leg up on it, get ahead of it, to make sense out of it. Wondering how in the hell did she find out so fast. Did they already come by? Did they call her? Play dumb was all I could think of.

"Where have you been?!" she yelled.

"I was at the mall." Trying to keep it short and sweet. She doesn't need to know more information than she was asking.

"Your work called. You didn't show up, why?"

"I called in sick. I just wanted a day off."

She was mad.

"You know we need that money. Why did you call in? Why did they call me if you called in? You wanted this job Rachel, you can't just call in because you want a day off." She was talking to me like I was a little kid and I hated her for it.

"I don't know why they called you. I told Mike. Maybe he didn't tell the manager."

"Maybe you're not responsible enough for a job then."

I felt my freedom slip away with that sentence and it scared me. Fight or flight. Do I plead or change the subject and get on the offensive. Ah, the latter.

"Mom. I took the day off because I'm worried." I took the tone of a very solemn child. It pulled on her, I saw it, but only for a second. She switched to the 'are you bullshitting me' look.

"What do you have to worry about?"

Then I pulled out the big guns and totally caught her off guard, "Are you addicted to drugs?"

You see, this subject was always off limits. We all knew that they were doing drugs, but it was taboo to talk about, ever. You just didn't mention drug use or how it affected our lives. For instance, you could never say anything like "Well, we would have food if you didn't trade all of our food stamp money for a weeks' worth of meth". That would have gotten you a slap in the face and more.

So attacking this subject on the front lines really knocked her down a few pegs. She knew I was straight edge and she knew exactly what that meant, which was the complete opposite of what she was in every sense. Asking this question so blatantly left no wiggle room, no explaining away, and I had the upper hand. I was secretly giggling inside with the notion that I had one on her. I was winning. She hadn't gotten a call from the school or CPS or the police, not yet, so I was in the clear, so far. I was winning.

Her face morphed into a contorted mix of a smile of embarrassment and frowning disappointment. She was confused on how to approach this with me. This was absolutely not a topic of conversation and I was not privy to such information, so how dare I ask such a clear, concise question.

"What are you talking about?" was all that spewed out.

"Mom. I Think You are Addicted to Drugs." I said sternly. Tunnel vision set in instantly.

She got mad at my repeated attempt of revealing her true self to the world. Making her say it out loud, making her know what she really is.

"Who do you think you are?! Asking me a question like that? Why would you even say anything like that to me? What is wrong with you?" She was stumbling over her own words. She couldn't even grasp what this situation was. I was confronting her and she couldn't handle it, like she never even thought it would ever happen, not ever.

"I think you are addicted because you hide in your room all the time and never come out and I can smell it on you." I said it as plainly as I could muster, trying to set her off. I was picking this fight and I didn't care anymore what could happen to me.

She saw my discontent and she started in on me with a string of screaming obscenities and accusations of "Who the fuck do you think you are? How dare you fucking say that to your mother! Fuck You! You fucking little ungrateful brat! I give you everything!!! EVERYTHING!! You Fucking Bitch! You Spoiled little Fucking Bitch! It's None of your Fucking Business What I do behind closed doors! You have no Right to talk to me this way!!! Fuck You! Fuck You Bitch!" and so on and so forth. I sat there and watched her try to scream her respect back into me. I didn't shed one single tear. The words were meaningless, had no value. I didn't believe any of them and saw straight through them to her fear of the truth. I had won when she sent me to my room, grounded me, and made me promise to quit my job. I won.

The next day after school she was waiting for me again in the living room. She informed me that I wasn't going to quit my job, but I wasn't going to get any of my check anymore, so I better find some other way to get to school. I doubly won. Sure, I wasn't getting any more money and basically working my ass off for free, but I still had my freedom and she was wavering on her punishment. And if she would waiver on this one thing, she would probably forget the other stuff once she was out of it again.

A few days went by and nothing happened. I went back to the counselor and he called the case worker and left a message. Nothing happened. Not one thing happened. No one came to the house. No one saved us.

I continued to go to the counseling at the school, talking to the advisors, telling them the truth. It was all for not. It was left up to me to save myself. As much as I loved my brothers and knew that what they were doing was all wrong and there was so much for them to accomplish in their lives, the hope for them was lost. I was on my own. Dog eat dog mentality set in. I couldn't help anyone but me.

Counseling was a joke. It was a group of whiny teenaged children complaining about why their mom or dad wouldn't let them have the car or how their lives are so peer pressured. I kept my mouth shut for a while. I even gaffed at some of the tears that were falling. These kids didn't have a clue what it meant to have a hard life. I didn't belong here either and I knew it.

One day the counselor asked me why I was smiling. All I could say was "I just wish my life was only worried with grades, parents and boyfriends". I demeaned every single group mate with that sentence alone. One girl who had a problem with not knowing if she should give up her virginity got snippy at me. "What could be so hard about your life?"

This was a loaded question and week after week of listening to these big babies I set off to make every one of them bawl. Hope was lost and I was about to prove it to them.

I strung out 15-minute sermon of a synopsis of my hardships, starting with the beast and the rape of my youth by not only him, but my family. I told them everything that had been swimming in my head, all my worries, all my anxieties. Everything that was building up over the weeks of this so-called counseling and listening to the menial tragedies these children were going through in their own separate lives.

With my disorder I am able to accurately remember strings of words, phrases, recount them, and use them to my advantage to prove a point. I spoke with such fever, such passion that it would have put the mini micro machine speed talker to shame. I shed no tears. In my speed rant, my tone demanding eye contact, my emphasis on points commanding full attention. It was not a debate, but a sermon on hopelessness and how each of them hasn't a chance in this world if they focus on their itty bitty problems. I climaxed, climbing higher and higher in my angriness, not raising my voice at all. All I did was let the little angry, bullshit-calling Rachel loose. She took over and let these kids know that what they were complaining about was not worth complaining about.

The therapist stood by, not saying a word, with tears in her eyes, she was stunned. The vileness of my life and lifestyle brought her down. This was not what she signed up for when she wanted to be a school counselor, I could tell. I will haunt her for always, because I was lost and never found. I slipped through the cracks and no one, not even her, not at this moment, had the capability to take it back and make it better. I was broken.

I finished my rant and took a deep breath in accomplishment. Tears by some, sobs by the rest. In that instance I realized that I created perspective in these children. I was living my second lifetime already and I knew my wisdom was bigger than theirs, including the counselor.

I never went back to the sessions with my group. I forced myself to go to classes and make eye contact with those who knew my secrets. I watched the eyes change when they saw me, they really saw straight through me and down to my core, my black, cracked core.

Chapter 19

No one ever approached me about it again. But the respect I had was immense, I felt it everywhere. I put myself on top, in such a fucked up way, I was better than all of them because I was still here, even after all this, I was still here.

Working at the pizza parlor wasn't enough for me. I decided to switch jobs where I knew I could get more hours. I got a crappy bagger job at the grocery store down the street, another crappy job, but one with a bigger pay scale and promised more hours.

School let out for the summer and my best friend had gotten a job that was opposite of my hours so I rarely saw her. I fell deep into depression.

My mom really got bad with the drugs and Bobby fed them to her anytime it seemed like she was trying to make sense of anything. She would sit on the floor of her bedroom separating a big pile colorful beads. It was just a task, not that she would do anything with them, like make earrings or necklaces to sell, even if that's what she wanted to do, it wasn't going to happen. She would start to talk about something, but was so drug-garbled that it was unintelligible. And in her frustration she would try to say it again only louder, like that would help, but it didn't. Bobby would reach for the pill bottle, dump out a handful, grab a Squirt pop and physically feed them to her until she had taken every last one of them. The window of "awake mom" would only last 10 minutes after that. She was officially Somatose.

Somas. A cheap high. Brave New World had it right. It is definitely a drug that sedates the user into submission. It is a drug that allows you to find happiness in even the worst situations. Bobby had a lot of back and neck problems and underwent a minor procedure to fix it, and his postoperative pain management included Somas. The real downfall to our family, Soma. It was cheap and readily available, especially if you go down to Mexico to get it where you don't need a prescription and there are no limits on how much you can get.

The summer rolled by without me even noticing. I slept it away. I was either at work or in bed. Because it was summer I was allowed to work 40 hours a week and I would pick up extra shifts anytime anyone needed it. I was the go-to girl if you wanted to take a day off. 40 hours a week easily turned into 50-60 hours. I didn't mind working that hard because it wasn't hard work. I did my job efficiently and without complaint just as long as I didn't have to be at home. Pushing carts, bagging groceries, accomplishing the go-backs, emptying garbage, cleaning bathrooms, whatever they needed me to do, I just did it. It was my life.

When I was at home, it was straight to my room for me. I didn't have a life there. My room was dark, safe, and cool, literally. Our house was equipped with only a swamp cooler, except for my room. Bobby had closed in the carport to make another room and because it wasn't officially a part of the house, it didn't have duct work, so there was a wall unit air conditioner. It was literally the coolest room in the whole house. Although I wasn't allowed to run it all the time, that summer they were so out of it they didn't notice that I had that fucker on high at all times. But to hide the fact that I was jacking up the electric bill, just in case they ever came out of their room to check on me (Ha!), I kept my door locked and a towel smashed in the threshold. I slept in peace. Cool, sometimes cold, peace.

I didn't see my mom that summer, not at all. I would go to work, come home and sleep, get up and do it again. I didn't care about anything; showers, food, brothers, the house, nothing mattered anymore. I was a workhorse and nothing more. On Fridays I would get my little paycheck and shove it under her door. No one checked on me and I never checked in with anyone. I was insignificant and it wore on me, so I slept it away.

School started in the fall and I still hadn't seen my mom. She was there, in the room with the door closed. I started my junior year and I didn't want to be there. I was still working 40 hours and no one at work noticed that I was in school, so I didn't say anything as it was against the law to let anyone attending school to work more than 25 hours a week. I kept my mouth shut and kept working. I attended my classes, got a boyfriend, went to work, and slept. Rinse and repeat.

I went through boyfriends every time there was a new moon. I wasn't going to end up like my mom, you know, falling for whatever comes along. Boyfriends were fun, but expendable. I trusted no one with my feelings and therefore never let one get too close to me and the second I heard those three little pathetic words of untruth, I let them go.

It was amazing how boyfriends think that a month is the time to say such things. I never said it back because I didn't believe that it was true and they were lying. I would never let myself get into a situation where "he" would need only me because it would be expected from my end to need only him.

I always went into a relationship letting them know that I didn't want to hear it, even if they felt like they needed to say it, I did not want to hear it. They broke that rule at the month mark, all of them, and so I would break it off. You can't have love in high school, it's ridiculous. There was more to life than a boyfriend who supposedly "loves" you. Puppy crushes were not on my to-do list. So I dated a lot of different boys, which was a nice distraction for a few weeks.

I never let a boyfriend see my home. I never shared my home life with them, even though most all of them took me home to meet their moms and have dinners with their families. Shit, I was just grateful to eat a meal, a real meal with food groups. How was I ever to measure up to that? I couldn't. My mom couldn't even come out of her bedroom long enough to say hi to me, let alone make a meal for a guest. That would be way too taxing on her. I kept my little secrets, which was easy to do because the boys weren't around long enough.

The store I worked in opened a bank branch in it. It was the "new thing", to have grocery stores with banks in them where you could do both shopping and banking in the same place. I thought it was weird. Who does "banking" and why is it such an inconvenient thing that it now had to be combined with your shopping? I thought the only thing the bank did was convert the paper check into money and kept it safe in an account for you to use later when you write your checks to pay for bills. I was completely naïve to the whole idea. Why not just cash your check at the store and keep the money in your wallet? I mean, that's what my parents did. They didn't have a bank account, that was for rich people who had leftover money that they wanted to save for vacations and stuff. It was just so foreign to me.

Then one day at work I was bagging my coworker's groceries. She was a single mom who still lived at home with her mom. She had two kids and was only 19. I thought she was so grown up. I still hadn't lost my virginity, and I wasn't going to, but still here she was, buying diapers and formula and some groceries and here I was, bagging them up for her. We chatted about this and that while she was being rung up and then the strangest thing happened. When the cashier told her the total, she handed her paycheck over. I was stupefied. The cashier took that check and cashed it for her without question, giving her the balance due after deducting the grocery bill. I literally froze up in awe. Without knowing it, I was making an open-mouthed, semi-retarded face. She was handed 20's and 10's as it was counted out. I felt like I was witnessing a crime, not a murder or child molestation, but rather a little "under the counter", "look the other way", "it's not hurting anyone" type of crime. So I bit my tongue and bagged up the rest of her stuff.

A few days past and I wondered about what I had seen. She got her checked cashed without an ID. After being at this job for a while I watched when someone would cash their check at the register, but there were always two pieces of I.D. that were needed. I didn't have one piece of I.D., so people with two pieces of I.D. were the elite and I wasn't in that class. So having her cash her check without question raised a huge question in my head; "How did she do that?" And the next time I saw her, I asked her. But thinking I was asking a taboo question, I made sure that we were not being watched and I spoke very softly, like it was a big secret and I was delving into an underground topic. It was silly really when it came down to it. The big secret was that you can take your paycheck to any cashier that knows you and she will cash it automatically because you work at the same store. I didn't need a bank account, no I.D., and you didn't need to be 18 (an adult). The rest of the day my head was spinning. The possibilities of my freedom became apparent, but I didn't know if I had the guts to go through with it.

That following Friday, with my paycheck in hand, I went and bought myself a pop. This is a luxury not afforded to me. I knew that if I went through with cashing my check I was going to have to have a really good lie to go along with it. I needed to spin it to make it look like I was doing them a favor by cashing the check and just giving them the cash. I devised a plan. And this wonderful little plan included buying a pop. It was my little treat to give to myself.

I went up to the cashier and she rang up my pop. I was terrified as I handed over my check. The cashier spoke up, I wasn't supposed to buy just one little thing in order to cash a check. She did it anyway, but told me to make sure to buy some groceries next time. I thought I was in the clear, I was about to get handed $240.00 of my hard-earned money, and a pop. The registered opened and she counted out the money to my eager open hand. It was so beautiful. I neatly folded it in half and shoved it deep into my pocket, grabbed my pop and ended my turn by taking the receipt. As I walked away feeling deviously proud of myself, the cashier called out after me. I was caught. I don't get to keep the money. I have to give it back so they can give the money to my mom. I was going to get in trouble, I did something wrong. I got tunnel vision.

She was standing there with my check in hand, saying something about a pen. I went back to her and she told me to sign the back. I did as I was told, waiting for her to ask for the money back. "Thanks" was all she said and she turned to help the next customer. I had never signed any of my other checks. I didn't know that was part of the process. I just didn't know.

I took my money home and went straight into my room. I had a plan, but still didn't know if I could go through with it. The money wasn't doing the proverbial "burning a hole" in my pocket, quite the contrary. It felt like a 50 lb weight calling my name to do the right thing and hand it over to mom, or really, shove it under her door. But I fought the urge to "do the right thing" because it wasn't right. It really wasn't. I earned it, it was mine, all of it. She would notice if I didn't give it to her, right? Would she really notice? I thought about it all night. I kept that weight in my pocket for 3 days when I heard a knock at my bedroom door. I knew it was Bobby, by the knock, I knew he was looking for the money. I was busted. I hadn't spent any of it, well except for the pop I bought.

"Rachel?! Open the door." He wasn't mad. He was inquisitive.

"Hold on a sec!" I yelled back.

I pulled the weight out, kept $30 for myself, shoving it under my pillow, went and opened the door with cash in hand.

"Hey, didn't you get paid this week?" He actually was worried about the money. He finally woke up and realized he didn't have any and now he was sober, somewhat, and needed it.

"Yeah. Here ya go."

He took the cash. He didn't even question how it magically got turned into real paper money.

"Thanks." Turned and walked away.

I locked up and went to the pillow and looked at my little $30. I had a fist full of money just moments ago and liked the idea of how it made me feel, free.

I decided I will just work as much as I possibly could, as much as they would let me and give them around $150 a week. They didn't notice if I worked more, shit they didn't even know when I was home or not. I sat there planning my future, getting an apartment, or living with friends, getting a car someday, then it dawned on me. I had $30, I'm going to Ayala's for nachos.

Ayala's was our little neighborhood Mexican food restaurant that served an insanely large portion of Super Nachos for 5 bucks. It wasn't just Velveeta cheese and some crappy chips, Oh No! it was the works with beans, real chedder cheese, jalapenos, taco meat, sour cream, guacamole, lettuce and tomatoes, and a large dollop of homemade salsa. I was going to Ayala's for Super Nachos and I was going by myself.

Then, a knock at the door. It was mom, I could tell, mostly because she was pissed and screaming my name as she did it.

"RACHEL! OPEN THIS FUCKING DOOR RIGHT NOW!"

Fearing for my life, I ran to the door and unlocked it as she turned the knob and pulled it open. She stood there, bag of bones. I hadn't seen her in quite a few months and the site of her physical state shocked me. She had wasted away to barely a human. Although she was skin and bones, weak looking, her voice was strong and demanding.

"WHERE'S THE REST OF IT?" She was seething.

"What?" I knew what she was asking, but I was playing dumb this time.

"WHERE'S THE REST OF MY MONEY? WHY DID YOU, HOW DID YOU CASH YOUR CHECK?" She was going to knock my block off.

Then it came to me, immediately and fluidly I spilled out the lie I had been rehearsing in my head for days.

"Mom! The water guy came over on Friday before I went to work and he was going to turn off the water. I told him I would give him the money today. I tried to tell you on Saturday but you wouldn't answer your door. You told me to go away, you were sleeping. I tried to tell you yesterday, but you didn't answer your door again, so I wrote a note and shoved it under the door. I was afraid the water was going to get shut off so I cashed the check and I was going to pay the man today." It was brilliant. It had all the elements of being a good child and therefore yelling at me made her look like the asshole. Her days ran together into weeks, she didn't have a clue of what I was talking about, because it had happened so many, so fucking many times before. She couldn't make heads or tails out of it because it seemed too real, so like her and her attitude and her character. It was truly brilliant. But it still left a question unanswered.

"Okay, so where's the rest of it." This time she asked me sternly but sheepishly in the same breath. She was wrong for even asking, but she did and she was ashamed. Her appetite was stronger than her virtue.

"That's all of it. I gave it all to Bobby." And this sparked something in her. I had said it so undeniably truthful, even if it was a lie, that she got paranoid. I saw it. I really saw paranoia. It had a face, a look, and I witnessed it and upon realization, well I ran with it.

"I gave him about $210. I didn't work that much last week, but that's what I gave him. He has all of the money mom." And to my surprise, my delight, I played the right hand because then she said this.

"You didn't give him $210. He said you only gave him $140." She was full blown paranoid and mad.

Bobby was such a little prick. That mother fucker was holding out on my mom and I had proof, yet that proof was going to get me into trouble. Tunnel vision set in. I decided that I was going to sacrifice myself to feed her paranoia and reunite my alliance in her eyes. I pulled out my pay stub. It showed that I had made $240. Yes, the math doesn't make sense, and she saw it too. But I had an answer for everything. I was calm inside, but I played the poor little girl card to the paranoid mom who was craving her fix and just realized that her husband was holding out on her euphoria.

"So where's the rest of it." She shifted her paranoia at me, but I had the answer.

This one always works; women will agree, and most men will too because this is an uncomfortable situation to talk about...I answered, "Mom I needed tampons, lunch money, and bus money." I did need those things, but I already had them covered. See, the school offered free lunches and bus tokens to those that needed them if you signed up. I had mastered my mom's signature, so it was easy. As for the tampons, well the machine at work needed to be refilled, right? Guess who did that job. Yup, me. So I never paid for tampons.

Mom knew that I got free lunches and free bus tokens, so she was still paranoid.

"They didn't kick in yet. They are still waiting for approval. I didn't know what else to do. Do you want it back? I can take the tampons back if you need the money."

This was a humiliating question for her. I watched her debate it in her mind as if it was a real way to get 5 dollars back, denying her daughter freshness on her hardest days of the month.

"No. Don't do that." She answered. I shamed her. It felt good.

I could see her still mad, but it wasn't at me. That also felt good. She scolded me about cashing my check and that I shouldn't do it and to just give it to her on Friday. I agreed with her. I was going to have to be smarter about this.

Falsifying my birth certificate came back and bit me on my ass. My schedule at work changed and they gave me the morning shift. I was officially 18 by my birth record, but in all reality I was only 16 and still in high school. That's why they were still working me at 40 hours. I weighed the options and came to the conclusion that work was more important than school, so I stopped going. Not entirely at first, just on the days I was scheduled to work. No one even noticed. I slipped through the crack. We didn't have a phone, so the school couldn't call to tell on me. And our address was linked to a cousin, so the notes home were discarded without regard. I was unattended.

Even after the warnings from my mom, I continued to cash my checks and keep the balance after rent, $150 I thought they deserved. I would shove it under the door and they never questioned me about it. I had to be smart about it, hiding food in my room, not wearing new clothes in front of anyone, not that anyone would notice, but just in case she emerged from her cave, I had to be good and smart.

I kept up my rouse for a couple of months, getting angrier and angrier at the time I was spending at work earning money for her lazy, drug-addicted ass. I skipped school all the time and didn't care. No one noticed, not even my best friend, who wasn't my best friend anymore because my life was too complicated to include outside people. I worked and worked and stayed elusive in my spending. Keeping my six-packs of Pepsi in my room, only coming out to take a quick shower or get some ice for my indulgence.

I saved my money and planned for a better life.

I came home from work one Sunday to find my mom in the kitchen. She was the walking dead. So thin and frail, a breeze could have knocked her down, or so I felt. It made me feel strong. All my anger and my bitterness had been shoved down and neglected for such a long time. No one was there to hear me, except me and I had had enough of it.

"Rachel, do the dishes." Not a hi, or how was your day. Nothing but a command.

"It's not my turn." I said, kind of loudly in my defense.

"I DON'T CARE, DO THE DISHES!"

I actually hesitated and contemplated the fact that the dishes did need to get done, in fact every dish was dirty and piled up with trash and rotting food. The stench was a slap in the face. And where the fuck did all this come from? I haven't even eaten here in weeks. I had stopped cooking food because the beggers would come out of the woodwork and guilt me into feeding them, including my brothers and his friends. SO I stopped cooking in the house, sticking to foods that I could heat up at work, or snack on in my room. If there was never any food in this house, how in the hell were there so many dirty dishes? And how did it get so filthy? And why am I the one to have to clean it up? Duh! I was there, and she was frustrated with the mess, therefore it stands to reason to tell the first and only kid you see to clean up the mess. I debated with myself. Fight or flight. Argue or do the damn dishes. I'm fighting this one. Tunnel vision.

"I haven't even been here? I've been at school or work all week. It's not my turn."

"Don't you dare raise your voice at me! You do these dishes, every last one of them!" She wasn't having the fight. She demanded my submissive respect, like it was automatic. I wasn't having it. My feathers ruffled. I had lost all respect for her and I wasn't going to do the stupid dishes. It wasn't my turn, she was being unreasonable, she was not of her right mind. So I walked away without a word, into my room and shut the door.

I turned up my stereo as loud as it could go and sat there waiting for it. Wait for it. Wait for it.

BANG! BANG! BANG! "Rachel EVE!!!! You tu...the....dishes!!!" she was drowned out and it was kind of funny.

BANG! BANG! BANG! This time I thought she was going to break the window in the door. Yeah, they might have made a new room out of the carport, they were just cheap on replacing the old carport door, so they just painted over it for privacy.

".....Cunt! You little.....out...re...RIGHT NOW!!!!"

I turned the music off and opened the door. I fluidly phased out and my mean, unrelenting, bitter self came through and accepted her rant.

"Who the fuck do you think you are?!!! I am your mom! You will do what I say! Get in there and do the dishes!"

I heard the words, but had no response. I stood there staring blankly without fear. It unnerved her.

"WHAT HAS GOTTEN INTO YOU!? YOU UNGRATEFUL LITTLE BITCH! HOW DARE YOU LOOK AT ME LIKE THAT! ARE YOU LISTENING? YOU'RE A

NOTHING! NOTHING! YOU WILL NEVER BE MORE THAN THIS! HOW DARE YOU TREAT ME LIKE THIS? HOW CAN YOU BE SO CALLOUS!? WHAT IS WRONG WITH YOU!? Are you so black-hearted that you don't even cry anymore? Do you even care about me, about how much I love you? I do everything for you! How can you just stand there staring at me? Are you that cold-hearted?! Where did you learn to act this way???!!!! Why WON'T YOU CRY?!" She was screaming so hard that it her voice changed from normal vocal sounds to a guttural raspiness. She was desperately seeking a way to emotionally engage me and I was so far removed from the situation that I might as well have been in Timbuktu.

That last two questions stuck with me. Where did you learn to act this way? And, why won't you cry? Those were loaded questions. And without hesitation I answered her.

"I must have learned it from you." It was a blank response and it was not what she was expecting. I saw the words pummel her gut and the air leave her body. I was digging my grave, but I didn't care. I was already dead inside.

Growing up we would get knocked around a lot by her. Punches, kicks, slaps, shoves, mean words, guilt trips of going to hell...you name it, it happened. And every single time that any one of us kids would start crying, her immediate response to dull her aching guilt was "Shut Up! Quit Crying or I'll Give You Something To Cry For." Along with other such hits as "Wipe Those Tears Away" and "I don't want to see you crying, get away from me".

So when she asked that question of where did I learn it? It was like I had to remind her. She didn't want our emotions when we had them unless they were what she wanted at the time. I only answered her question to the best of my ability with the utmost truth attached to it. I learned it from her. It does no good crying, so I didn't. Well, this enraged the bull in her.

She cocked her hand back and I stood my ground waiting for the impact. Let her hit me, I wasn't even there. I was standing behind her at the door watching the look on my face as I scrunched it up for the impending contact. I did not flinch. I had brothers, they taught me the hard way how not to flinch. Her hand flew forward and my face absorbed the blow. Head thrust back so far that the momentum knocked me off my feet and my ass landed on the floor.

I felt the pain in my teeth and lips. I definitely was bleeding. She knocked me right back into myself.

As fast as my ass hit the floor, I was up on my two feet again in the same spot. I responded in a whisper,

"You stupid Bit." I stopped short. I didn't finish my sentence. Instead I went back to the doorway and watched me go zombie-eyed. My lip was swelling by the seconds and there was a trickle of blood starting down my chin. I told myself to let it be, let her see her damage. Don't react. Just let it be.

"WHAT!? WHAT!? GO AHEAD! YOU THINK YOU ARE SO MUCH BETTER THAN ME!? GO AHEAD AND SAY IT, SAY IT YOU LITTLE CUNT! TELL ME I'M A BITCH!" She was a raging demon now.

I kept telling myself don't engage, but I wasn't listening, my mouth hurt and I wanted to tell this bitch off. But instead I said,

"No mom. I have too much Res-pect for you." Emphasizing the word respect with a spittle of blood popping off just to make sure she understood.

Her hand cocked back again. I let it. I kept my arms at my sides and stood with my feet planted. This time I knew how it was going to feel. I watched from the doorway when she contacted again. Right in the same spot. Fuck! That hurt. But this time I didn't even step back. I was a formidable pillar of strength. I took my blow and kept it. She felt it and withdrew her hand as quickly as she threw it out. This time my mouth hurt her hand and she whimpered and sucked air in through her teeth in pain.

I stood there watching the back of her head go down to inspect her knuckles. I looked over and now my lip was gashed and gushing crimson. I had that same blank look. I will not be dragged into this. She had lost her mind and I wasn't going with her on this trip to emotional hell.

"You think you can make it on your own?! Do you really think that You could survive without me?! Go Right Ahead and get out of my House! I don't want you here! I HATE YOU!" I had won.

There it was, my out.

The joy of the shackles falling away, at her doing no less, jolted me back into the situation. I was sucked in at the thought of freedom. Pure freedom from oppression. A smile came over me. I couldn't help it. I smiled.

"Okay. I'll leave." The words were almost giddy. She sensed it and panicked.

"OH NO YOU DON'T! YOU ARE MINE UNTIL YOU ARE 18! YOU WILL NOT BE GOING ANYWHERE! YOU STAY IN HERE AND THINK ABOUT WHAT YOU DID! YOU ARE NOT ALLOWED TO LEAVE UNLESS YOU ARE GOING TO WORK AND YOU WILL NOT CASH ANYMORE OF YOUR CHECKS EVER! YOU WILL BRING ME THE CHECK AS SOON AS YOU GET IT, EVEN IF IT'S ON YOUR LUNCH BREAK!"

I was screwed. That wiped the smile off my face and put it on her's. She stormed out, slamming the door in her wake.

I waited a whole 5 minutes after I heard her bedroom door slam on the other side of the house to grab my backpack and stuff it full of my personal items. I was really doing it. I was getting away. I wiped my hand across my mouth and pulled my hand back in horror at the pain. My hand was full of blood. I didn't have to be here anymore. I didn't have a plan, but I didn't care. I have a job and I can take care of myself.

I opened up my window, jumped through and made a break for it down the street. I ran so hard my lungs were burning, my throat was dry, and before I knew it, there were tears streaming down my cheeks. I was devastated. Everything I had ever known was being thrown away by me. Love really didn't exist, not even unconditional love. I was truly, utterly alone in this big world. I ran bawling away from my life for my life.

It was Sunday. I had a pocket full of bus tokens and cash. I sat at the bus stop waiting to go anywhere. But it was Sunday. I was so in my own bewildered mind that I hadn't noticed what day it was. No busses on Sunday.

Chapter 20

I would like to clarify something to the reader. To this day my mom says I ran away and I like to say that she kicked me out. While yes, I did physically run away, wouldn't you agree that I was kicked out simply for the fact that she drove me away with abuse? I hope she reads this far.

I was sitting at the bus stop for about an hour or so crying my little green eyes out, trying not to focus on the pain in my lip when I realized that it was Sunday. No busses on Sunday. Okay, well then I guess I'm not going to my friend's house. I can't walk 12 miles, I mean, I probably could, but I wasn't going to. So I walked to the park. I thought about calling my best friend, but I thought of my mom calling her first trying to find me and that I wouldn't be safe going over there. I went into myself, frantically trying to figure out what to do. I had decided no more school. Fuck that noise. I wasn't about to go back there. There was no need. Work was all I needed. I had a couple hundred bucks to tide me over for food and whatnot, so that was okay. Now all I needed was a home.

The lights came on at the park and I watched as families came together for barbeques and flag football. They were going about their normal lives and I hated them for it. How could they just be having such a great time when I'm sitting here under this big tree completely shattered. My whole world was just taken away from me and they were gallivanting about unaffected. The world was bigger than me, I figured it out.

It got later and later and families packed up and left. It was quiet. It was 10 o'clock when the lights went off.

I walked over to the inside edge of the park and found a nice big oleander bush. My brothers and I used to play in bushes just like this one when we were younger. They were perfect for making forts in. They were mostly hollowed out and provided the perfect cover for anyone trying to hide. I went in. It was spring time so, though it was not freezing at night, it was still a little chilly, but the oleander felt like a cloak of warmth. I laid down and propped my head up on my backpack full of incidentals.

I awoke with a hand over my mouth and a forearm against my chest/neck area. I felt like I was dreaming until he spoke. Garbled noises was all I heard. The stench of alcohol was all I could smell. It was so dark and he was so big and strong. His hand smashed my lips into my teeth, burning, searing pain. His weight on top of me made it hard to breath. I tried to scream, but it was met with force on my neck. He stifled me.

"Just be quiet. I'll be done in a minute."

I tried to kick and wriggle. I tried so hard to push against him, but he was a doughboy. My fists and feet met nothing but gooey fat. My blows did not deter him. He sat down on top of my pelvis as his protuberant belly squashed down on my chest. I was crying and couldn't breathe. Tunnel vision. Darkness.

I woke up again this time with him entering me. In my frantic state, I fainted. In my unconsciousness he had taken my pants and panties off. My knees immediately clenched, trying to close and force him out. He reared up and came down hard with both fists into my gut, knocking the air right out of me.

Flash of a sparkle of light off of something. It was on his shirt. I couldn't see straight. Was I just seeing stars from the pain in my body?

He thrust into me, holding my hands down tight with his, all the while whispering "just be a quiet little girl. Oh you are such a naughty little thing. You feel so good inside. Just be quiet…oh fuck you feel so good inside." I stopped fighting and took it.

When he finished he collapsed on top of me breathing a sigh of relief, of accomplishment. I vomited.

He got up onto his knees and looked down at me and the sparkle was back. It was on his shirt. I saw it but didn't believe it. He was a rent-a-cop. I knew that badge and it scared me.

He looked down at me and put his finger to his lip, telling me "shhhh". It was dark, but I could make it all out. His eyes, his body type, his ethnicity, his badge. He half stood up, crouched over under the bush and pulled his pants back on. I laid there stunned, half-naked. I didn't know what to do. He left. I watched.

I quickly got dressed and made a break for it, like he was going to chase me, but he didn't. I kept my eye on his little truck and he just sat there, satisfied. I never went back to that park and I never will.

Chapter 21

After my first failed marriage of only a year, I found myself living back with my mom and Bobby. It was a sad situation. Our home in Maryvale had burned to the ground after the dryer had caught fire in our laundry room, which in turn burned the 6 foot tall high pile of dirty clothes stacked in the room. It was really quite a site, that laundry room. It never was cleaned out completely, always a new stack of clothes thrown on it daily.

Mom and Bobby were infamous in the old neighborhood for being "dumpster divers". Every night they would go out and scour the dumpsters at the stores to find the ultimate deals. Hardly stained clothes, old furniture that could be repaired with some effort, half used paper towel rolls that if you only peeled off the first fifty stained and ruined, you could get down to the good ones underneath. It was ridiculous half the shit they would bring home.

Even now, when I watch that Hoarders show on TV it gives me flashbacks on how we lived in the sea of "another man's trash".

The laundry room was no exception to the rule of piles, in fact it was quite the contrary. It was the place where all the clothes from the expeditions would end up and it was tall and dense, growing ever bigger day by day. So when the dryer overheated and caught fire, well that pile just intensified the burning of our house. I didn't live there at the time, but I was affected by it.

In one big swoop mom and Bobby and all the kids were homeless. Mom and Bobby had found a hotel room they could afford, but by themselves only. So the boys ended up at my house with me and my husband. She promised that she would have a new apartment within a week when they got their check from the State. Of course I couldn't turn my brothers away and my husband was very accepting of the fact that we would take care of them because I would do the same for his family if they needed it.

The problem was that after week one the boys started to go through withdrawal. All of them were fucked up on one substance or another. The fights and the disrespect was overwhelming. They actually demanded things, such as rides to get their fix. I flatly refused every time and that would turn into a fight. My mom had turned them all into monsters.

When we were deep into week two I started to worry. Days had gone by and I hadn't heard from my mom. I tried to call friends from the neighborhood to find out where they were staying and called different hotels in the area, but to no avail. They had disappeared. I was crushed.

Week two ended and well into week three I was frantically cruising different parking lots of different hotels, motels, inns, and by friends' houses looking for their car. I made dozens of phone calls and no one had heard from them. My brothers started really craving and my husband and I had had enough of them.

Finally, in week four I found them. Their car was parked in a hotel lot on the other side of town. I did the only thing I could think of. I went straight home picked up the boys and all their crappy attitudes, drove over to the hotel, found out what room they were hiding out in, banged on the door and walked away. I didn't even stick around to find out what happened. I didn't care. She went on a binge and dumped her responsibility on me and I wasn't going to have it.

When I got home the phone was ringing off the hook. I finally answered it and it was her, she was pissed at me, screaming at me to come pick up the boys. She couldn't afford to have them stay at the hotel with her. When I asked what happened to her check, she had a sorry excuse. They had driven down to Mexico, loaded up on Somas to sell back here in the States. But then the car broke down, they ran out of money, didn't want to get caught by the police, yadda, yadda, yadda. I had heard so many excuses so many times that I just didn't believe any of them anymore. I knew in my heart she was just a selfish person.

I refused to take the boys back and hung up the phone. She was just going to have to figure this one out on her own. I wasn't her mother, I wasn't the boys' mother, I was just the most responsible person she knew and I was only 19 at the time. I was wise enough at my young age to realize when someone needed to lie in the bed they made and I wasn't going to help her anymore.

But then my marriage fell apart and I needed help. You know that old saying "you can never go home again", well it's true. Although I moved in to her home, it wasn't the same. The control has shifted. You're an adult, you've lived an adult life, but when you rely on your parent again they want that control because obviously you can't deal with it on your own, you're a failure. Yeah, that was the attitude.

The house they were renting was a very small 3 bedroom. They had turned it into a flophouse. Their previous home had been a flophouse too, but this time it was really bad. Not only were my three brothers and I living there, but my uncle and believe it or not, my real sperm donor of a dad. Yes my stepdad and biological father were living at the same house, not under the same roof though.

It turned out my homeless dad needed a place to stay and of course in my mom's drugged out haze had agreed that he could live in the backyard. So he built a makeshift shanty between the block wall and laundry room wall with tarps, warped plywood, and rugs. It was weird.

I was still clean and sober and I had to share a space with a houseful of drug-induced lunatics. I slept in beds that weren't ever mine, just empty. I ate whatever I could afford and hid my food constantly. When I washed my clothes in the bathtub everyone would come in asking if I would wash something of theirs and when I refused, I wouldn't be left in peace to do my task until they would throw their socks or underwear in the water with mine and walk away. I never did any of their laundry, never. I would leave it in the tub for them to find still dirty and wet. I would literally have to sit on the back porch and guard my clothes on the line. It wouldn't have surprised me if they would steal them to either wear an item, such as socks, or sell something, like a pair of jeans. I was on watch 24-7 with my stuff in that house, it was unbearable.

I had found solace in a new boyfriend. He was someone I had known from high school and ran into him at the grocery store. I spent a lot of time at his house with his family. I didn't have a job anymore and had nothing to do all day. He was going to college for art design and I admired him for it. I tried not to be home as often as possible, even sitting in his car in the parking lot in 100 degree weather while he was going to class for 3-4 hours a day was better than the flophouse. He was so great to me. He knew my situation at my mom's, had seen it firsthand, and took pity on me. He got an allowance from his parents for food and gas and he would share his daily lunch money and buy me food too. It wasn't much, but it kept me alive. He kept me alive.

I started to get antsy with my living situation, but the only other person I knew who could help me wasn't answering her phone. She was a close friend I had made when I worked a local gas station but had quit right before I had and I lost touch with her. I hadn't called her in months, but I really needed to talk to her and see if I could just stay with her until I could get on my own two feet.

We didn't have a phone at my mom's, that was a luxury that was not afforded to us. So making phone calls meant getting on a bike and riding down to the park and using the only working payphone in a 2 mile radius. I knew she had gotten a new job, but I didn't know what hours she worked, so I guessed. If she worked days, I would call her at 6 am and 4 pm, but if she worked nights, I would call at 6 pm and 2 am. So I was riding that stupid bike back and forth to the phone 4 times every day. This went on for 2 weeks straight, every day, riding and calling. Finally! She picked up the phone.

It had turned out that she was living with a boyfriend and he was extremely abusive to her and had broken the phone in one of their violent fights when she tried to call the police. She was so relieved to hear from me and was really excited at the thought of having another person come to live with her to help with the bills who wouldn't kick her ass every night for not doing the dishes just so. She told me to call her back in a week and she would come pick me and my stuff up. She would even arrange a real job for me and I would get to use her car whenever I wanted as long as she didn't need it. She opened the world to me. The independent world. It was possible to live on my own, sort of, and be completely responsible for myself. I was so relieved I cried. I could do it, just one more week, I could do it.

I told my boyfriend I would be moving across town and he got real upset. I tried to reassure him that I would be able to see him just as often, but that I needed to move. He understood, but he pulled away. I felt it change after that, I had lost him. I didn't take it too hard, after all a whole new life awaited me.

The day Crista came to pick me up I didn't say a word to anyone about me leaving. I packed my clothes up in my little suitcase and climbed in her car and never looked back. I was giddy. My heart was so big right at that moment. I was free, really free.

The first two months were awesome. I got into the swing of working and helping take care of her two wonderful children. We ate food every single day, with mealtimes and food groups and I was helping with grocery shopping and cleaning house. We even went on little trips and had friends come over. It was "the life" that I never even knew I really wanted. I was independent and was loving every moment of it. Then I missed my period, twice.

I had always had messed up cycles. I would miss one month only for it to come back with a vengeance and make me bleed like a stuck pig the next month. But I never missed two periods back to back. I thought to myself about recent ex-boyfriend and how we used protection every time. I couldn't be pregnant. I just couldn't be pregnant. But the test proved me wrong.

I took three of them in a row just in case and they all said the same thing. I even went to Planned Parenthood so they could do it right and tell me I wasn't, but I was. Damn it.

I was 20, living with a friend and her two kids, not in any relationship, in a new job that would be threatened with a baby on board, no plans for a future, and now this. I wasn't ready to have a baby, I couldn't take care of a newborn, I was just learning how to take care of myself. I debated if I should tell the father.

When I did finally make the call, he was surprised. The conversation was awkward. He had all kinds of reasons why we should abort and that solution, in my mind, was just not an option. I shut down and shut him out. I refused his calls after that. He was literally afraid of his parents finding out, as he still lived with them. He was a young adult and he was afraid of his parents still. It was absurd. So I cried for all of 15 minutes, pulled up my bootstraps, and decided this child deserves a loving stable family. Adoption was my only option. I would've loved the baby, but I would have never been able to give it a life it deserved. Love doesn't buy diapers or formula. And after living a life on government help, I refused to put a baby through that. I convinced myself I wasn't worthy of having and raising a child yet, I wasn't mature enough.

When the father found out, he got mad, but accepted it. He signed all the papers without hesitation and I never saw him again.

Over the months my tummy and boobs grew. I tried to hide it from my job and I did a real good job at it too. I was working in a warehouse, picking orders for an office supply company. It required being on your feet for 8-10 hours, walking up to 15 miles a shift, and lifting max of 60 lbs. I had gotten into really great shape with that job, even though I was growing, I was also stronger. Then one day I had to come clean. I lifted a case of paper and felt a warm gush between my legs. It was too soon, Three months too soon. I went to the bathroom and saw blood, something was wrong. My belly began to ache and cramp. I actually sat in the stall contemplating going back to my station and finish up my shift, but the pain made me tell the truth.

The shock and horror in my boss' eyes led me to believe that tomorrow night I won't have a job to come back to.

At the hospital they ran their tests and concluded that everything would be fine, but I couldn't keep doing the same job anymore. I needed to take it easy from here on out. Up to this point I had been doing everything as I normally would have without a second thought. I woke up. I came to, if you will. I wasn't alone in my body anymore and I needed to really take into account that I couldn't avoid being pregnant anymore. I really needed to find a set of good parents and prepare for the separation. That time in the hospital really did a number on my emotional state. I was really the only one who was going to have to take care of this, go through this, and I needed to get on the ball and do something. I couldn't push it out of my mind any longer.

My boss was awesome. He got me an "inside" job, out of the warehouse and into customer service. The hours were great and it was an air conditioned, sit down at a desk job. He went out of his way to make sure I was taken care of and I really appreciate it as my tummy got bigger and bigger.

Crista also jumped onboard with me and helped me with finding parents for the baby. It turned out that her aunt wasn't able to have children, but always wanted children. It was the perfect setup. She would let it be an open adoption, keeping me involved in its life. It was all falling into place. I was thrilled.

Then one day my ex-husband called me. He wanted to talk and asked me to come over to our home. It had been months since I had even talked to him, let alone see him, or rather him see me in my "condition". I was confident that he wouldn't want anything to do with me once he knew what I was about to go through.

I went over simply to talk. We weren't officially divorced yet, but the papers were drawn and I had it in my head that we were already ex's. He had prepared dinner and we chatted a bit. Then he asked me to come back to him. He had admitted he was wrong, that he couldn't imagine his life without me in it, so on and so forth. I really believed him. I witnessed hope in his words. But, big but…would he still want me after I told him I was pregnant with another man's baby? It was obvious that he hadn't noticed my little belly. Maybe he just thought I had put on weight, I thought to myself. He spoke such kind and loving words to me and I wanted to believe that we would work things out and life would or could be better for me, for us. I didn't want to be a divorcee like my mom. I wanted to have stability and a foundation to build from. But I couldn't do it dishonestly. I started to tell him.

"There's nothing I would like more than to be with you, to come home and start anew, but"

He finished my words for me

"You're pregnant, right?" he said with a smile.

I was surprised at his smile. He wasn't upset. It turned out he had been talking with Crista and knew all about the situation and still wanted me to come home. Although my freedom with Crista had been fun, I missed my little house with my husband. So I decided to come home.

A few weeks after coming back I got a call from Crista, her aunt didn't want the baby anymore. She was too chicken-shit to call me to tell me herself. Her husband said no way is he going to raise a kid in this world and that God didn't want her to have children for a reason…blah, blah, blah. The news devastated me. I had trusted that this was going to work out, I trusted them so much with the baby's life. So when her aunt called me back to tell me that she still wanted the baby and that her husband will come around eventually, well I told her to Fuck Off. There was no way I was going to hand over a baby to a family who only half wanted it. I sat and cried and my husband held me tight in his arms.

He was so wonderful to me. He immediately said he wanted to keep the baby with us and that we could raise it together. I actually entertained the idea for a few days, never actually committing to his reassurances. I kept internalizing it and came to the conclusion that we were not stable enough yet to have a child come into our lives and what if this time it really didn't work out between us, then where would I be? A single mom raising a child. I just couldn't do that to the baby. I made the decision, I had to find parents for the baby.

I searched the newspaper want ads every day, hoping that I would see the perfect ad that would just stick with me. Nothing ever popped out and caught my attention. They were always the same old, same old.

"Loving couple who will love and cherish your baby, give it everything it ever wanted, and will help with mother's expenses."

So strange I would think. How people who can't have babies themselves are willing to tempt you with money. So strange indeed.

After a week of perusing the want ads, I got a call from my mother-in-law. She had explained my situation to her best friend, another woman who couldn't have children, but always wanted them. I knew her very well. She was in her 40's and lived back east, but always came out to visit my mother-in-law at least twice year for a couple of weeks. We would always get together and visit. She was really a very nice woman. I had never met her husband, but had always heard nice things about him. Well, it turned out that she wanted to adopt the baby. I was elated. Now this was a very close friend of the family, very well off, super nice, and her virtues and morality matched what I was looking for. Yes!

I was in touch with her on a very regular basis, talking about the baby and my growth. It was so reassuring to have someone so interested in this little bundle on its way from heaven. My mother-in-law and my husband were very happy about the whole situation as much as I was. I felt relieved that it would finally be settled. My heart could rest in this decision soundly.

It only took 3 weeks before my heart was smashed to pieces in hopelessness again. I got the call. She had called to let me know that her husband said that he didn't want to raise a bastard child and that he would divorce her if she did it anyway.

Okay, it's hard enough to deal with hormonal emotions when you are pregnant, but shit, it really sucks when there are these rollercoasters that I kept getting on. I was once again screwed. No room at the inn for this little one.

So I bawled my eyes out and my husband held me tight and reiterated the offer that we could do it together. No way, I thought. It's just not possible. We were not in a place to raise a child; emotionally, financially, it just wasn't an option.

I picked up the paper, went for the ads. In the sea of pleas, I saw it. The perfect wording, verbiage, context, it just rung out as truthful and loving. It was there, that one ad, that was calling out to me. I knew it would happen, but I didn't think it would be so obvious. Had I gone through this rollercoaster ride so I could end up right here, at this moment, reading this ad? Yes.

I called.

They were so perfect. Everything about them, perfect. The struggles, the triumphs, the life they led, all of it was perfect. They were going to be great parents. Mary and Jim, perfect.

My water broke in the middle of the night and my husband drove me to the hospital where Crista was waiting for us. The labor wasn't too bad. The cramps sure did hurt, but I put the pain aside because the fear of something so huge was about to burst out of my vagina. I started to believe that I was going to split in two and the anxiety took over and I flipped out, crying, babbling. I just wanted to go home and go back to sleep. Then the contractions got really painful and they gave me the epidural. What a lifesaver that was. I actually fell asleep for a while, but just a while because then its heartbeat took a dive and the next thing I knew I was in an operating room swarming with nurses and doctors yelling at me to push. Crista stood by me the entire time helping to count. If you've ever had a child you know that when they count to ten it's a really slow ten, more like thirty seconds.

Anyway, I pushed and pushed until his heartbeat slowed way down and the doctor demanded a C-section. That right there, a C-section, I knew what that meant. I had seen videos, heard horror stories, and there was no fucking way I was going to have a C-section. Nope, not me. I cut him off as he was trying to explain it to me. I told him no way. Fuck No! were my exact words.

They did it anyway. They knocked me out and removed the baby from my belly. I woke up alone in my body again. My husband, holding my hand, told me how much he loved me and then made one last attempt at changing my mind. In my stupor I explained again why I just couldn't. He finally accepted my decision.

I made the call to Mary and Jim and they were on the next flight out.

I avoided visiting with him until the last day in the hospital. My mother-in-law insisted on taking pictures with me and him. And although I protested, she was a traditional mother-in-law and she got her way.

The second I laid eyes on him I was instantly in love. He was so beautiful and the thought that I had made him all by myself, something this good was made by me, it was amazing. I held him and cried because I knew he didn't belong to me anymore. I made a promise and I had to keep it. He was just so perfect. I loved the little baby boy.

I left the hospital empty-handed with a heavy heart. I made it home in one piece and he will live a life that I could not give him. He will be loved, cherished, spoiled. They all deserved each other. I deserved to give it to them.

Chapter 22   The Stalker

After having lived the quiet little suburban housewife/mother role for a while, I found myself divorced, living in a crappy little condo with three small children. I was working 60+ hours a week transcribing medical documents from my kitchen and working at my family's pizza shop on the weekends to keep all of us above water. The money was great, but the stress was overwhelming. The kids weren't in school yet, so I was pulling double duty constantly. I averaged 4-5 hours of sleep for 2 years straight. How I did it? I have no idea. I just knew that I had to do it. There was no choice.

Pushing myself to constantly rotate priorities and the scrambling anxiety that accompanied each task made me cope. I had to be a mother and a mom. I had to be a business owner. I had to be head of household. I had to be sole-provider. It was only appropriate that I was a different person for each one of these roles I performed daily. Everyone does it. You aren't the same person when you talk all professionally to a coworker as you would be if you were talking to your spouse. Those are split. You instinctively know that you can't say certain things to certain people out of fear, pure fear. You do it to protect yourself, your environment, and your feelings.

I had so many roles that I was performing and I had to keep them all straight. The stress was whittling away at me, but I would find a new energy out of nowhere that would make me dig my heels in and fight for our little family and our survival.

I still craved being in love with someone. I knew that that was the way it was supposed to be. You are supposed to be married, at least that's what I was brainwashed to believe. So, I dated, a lot, trying to find that one, "the one".

After my many failed attempts at love that equaled close to 15 men in two years and after the last one got me pregnant and said he could never love me, and the stress from losing the baby, I gave up. I finally succumbed to the idea that life isn't about sharing it with someone who would make me a better person, but in fact, it was meant to be something that was all mine. My life, my ideas, my way of living. I wanted to be selfish, not realizing that in every failed relationship I was just that, selfish. So I took my vow of celibacy. I figured I needed a year off, a sabbatical to find who I truly was. I had this grandiose idea that if I just found a way to be happy with myself, love myself as I was without a man, to truly be content with the life I lead, **I lead**, that the right man would eventually rear his head and find a way into my life without compromising me, my children, and my way of life.

My best friend and I started hanging out a lot more. You could say we had a relationship, not sexual, but I fell into the same old routine with her that I would have with a man; calling her a million times a day, clearing my schedule at the drop of a dime to spend time with her, making sure that she approved of random things. I spent more and more time with her, until she found a girlfriend, a real true love girlfriend and then my time with her dwindled away. Little by little I was being excluded from the fun stuff we used to do together. I was jealous, but I knew that she deserved to be happy and that this girlfriend obviously could give her so much more than I ever could. I accepted the relationship, but I wasn't happy about it. I had spent months doing everything with my best friend. Every little bit of extra time was spent with her, and now it was slowly dissipating to more free time by myself. I was so sad. I had inadvertently put my emotional dependence on another person without realizing it. She wasn't a man, I wasn't "dating" her, but here I was, broken-hearted. I had wrapped myself up in her and we had created a life together, so when it was appropriately taken away from me, I went numb. Cynical is a better word for it. I couldn't handle the idea that I had done it again, created another failed relationship. How could I be so dumb? I really was a codependent type of person that had no idea of how to get away from it. So while wallowing in my own tears one morning I figured it out and got mad and let go.

Putting your eggs in one basket is never a good idea. Never. And I will never ever do it again.

I let go, or rather I tried to let go. She would still call me for little things here and there, such as a ride to the airport. And she felt me letting go because I started to purposefully not answer my phone when she called or I would lie and tell her I had plans that I couldn't break when she wanted to hang out. If her life was going to be busy, well my life was going to be busy without her.

One day she invited me over to watch a movie. I thought that would be a great idea. She was earnest in her invitation, sounded so sincere that she wanted to spend time with just me, and since I was in somewhat of a good mood, I accepted. But there was a catch; she wanted to watch the movie over at a friend's house. Dang it, I had already accepted, so I tried to get out of it. The truth of it was that she was trying to kill two birds with a stone. She needed to feed their dogs and check the mail and water the plants (housesitting) while they were away on a trip. I saw right through it and was deflated.

She insisted that I come over and watch some movie that she really had to show me because for some reason there was a character in it that reminded her of me and it was really cool and I would really like it and I will laugh, yadda, yadda, yadda….

I met her there.

The house didn't belong in Arizona. The architecture style was all wrong for downtown Phoenix, but it had a charm about it that made me think of Hansel and Gretl and the moment of relief they had when they saw the gingerbread house after being abandoned in the woods by their own father.

She was already waiting inside when I let myself in. I found her watering the plants out back. She was excited to see me and my heart swelled from her attention. It was just me and her again, at least for a few hours.

She had a few chores to do still so I made myself at home. I snooped. Yes, I snooped, but not in the menacingly way. I wasn't out to steal their identities or help myself to their pain killers.

My best friend had told me a number of times how much I would get along with these people. They had been close friends of hers for years and she really thought we would hit it off. I always took it with a grain of salt when she would tell me about them and how "cool" they were. It was as if she was trying to pawn me off to someone else because her time had gotten so filled with her new girlfriend. I read into it, as all women do. She wasn't trying to make a connection for me, she was trying to give me away to clear her conscience and I saw it. It made me sad.

I walked down their hall lined with bookshelves and read the titles of random books and movies and was all of a sudden in a familiar place. Everything I was reading was something that I already owned. It was like they had gone to my condo, peeked at my inventory, and went out and bought every item to stock their own shelves. I kept saying "No Way!" and "What the Fuck? No Way!". My words got her attention.

"What?" she would call out from a random room.

"Oh Nothing, I'm just surprised." I would reply through the house in her general direction.

I stood there for a solid 20 minutes reading titles, picking up books that I owned also and read the backs to remember why I loved it. She would call out to me asking here and there questions, but for the most part I would just call back an answer that was easy and quick. I was in my world there.

We finally sat down to watch the movie when she finished up. Hedwig. It is a movie about a transvestite who just wants to be loved for who he/she was. She said I was Hedwig. I never told her about how that hurt me. That was the nail in the coffin that was the end of our relationship. I went home and cried. (p.s. Hedwig isn't even a "pretty" or convincing transvestite.)

A few days later she called me, of course she needs a ride to the airport. It was Christmas Eve and my kids were with their dad this year. I didn't have work and had been wallowing in my own sweat stained shirt for days. My depression had gotten the best of me. I didn't want to leave the house, except for the short trips to Jack in the Box for their cheap tacos and to the little store to get my fix of pop and cigarettes. I had been on a solid three-day binge of eating crappy food, not showering, and chain smoking. I reeked. My hair was so oily it could've stood up on its own. But she needed the ride, so I agreed.

I didn't bother "getting ready". I didn't even bother to put shoes on, which is actually against the law in Arizona.

Arizona law states that you must wear your shoes while driving in case of an emergency or a breakdown and you have to walk somewhere. I would agree with this because in the summertime here you don't want to walk on the 150+ degree sidewalks in bare feet.

I picked her up and while loading the car she mentions to me that we have to stop by Salina and Todd's. She didn't mention it on the phone, it wasn't the plan from the get go. I was a little perturbed. It turns out that she needed to drop off her presents for them because one was time-sensitive; a basket of sausages and cheese or something. So of course I obliged. It's not like they lived far from the Airport, so why not. I didn't even need to get out of the car, right? So, why not? Fuck it. I'll do this one thing and go home and sleep the rest of the day in my dirty clothes watching bad movies, avoiding the whole Christmas day without the kids thing.

We pulled up to the front of the gingerbread house and she asked me to help her bring in the presents. No way! She was going to have to take multiple trips into the house with them. I was a total scrubamuffin, a mess. I hadn't brushed my teeth and could feel the grime on my scalp every time I scratched at it. Even my armpit hair had gotten out of hand. I wasn't going to go meet people for the first time looking like that and with no shoes to boot. We must have sat in the car for at least 10 minutes arguing about it when Shannon, the middle daughter, came out to see what was going on. I was going to have to meet a new person, looking like this. I did not want to be there. My unhygienic appearance hit me like a ton of bricks. My humiliation came to light and I was forced to come out of my fog of autopilot depression and into the world of people and compare their freshness against my rankness.

Shannon was a sweet looking sprite. Her eyes sparkled as she grabbed my hand to shake it. My mind switched to "customer service mode". The façade took over and I pretended to be jovial and polite even under the circumstances that I looked like a homeless person who just stole a brand new Santa Fe.

My best friend and Shannon ganged up on me. And out of politeness, I accepted and went in, no shoes and all. At least I had socks on.

I walked into the house that I was just in days earlier, trying to be invisible, but to no avail. The house was filled to capacity with the family. Salina and Todd had just gotten home from their trip just hours before and the entire family came over to spend Christmas Eve with them. Parents, grandparents, children, aunts, and uncles it was surreal. I don't have family like this and never really experienced such a largely related group. My best friend was beaming. She was so excited to introduce me to Salina and I was in a small part excited too. I wanted to see who this woman was that had all the same media I had.

Salina was the elder version of Shannon. Sprite-like, petite, and with the sparkling eyes that made you feel like you are welcomed whole-heartedly. It was genuine.

Salina took me around to meet various people, introducing me as my best friend's best friend. And she had a little synopsis about me that was surprising to hear, since I had never met the woman before. Apparently I was a successful business owner who has three small kids and loves all the same stuff Todd likes. I made the rounds with her and made sure to put on my smile and seem interested in all that was being said. Now, mind you, in the back of my head I was wondering what kind of horrific odor I was putting off, but I kept my arms close to my sides and made sure I wouldn't step in too close so as not to O-ffend.

After a few minutes, Salina excused herself while leaving me with one of the son-in-laws who had engaged me in a conversation about my job and kids. He was pleasant enough, but I wasn't really interested in keeping up the conversation for fear he might get a true whiff. I excused myself to the restroom.

I knew this room and it was void of people. I quickly took a whores bath and stole some of their toothpaste to do a camping-style brushing of the teeth. I even used their brush without fear of getting lice.

I came out determined to find my best friend and get the heck out of there. After wandering around smiling I found her in the nook of the kitchen, deep in conversation with Salina. I walked up knowing I was interrupting. She let me know that we would leave in a few minutes, but there was something important she needed to talk to Salina about privately. Satisfied with the answer that we will be going soon, I let them have their privacy and made my way back to the hall. There, I was free from people crowding my personal filthy space.

I stood for a while reading the shelves I had not gotten to on my previous probing expedition. I felt comfortable enough to take things off the shelf and flip through them. They obviously knew enough about me to know that I wouldn't steal from them and that I am not a total klutz and wouldn't break anything. I was content in this moment in my world in someone else's home.

I felt a presence, but I didn't want to look up for fear of having to commit to a conversation I didn't want to keep. I figured he was just waiting for the bathroom and I didn't need to engage him anyway. Keep reading.

I put a book back where it belonged and skimmed. There, on the shelf, was a movie I hadn't seen in years. In a quick fluid motion I snatched it off the shelf and giggled. Fire Walk With Me. I was dumbfounded. No way in the world did they actually own this movie. I owned this movie and loved every minute of it. How is it here, in this house? There was only one other person in this whole wide world that I knew that loved this movie as much as me and I had lost touch with her years and years before. The memories and delight of finding it right there was immense and I was surprised that there was someone out there that actually owns it too. It blew me away.

The presence was still standing at the end of the hall. In my moment of excitement at finding this one simple pleasure I felt the urge to share it with anyone standing within shouting distance, so I decided to share it with the presence. Without looking up and with a huge grin on my face I said to him, "Have you ever seen this movie?" He didn't answer, so I looked over to him.

Standing there was the man that will change my life and the lives of my children forever, although it wasn't apparent at the time. He was frozen to his spot staring straight at me. My blood ran hot. He was extremely handsome. My mind quickly ran through the faces I had met today and he was not in the line-up. Had he been standing there staring at me the whole time? How long had time passed when I first felt him there? 5 minutes? 10 minutes? Crap! Where was my best friend? Why haven't we left yet? It's amazing how the mind works. In a millisecond you can think of a thousand questions and answers, and there he was still staring, not answering my question. It would have been awkward if I hadn't been so attracted to him.

I'm a woman, I know things. I know why a man has that look on his face. All women possess the knowledge of what a man wants the second you set eyes on him and he makes eye contact with you. They are not mysteries or conundrums. I saw it right there in that moment, he was awestruck. I have never had, to this day, a man look at me the same way as he did right then.

Embarrassed that I was being admired in the state of my appearance, I tried to repeat my question when I got a stupid fucking crack in my voice that made me choke on my spit for a second. So, I cleared my throat and asked him again. It was kind of creepy because he hadn't moved and just stared at me in the time between the first and second inquiry.

"Have *you* seen this movie?" I asked.

When he answered his face lit up with a beaming smile "Yes. It's mine."

Of course. Karmic irony does exist. It was Todd, Salina's *husband*. Damn it. Of course this man belonged to someone. Why I thought he didn't would be confusing to most, but I figured it out. The look in his eye and the expression on his face and the tether between us spanning 25 feet down the hallway when we made eye contact gave me a sense of hope that all was not lost in love.

"Oh, you must be Todd." I said with a smile of freshly camp-brushed teeth.

He ignored the statement, "Have you seen Fire Walk With Me?"

I recognized his one-track mind, he was really astounded with his question to me, like it wasn't possible that I had seen it.

"Yes! I've seen it like a thousand times and I love it/own it." I said taking his lead of moving on past my acknowledgement and attempt at introducing myself.

He closed the gap between us. Each step closer to me my heart raced a little bit faster. He asked me questions that I knew all the answers to and I did the same to him. We both would exclaim "No Fucking Way!" when we answered or got onto a topic. He was my split-apart. It was only when Salina and my best friend walked up did we half attempt to stop talking to each other. Salina introduced me with my little synopsis and we shook hands.

Have you ever shook hands with someone and after the appropriate timing of the shake you let go, but they are still holding on and so you give one last little squeeze to "end the shake" and it's a little awkward? Yeah, that happened, sort of. I went to let go, realized he wasn't letting go, so I regripped and gave the "last squeeze" and released, but he was still holding on and talking. He continued to talk to me while holding my hand. Now what he was saying at the time I really couldn't tell you because my mind immediately was thinking about how I was going to get out of this. Not that I wanted to, really I could've held his hand until the day we died, but his wife was standing right there and my best friend had this look on her face like "what the fuck"?

It was brought to his attention that we had to go because a flight was going to be missed, and that's when he let go.

We walked to the door and everyone came around to say goodbyes. I felt so welcomed into this family. They had genuine smiles and sincerity in their voices. I was asked to come back the following weekend for a going away party for their son who had been accepted to a university in Chicago. I accepted, knowing full well that I won't be coming to it.

After the airport, on my drive home, I reveled in the thought of Todd and his smile and his handshake. I knew right then what it meant, but I also knew that it was off limits. My best friend was starting a whole new life with someone and the transition to the new "family" was becoming more and more enticing the more I thought about it. So, I would not entertain those feelings about another woman's man.

My best friend returned home from her trip and disappeared into her life with her girlfriend. They decided to move in together and I was almost completely cut out. I complained and voiced my concerns, but they fell mostly on deaf ears. I was alone to fend for myself for the most part. There were invites to events and gatherings, but never any real best friend time for just me and her anymore. I had lost her.

I came to the conclusion that being with her in a group setting was better than nothing, which is what it was without her, nothing. I hadn't made an independent life outside of her and I knew that needed to change. So I started hanging out more and more with the group. Usually it was the girlfriends and the married couple, Salina and Todd, and me. I was always the odd man out and they tried really hard to not make me feel that way, but at the end of the gathering, it was what it was. They went home with their respective partners and I went home alone. I was really trying to stick to my guns with the whole celibacy thing. I wanted a relationship-free life, but I didn't want to have a friend-free life. I wanted to have friends like on a phone tree. Without a relationship taking up my time, I had lots of time to spend on whatever I liked, so having a ton of friends made sense.

More and more time was being spent with Salina and Todd and their family. They had three grown children, two girls and a boy. Actually, what should be said is that she had three grown children from a previous marriage, but Todd had been involved with them since their early childhood. The two girls had children of their own. So it was in essence a huge family in my book. All of them started calling me on a regular basis, asking me to go here and there, involving me in everything they took part in. They weren't Mormon, but it sure felt Mormon-like in the way that they believed heavily in family participation and that family came first. All free time included everyone, even the odd man out. I found myself busy with no free time to wallow. I had multiple best friends now and they all had an egg. Different baskets was the way to be.

Months had passed and life was going smoothly. I had come to accept my life for what it was and I loved it. It wasn't easy, but it was all mine. I hid my true feelings, quashed them down into the pit, and played nice with everyone, including Todd. I realized that he was just an extra friendly person when it came to me, at least that's how I would like to explain it away. Although, sometimes he would overstep his boundaries and make awkward moments for anyone who was around us. It was like he had different rules on how to behave with me than anybody else. An excellent example would be that he would take food from my plate, but no one else's. Or in a group he would just talk to me/at me, even if I wasn't the one who was asking the question. All his comments were in my direction. He would prefer to sit by my side even if there was a spot next to Salina. I recognized these awkward moments and would quickly try to correct them by moving seats and inviting Salina to come sit by her husband, making sure I didn't fill my plate full and eat quickly away from him, or even excuse myself from the conversation to get a drink or go pee so he would have to talk to the person who he was in the conversation with.

Okay, now don't get me wrong, I would go home every time after every gathering and run through the events of the evening in my mind and smile at the thought that this man was seeking me out, in public no less. Not trying to hide it or not knowing how to hide it. But if he wasn't trying to hide it, then maybe this was just his character. I had to convince myself that I was building up and reading into something that just wasn't there. I had to explain it away. I was getting more and more involved with the family as a whole and feeling the love from everyone, that there was no way I was going to screw this up by becoming involved in a seedy, torrid affair with this man who was everything and more than I ever wanted, but belonged to a woman who I dearly loved and respected.

Salina took a job down in Tucson, she had to due to financial reasons and the unavailability of jobs here in Phoenix. She got a sweet job at a hospital and would be working double shifts most of the time, so both she and Todd decided it would be best for her to rent a room down there instead of trying to make the 120 mile commute on no sleep. It was arranged that she would work and stay four days out of the week in Tucson and come home for the other three.

At the same time Salina took the job out of town, her son moved out of the house to Chicago to attend university. A few weeks after that her daughters and respective partners and children finally got their shit together and moved into their own homes. Todd was left to his own devices in a now empty house that had been filled to the brim with kids and constant activity.

One quiet evening, after the kids had gone to bed, and I was just sitting on the couch watching a movie, I got a call. It was Todd. I had talked to him hundreds of times in person, but him calling me on the phone seemed somehow wrong. It was a private thing between two people only when you talk on the phone. At least that's how I see it. Before I even hit the button I had already made the decision to make sure to mind my P's and Q's. He was just bored and wanted to borrow a couple of my movies that we had talked about previously. I didn't think anything of it, so I told him to come on over and get them.

I knew I had to be good, I knew it, so why then did I run to take a shower? Make sure that I had clean, cute, casual clothes on, and why did I put on "cool chick" music?

I opened the door to let him in and I took immediate notice as he passed me that he had also recently taken a shower and smelled so god damned good.

We made pleasantries as he took a seat on the couch and I grabbed out my special box of movies. The special box has to be put away because these are the fucked up kind of movies that you don't ever want your children to come across, or even watch when they are adults in their own homes with their own lives. Yes, truly fucked up movies, and it was so cool to find another person in the world that liked them as much as me.

It was an uneventful visit. He took a few movies and went home to watch them.

When he called the very next day to tell me what he thought, well, I was shocked. He had watched all three movies the night before and he wanted to bring them back to me. I told him how I had plans with one of the daughters to play a game of Settlers that night and he said he knew, that it was his game and he was bringing it over to her house so we could all play together. It's not a partners game, so I wasn't his partner. But since Salina was out of town working and their daughter has a husband, and Todd and me were the oldest, well, I was included behind my back by him to have her invite me. I can't help to laugh at this thought, even now as I write it down. Sneaky little bastard.

That very night, I saw it, felt it, knew it, and had to find a way to stop it before it got started. There was no explaining it away. The daughter and husband were completely oblivious to it. While we played our little game I created alliances with the daughter and ganged up on Todd. He shifted in his seat every time I took a striking blow to his farm and I wouldn't share my wheat with him. You really need to know the game to understand what I'm talking about here, but just know that I played completely unfair and I watched him grow frustrated and aggravated with my every move. By the end of the game, that he lost, he was ready to leave and so was I. We got in our cars and drove away. I knew that I had done my best to keep him at bay and was successful, at least until my phone started ringing.

He was calling me and I had just driven away from him, what could he want? He had forgotten to give the movies back to me. I told him to keep them until next time we see each other, but he wanted to pick out a couple more, so, well, I invited him over.

This went on for weeks. Every couple of days he would call and want to borrow more movies and I would oblige, happily. Every day I would get calls from someone in the family, inviting me out to do things and of course when I accepted and show up to meet them, Todd mysteriously also came along, or he would show up out of the blue. I would never ask if he was going along when it was supposed to be a me and the daughter thing, but it was like he was finding out behind my back if I was going to be there and he would just walk into whatever establishment we were at and join us. Of course, it didn't bother me one bit. I was not the one doing the seeking. I tried over and over again to explain it away, that he was just bored and lonely, but he would always gravitate to wherever I was at. And if for some reason, like not finding a babysitter for the night, I couldn't make it, I would get a phone call that more movies were needed.

Salina knew everything. She knew about all the phone calls, the outings, the movies, everything. I made sure of that. And her tone when being told was acceptance. She was okay with all of it. She even suggested that Todd and I spend more time together. I was a little disturbed by it, but the way she said it made it sound like Todd has found a new best friend and it was me. So with this information, knowing that she knew, knowing she was okay and that Todd's character is really just what it was presented, that he was a lonely soul who is now my best friend, well I opened the door a little wider and let him in.

I told him about my favorite bar and that was the beginning of a real true best friendship. I invited him out one night to go drinking. He was totally up for it.

We met at MonkeyPants, got a couple of beers, and I made myself comfy on the couch. He stood over me for a second and took the seat right next to me. Literally, right next to me. I was uncomfortably close, so I scooted over and made some smart-ass remark about how I have a body bubble and he should stay out of it. We talked, laughed, drank beer, and smoked cigarettes until the bar closed. It was hard to say goodnight. We had touched on so many topics, almost nonstop conversation about everything, so we continued it in the parking lot. It was like trying to end a conversation with your grandma on the phone. Even though you say I gotta go Grandma, she continues to talk about something or asks you a question that you just have to answer out of respect. But with Todd, well he just kept wanting to know more about the stuff I knew and I was more than willing to share that with him. We finally said goodnight when the staff was staring at us.

I went home and dreamed daring dreams of things that should not be thought of about another woman's man.

Before I knew it, we were talking on the phone 5-10 times a day, texting all day while working, emailing, and seeing each other practically every day for at least lunch or out for drinks at night. We talked about everything, almost everything. I did make the effort to keep it light and never really spoke about my past or my personal life, except that I don't date anymore. He would ask personal questions, especially with liquid courage, but I learned a long time ago how to avoid those questions and turn them around while explaining them into a bigger question to be answered and in turn he would eventually end up talking about himself all night long. It was easy, it's always easy. It's the best way to keep you safe and secure.

But because he was Todd, an exceptionally smart man with a desire to actually know more, he figured out what I was doing and how I did it. It took him a while, but most people never figure out what I'm doing. So one night, halfway through him answering my redirected question he stopped, looked at me and said "you're not going to trick me tonight". I froze. I knew what he meant, he knew I knew what he meant, but I still played dumb.

"Why, whatever do you mean?" I said in the slyest way I could with an evil grin attached to it. Also it was another question and he couldn't help but answer it.

"Oh, no you don't. I have talked enough about me. You know everything about me and we always end up debating about topics all night until we leave, but you still haven't said anything about you." He wasn't playing around and he wasn't taking my bait to play around with words. I was caught. Damn it.

I continued to play dumb, but he wasn't having it. He wanted to know more about me and he was determined.

The thing about Todd is that he is a student of life. Everything in life that intrigues him, he must know all about it. He is a great researcher and has a thirst for all information about everything that he finds interest in. At this moment, it was me. I was screwed, but I still held all the cards. He knew practically nothing about me and it was in my hands what I would let spill out for him.

To placate him I bought us a couple of shots each, and told him to go ahead and ask me a question and I will try to answer it the best I could. He started off easy, family, my family. Oh good,, I thought, this will take up the entire night and can go on for days.

Most people ask questions and then put questions in the original question as it is being answered. And he played along with what most people do, which dragged out something so simple into a complex wordy nothing tale. It never ended. I could talk about my family for weeks, and I did, but not unless he propositioned me. It didn't matter what the question was, if I felt it was personal, I routed it back to my family. He could know all he wanted about my family, but I wasn't going to get all emotionally involved with him, knowing that he knew my personal stuff. That's what husbands are for, not husbands of respected friends whom you love and wouldn't try to desecrate a union between such.

Let me remind you, that during this time I made sure that everything we talked about and every time we connected was relayed back to Salina. The weird part was that when she would come home from Tucson she would call me within minutes of being home to ask me to go out with her and Todd. I would try to beg off, telling her things like she should go have some alone time with her hubby and that it's okay, I don't mind staying in. But she would just hand the phone over to Todd who would relay what she was saying, both of them trying to convince me to hang out. Eventually I was spending every day off with Salina and Todd and every day that Salina was out of town with Todd. We were entangled. Our lives were one together.

All of a sudden I was a part of the hierarchy. The heads of household and of the group was Salina and Todd, but now it included me. I was approached with queries of advice that should be coming from the mom or the dad, but I was a mom and a dad to my own kids, so they all just lumped me into the Todd and Salina coalition. It was weird and I didn't know what to do, except go with it. I was included in party planning and I was the first to find out stuff. It was like we should be called Todd and Salina and Rachel. And when Salina was out of town, it was called Todd and Rachel. We were best friends after all and that's how it was introduced to new people. I was Todd's best friend.

Months and months had passed and all of my time had been taken up by the family and Todd. I hadn't been lonely at all, but what I hadn't seen was that my eggs were gradually all put into one basket, a big basket with many compartments, but one just the same.

Me and Todd spent all of our free time together when Salina was out of town. And he had figured out how to get information out of me, little by little he had most of me figured out. The problem was that I was drinking heavily, it was fun, but I couldn't see how he was piecing things together. Over the course of 6 months of seeing each other on an everyday basis, he managed to ask unrelated, non-chronological questions and he put it all together and knew so much about me that I had lost sight of trying to protect myself. I would wake up in the morning and kick myself for telling him this or sharing that with him. He didn't need to know this information about me, it was mine to keep.   But he knew it now nonetheless and I needed to stop drinking so heavily.

With our time alone being spent regularly, we had become extremely comfortable with each other and our language with each other was a little bit loose when it came to appropriateness for family and what they were thinking of our relationship. On more than a few occasions I was directly asked if I was sleeping with Todd by one family member or another. Even my previous best friend, the one who abandoned me and left me with this family for her girlfriend, came to me and said that it was weird the way we acted towards each other. I was pissed. How dare they think such a thing? He was my best friend and yes, we were a bit crude sometimes, but it was the way we were together.   I reassured any who asked that there was absolutely nothing going on between us. I had to say it over and over again and even threatened Todd that I was going to stop taking his calls and stop hanging out with him if everyone thought this way about us. Even Salina was on our side that nothing was going on, because it wasn't. I didn't even hug him, ever. The only time we had ever touched each other was when he shook my hand the first time, and the time he punched me in the arm because I made a goofy joke. And the time he punched me in the arm, well I looked at him straight in the eye and told him that he doesn't have the right to ever enter my body bubble and I do not feel comfortable with touching, even on a casual basis.

So, everything that people who were concerned for the validity of Salina's marriage were getting their information solely on what they were hearing coming from our mouths and the context in which we spoke to each other. It was unfounded.

With all the speculation looming and pissing me off, I had a serious sit down talk with Todd. I asked him straight out if he told Salina about all the times he calls me, texts me, talks to me, sees me. He said "No, that's ridiculous". I asked him "Why is it ridiculous? She should know.".

He got a sheepish look on his face, I knew that look, he was lying to his wife. I was mad. I flat out told him, "If you can't tell Salina everything, you are lying by omission, and that's wrong."

He didn't have an answer. I looked into his eyes and said "I think we should cool it for a while. Let's not talk for 3 days. No phone, no email, no meet ups." He went dark. I could see him break a little bit.

"Why? We aren't doing anything wrong. We haven't done anything that would be wrong." He tried so hard to bargain with me. My mind was made up, we couldn't see each other anymore. I loved the family so much, it was my whole life now, I was sucked in and I didn't want to compromise it. So many of them were coming to me with concerns and my foundation in the hierarchy was wavering, cracking from suspicion. It wasn't fair to me.

He reluctantly agreed after about an hour of arguing. Three days no contact.

The very next day after the "talk" he called me. I didn't answer it. I wanted to, it was second nature by this point to just automatically hit that button and say "hey". But he was breaking the rules. So he texted me "want to go to lunch? I'm hungry."

I'm so stupid.

I texted back "yes. Wassabe's?"

He texted back "yes. 12:15?"

I texted back "yes".

So much for the three days. We met up and he explained to me that he talked with Salina and she was going to talk to everyone and tell them to cut it out because there was nothing going on and that he shouldn't have to lose his best friend because of what people are thinking is wrong.

That very next weekend we went to our new place, Rogue. It was a great little bar, mostly empty on weeknights and we could put $10 in the jukebox and listen to our music all night long. Drinks were cheap, it was dark, and the booths were really comfortable.

I told him I couldn't stay late because I had to work in the morning, but he bought me a couple of shots anyway. I knew what he was doing, this was the setup to learn more about me. He had an important question and he knew that I wouldn't answer it fully unless I was lit. So we sat and drank for a couple of hours, chit chatting about this and that, mostly about why people think we are more than what we are. And we deduced that it was the way we talk to each other and how he never misses an opportunity to sit right next to me. It's kind of like the urinal rule: If there is a guy at the urinal and there are a line of urinals, you don't go up to the one right next to him, you leave at least a one urinal space between you two. He didn't have an explanation of why he does it, just that it's comfortable to sit next to someone he's comfortable with. So he chooses me. I told him to cut it out from now on. I also told him to stop following me around, and he didn't even realize he was doing it, at least that's what he said. I explained about how when we are at a party, gathering, or wherever, if I leave the room he follows me to wherever I'm going. I hurt his feelings on that one. He sincerely didn't think he was doing it, but I told him that other people, family have seen you do it. He ordered a couple more shots. I tried to decline, but he was sneaky about it, getting them while pretending to run to the bathroom, only to come back with four shots, two for me, two for him.

I really did need to work in the morning and I had to get home to the kids and relieve the babysitter. "Just another hour" he promised." We downed the shots and smiled at each other because once again I swallowed mine before he got done with his. Now it was my turn to run to the bathroom, and I came back with more shots. If we were going to let loose, might as well do it right. He asked me some questions about dating men and I let him in on a couple secrets that I wouldn't have otherwise shared without alcohol onboard. A kick ass song came on the jukebox and we both settled back in our seats and sang along with it. The room was ours.

I started to really feel it and I looked up to see him staring at me in that familiar way, like the day we met. So I called him out on it. "What?" I said.

"Nothing." He replied.

"No, it's something. I know that look, I've seen it a couple times before and I want to know, what are you thinking?"

"Really, it's nothing." He tried to sound convincing, but I could see the smile attached to it (it wasn't that dark in the bar).

"Why won't you just answer the question?" I wanted a debate, he was good at them and I loved fighting with him.

"Because, it's really nothing, I just like this song." He was lying.

"Okay, then." I conceded. I did this all the time. If I played like I didn't care, he would bite. It works with most humans. Try it.

I finished my beer and asked him to get me a pop from the bar and he complied. When he came back, he had more shots and a couple of beers, no pop. I called him a mother fucker while smiling. Knowing full well that he was trying to get me drunk and it was working. We sat in silence with music filling our ears, completely comfortable with each other, enjoying the groove of the inebriation.

I reached for my purse and checked the time. I really needed to go home soon. Putting my phone back I saw my pack of gum, grabbed a piece, popped it into my mouth and started chomping away. I looked up and he was just sitting there staring, I had grown used to that stare, but still appreciated it for everything it meant. I loved that I was being admired by my best friend. He asked a question, I didn't hear him.

I leaned in "What?"

"Can I have a piece of your gum?"

"Sure, I'm sorry I didn't ask you." I grabbed my purse reached in and pulled out a piece. I tried to hand it to him but he didn't take it. In that drunken stupor moment I thought I might have misunderstood the question. "Here" I instructed him to take it. He didn't.

He leaned in and asked again, "Can I have a piece of YOUR gum?"

No, I heard him correctly. Why won't he take the gum I'm trying to hand him? "Here." I said again trying to hand it to him. He smiled and gave a chuckle, "No, Rachel, can I have your gum?" I thought that was weird, but whatever. I reached up to my mouth and went to grab the gum out of my mouth all the while staring at him and the millisecond my fingers grabbed the slippery wet sugary goo it dawned on me. He wants MY gum. Duh! He wants to take my gum from my mouth to his; hence he is in a roundabout way asking to kiss me.

I wish I was a fly on the wall at the moment, to watch all the pieces fall together and witness that stupid fucking light flicker on above my head when I came to realize what he was really asking me.

"Oh! You want *my* gum." I said with the biggest smile, like I won the lottery.

"Yes, can I have your gum?"

"Yes." I answered honestly. I wanted him to have my gum.

He scooted in close to me, took his hand and placed it on the nape of my neck as he leaned in and passionately kissed me. The world slipped away. Nothing existed in that moment but this union of lips, tongues, hearts, and souls. We found each other in the darkness of the abyss and locked on.

It took me a few minutes of breathtaking silence to come back down to earth. I literally felt tingly all over and I could feel my heart burst into stars, racing blood to every cell of my being. I was warm and gooey. I leaned back and opened my eyes. He was there right in front of me looking squarely at me with a huge smile on his face. He held my hand in his.

"Wow." Breathlessly escaped me.

He chuckled and repeated "WoW."

I couldn't stop smiling and laughing. I didn't think of the repercussions, I didn't care to. I just had an amazing kiss from an amazing man who is my best friend. He leaned in and kissed me again and again and I scooted closer and our arms embraced each other as we pulled our chests together and smashed so deep, so feverishly. He held me tight and I matched him. He tangled his fingers into my hair and held my mouth to his. I never wanted to let go.

The lights came up and it was time to go. I walked out to my car with his hand in mine with no words being said between us. We climbed in and I drove around and down the street to a quiet spot, turned off the car, climbed over to his lap. I kissed him with all my might, making out like teenagers. He reached up under my shirt and held my breast in his hand and I leaned over and nibbled his ear, bit his neck, and pulled him in close to my heart. We melded into each other.

I only came to when my phone started ringing. It was the babysitter. She needed to go to work so I needed to come home. The sun was going to be up soon and I looked at him and said "I don't want this to end."

He smiled "Take me home with you".

I raced home, blaring the stereo, completely happy in this moment.

I brought him in after excusing the babysitter. I led him quietly back to my room and shut the door. He grabbed me and kissed me with a passion that would light a thousand fires, but it was only my fire he wanted lit. He whispered sweet words into my ear.

"I have wanted this for so long. I want you so bad. You are so fucking cool."

I undressed unabashedly in front of him and climbed in bed. He removed his clothing and climbed in under the blanket, on top of me. Spreading my legs with his knees, and resting above me to look into my eyes in the light of the dawn creeping through the blinds. I saw his soul in that glimpse of a second. We kissed as he leaned in on me, flesh on flesh, pressing so hard and so warm. His head at my mouth, I stopped and pushed him up. Took his face in my hands and stared right into his eyes. I had to say it, it had to be said:

"Right here, everything changes. This is the point of no return and we have the option to take it back right now. If we go through with it, nothing will ever be the same again. We can never be just friends. Everything we know will be different. You have to be sure this is what you want." I had the stern, but loving mother voice turned on.

He smiled, kissed me hard as he thrust into me. I whimpered at the sheer size that was filling me up, especially since I hadn't had sex in nearly a year. That night we threw caution to the wind and took our fates into our own hands.

We were wrong. We should have never started this. It's a one-time only kind of thing. It wasn't a mistake, but it was not right either. I told him it could never ever, ever happen again and that we have to take this to our graves. In my haste of lust, I didn't resist. I wasn't the strong person I thought I was. He agreed with me, but not because he wanted it to just be a one-time thing, he was placating me so we didn't have to argue about it. He knew me and he knew how to push the right buttons and when not to push those. He knew me well.

We agreed to not do it again and to just take it back a step. No touching, kissing, sex. We needed to pretend it didn't happen, especially around others. We were not to talk about it even with each other. Rules just plain don't work for him. Just when I think I have a handle on something, he goes and fucks it up, almost on purpose.

He started with the texts. Telling me intimate things about what he was thinking about and if that wasn't bad enough, he would send me these texts while he was using the restroom at a restaurant where the whole family was gathered to have dinner and he would wait to hit the send button until he was sitting down next to me at the table. And my phone would go off and I would get a text from him right there in front of everyone stating details about our sexual encounter and it would immediately take the breath away from me and I would choke and smile and blush. He would be sitting right there, next to me, kind of reading over my shoulder as I was reading it. My reactions would silence the table and someone would inevitably ask the dreaded question, "what?". I had to be quick to come up with something that sounded believable. Usually it was something about my ex-husband. Todd would sit there all smug, smiling, knowing what he just did.

Then when we would go out to a club and he would wait until I wasn't paying attention and he would grab my ass, even if Salina was standing right there. He didn't care anymore. He was being sneaky and living in the moment. A Thrill-seeker. Any moment he could get me alone anywhere, he would steal kisses, full-on smashed mouth, bodies pressed up against each other, grabbing assess, mussing hair kisses. Of course, I played along. I was getting all the attention I wanted, but it was getting really scary at the lengths in which he would be so bold. I had to constantly put him in check. It was tiring.

Finally, I had had enough. Although it was exciting and made me feel good, I had to put a stop to it. On our next outing I told him that we had to stop seeing each other. I was going to start going on dates and making time for myself. I wanted to have what he had, which was a significant other. He had someone who he could openly care for, but I had to hide my feelings. It wasn't fair and I was stopping it right then and there. He tried so hard to debate it. I stood fast. This time it was going to be different. I wasn't going to go out with just him anymore, it would have to be a group and I wasn't going to drink around him at all. He was crushed. He asked a simple question.

"Can I at least take you out one time? Just one more time, but this time I want it to be a real date. I pick you up, take you to dinner and a movie or something? Please? I just want to be able to have one last real date with you. Can I have that, please?" He was so sweet and convincingly sincere. I agreed.

We continued to text and talk on the phone during this time leading up to our real date. He would try to push my buttons, but I would cut him off at the quick. I wasn't going to have it. I deserved more than someone else's man. I truly loved him, but I also loved Salina and the family. I was wrong to be so selfish.

The night of the real date I wouldn't let him pick me up. I felt like eyes were on us all the time, paranoia had the best of me at this time. So I met him at the address he gave me. It was some sort of office building with a bar/restaurant on the bottom floor. It was really nice. I hadn't been taken on a date this nice in years and I was happy to be there with my best friend. We had dinner and then moved to the bar for a drink, one drink. Then he said,

"Okay, time to go."

"Where are we going?" I asked, kind of excited that there was more than dinner.

"It's a surprise, just come on." He was so giddy, I could see it in his eyes.

I trusted him with every part of my being, so I followed him hand in hand. We walked out to the parking lot to his car, but before I could get in he swung me around into his arms and kissed me. I released my whole body into his and kissed him back. He pulled back and said

"I actually forgot something."

Kind of bewildered I said "Okay. At the restaurant?"

"No. It's in our room." He smiled that devious little I-got-something-up-my-sleeve smile.

I stopped, looked up at the office building and magically saw it for what it was, a hotel. In my haste of being late to meet him, I just saw it as an office building, and in my defense, it did resemble one.

Ding! That light bulb sparked on and all the pieces fell together. I actually threw my fist in the air and yelled "Yes! Score!" (Yes, I'm that much of a dork.)

He laughed and grabbed my hand and pulled me in close for another kiss. Lifted me off the ground, still kissing me, he carried me to the door of the hotel. We walked into the lobby, past the pool, and up to our room. He opened the door and inside it was already fully prepared.

He had worked on the room before I had got to the restaurant. Candles lit everywhere. Champagne chilling in the bucket. A platter full of prosciutto, strawberries, crackers, fancy cheese. He had Portishead playing in the background. A full 3 dozen red roses in a beautiful vase graced the table. I stopped short at the sight of it all, trying to take it all in. It was the absolute most romantic thing that had ever been done for me. I spun around threw my arms around his neck and hugged him with great force. Then without a thought of what it was I was actually saying, I found that I was saying "I love you. I love you so much!"

He reciprocated with a hearty "I love you so much too!"

We spent the entire night together, barely sleeping. The end wasn't the end.

Over the next 5 months we continued to see each other on a regular basis. I loved him so much that I couldn't see straight when he was around. And he made sure he was around a lot. We spent every minute we could together. And when we were with the group, he continued to be out of line. It was so exhausting keeping the distance between us. I was so tired of thinking about how I was getting the short end of the stick. I wanted him, but I didn't want him at the same time.

One day I ran into an old friend. Someone I had known through my previous marriage. He was actually the best friend to my husband until they had some sort of falling out. But running into him was like old times. He was still the same old guy I knew and he looked so healthy and happy. He asked me to come out with him some time and I was thrilled to.

When I mentioned to Todd that I had run into a long-time friend, well he was upset to say the least. His jealousy ran through every vein and out his mouth at me. He was so sad that I was going to hang out with this guy. He didn't trust this guy. He didn't know this guy. This guy wasn't a part of the group. He was unnerved. But I tried to explain to Todd how he was just a friend. Todd had a great point, he was just my friend at one time.

"I don't see a ring on this finger, do you?" I was being mean. It's not like I was going to run off and have sex with my old friend, I was actually going to just hang out and have some laughs. Really.

Well, that question set him off. He was so mad at me that he started crying. I had to continuously reassure him that I loved him and that there was no need to worry. He calmed down and accepted the fact that I was an adult and I can do whatever I please. He wasn't happy about it.

I went over to my friend's apartment and we talked nonstop while sucking down two bottles of wine. It was getting super late and I went for my phone to check the time and realized I had 6 missed calls and 6 new messages. It freaked me out. The kids were with their dad this weekend, so what could it be. Well, it was Todd. He was really upset, crying and wondering where was at. He was checking in with me to make sure I was safe. While I was listening to the messages he called, so I answered and walked out to the porch to have some privacy.

The conversation had was intense and ridiculous. He had a wife he needed to be worrying about. I answer to no one. So I hung up my phone and turned it off.

I stayed on the couch because I was drunk off my ass and needed to sleep it off. The next morning I went home and there in the parking lot of my condo was Todd sitting in his car waiting for me to get home. This didn't look good on my part.

We had a huge fight and I told him three days, I needed to think about stuff for three days. I will not be answering your calls, your texts, your emails, your contacts. Stay away from me for three days. He wasn't to contact me until Tuesday, not a minute before. I needed to breathe and think all of this through. He was really being childish in his behavior.

I didn't hear from him the rest of the day or the next day (Sunday), but on Monday, he just couldn't stay away. He showed up at my door on Monday at lunchtime with tears in his eyes. He couldn't stay away for 3 days, 3 measly days. He looked like shit. He hadn't slept since Friday morning and he was hallowed. I told him to meet me the next day, the third day, at the park. He asked why we couldn't just talk right then. I argued that we both agreed to three days, so give it to me. He agreed.

Tuesday morning he texted me to confirm. I met him at noon. It was going to be a clean break. He couldn't argue or debate his way out of this one, but then he floored me.

"I'm going to leave Salina. I'm leaving her today, right now. I've thought it over for the last few weeks and I don't want to be with her, I want to be with you". He was so determined.

I was shocked, "No! NO!" was all that escaped me.

"Just listen, please just listen to me."

I couldn't speak. Those words just didn't make any sense to me and I didn't know how to respond. Frozen to my spot, I listened apprehensively.

"I've won a ton of money from poker and have been squirreling it away. I have also cashed in some of my investments. Salina has no idea about this. She never even knew that this money existed. You never have to work again. We can leave today, get a house together, anywhere you would like. You and the kids don't have to worry. I'll take care of you. I love you so much and I can't imagine my life without you in it. Please say that you'll stay with me."

I didn't even have to think about it. I knew my answer before he even had his spiel. "No. Todd, No. It's not right. You love Salina, there is nothing she has done so wrong to you that would make you feel otherwise. I will not be the one who breaks up a home. This is why we need to end it. You can't leave her. You belong to her and she belongs to you. I can't be the reason why you are leaving her or you will resent me someday for doing this. Please don't ask me this. Please don't leave her."

"Okay, now really listen to me Rachel. I'm leaving her no matter what. If you are with me or not, I'm not staying married to her. I want a life with you and the kids. I've got it all planned out. You just need to say you will be with me."

"I can't. I just can't. I won't. If you are going to leave her, fine. But I won't have any part of it. I will not support you on this. I will wait for you, but I will not be in the middle of this. If it takes six months, if it takes a year, if it takes 2 years, I will wait for you. But please don't do it."

"You really won't be by my side when I do this?" He was crushed.

"No I won't. I don't believe it's the right thing to do." I was determined.

We sat there quietly. No words left to say. It was done. He was going to do what he wanted to do, and I was too.

I gave him one last hug and said goodbye.

I turned off my phone, made dinner for the kids, and painted a lovely picture. Later that night after getting all comfy in bed, my house phone rang. Immediately I was pissed. No one is allowed to call that number after 8 p.m. because the kids were sleeping.

I grabbed the receiver and firmly answered with "Somebody better be bleeding or dying to be calling this late". It was my ex-best friend, you know, the one who abandoned me for her girlfriend. She was frantic, asking if I had seen Todd. I lied. Apparently he had left a simple little note instructing Salina on how to access bank accounts and such. He was leaving her. I was devastated at the thought. I was crying and so upset at the thought of them splitting up. I was genuinely sad for Salina.

After we decided to go out looking for him, I turned on my cellphone only to realize he had left me a message earlier in the evening. I listened to it and it made my blood run cold.

"Hi Rachel. I just wanted to let you know that you are the most incredible woman I have ever met. I love you so much and I can't imagine living my life without you. If you get this before morning please call me. If not, I'll be dead by the time the sun comes up. I wish you all the best in what you are looking for. I hope you find it. I love you. Goodbye."

I listened to it again and heard the "dead by the time the sun comes up" part and hung up and called him. I continued to call him as I grabbed my purse and keys. I raced around the city to all of our haunts trying to find him. I kept calling and leaving desperate messages. He wasn't listening to them because before too long his voicemail was full. I looked everywhere for him, even up to Payson, 120 miles away. I drove all night, making frantic phone calls to everyone. I kept my personal voicemail a secret from everyone. I lied about not seeing him for a couple of days. I lied my ass off, I was wrong.

I called into work and went up to Payson again looking at our secret spots, nothing. My phone doesn't work out of city limits, but when I got back in cell range my phone rang. I saw it was him, answered it, but had missed it by a split second. I called it back, but it went to voicemail. It wasn't full, so he must have emptied it.

I went home to wait. The sun had been up for over half the day and he called, so he didn't go through with it. Then Salina called the house phone.

"Rachel, they found him. He's dead. He was in a hotel room at the Clarendon." I collapsed. Screaming "I'M SO SORRY! I'M SORRY SALINA! OH GOD, NO!"

My brother was with me, watching the kids while I ran around looking for him, so he picked me up in his arms and carried me to my bed. I died that night. The Rachel that existed to love died. She mourned for months. Leaving her bed only to work, get her daily bottle of Nyquil from the Walgreens, and open the door for people who came to visit her.

She was lucky to have her brother live with her. He took care of the kids and household things, such as grocery shopping, as she couldn't go to the grocery store because it was too much of a memory for her. She actually collapsed screaming in the bread isle when she had to get hotdog buns, so she stopped going to the store. She needed to get her cigarettes, but she couldn't bring herself to leave the house and would ask people to do it for her. She couldn't take a shower and she would pee the bed because it was too hard to get up and function. She didn't care anymore. The world died that night with Todd and everyone around her was going about their business.

The few days following the death, Rachel couldn't bring herself to go to Salina's house, but she knew she needed to. She needed to face what she had done and take her lashings. Salina must have known what was going on. She must have. There was no way that this would go undetected.

She got up from her bed, brushed her nasty hair and teeth, walked out to the car and climbed in. Immediately she lost it. She cried and screamed the whole way to Salina's. That was the car that she had given the first kisses in, the many rendezvous, and every song that every station was playing somehow was speaking to her and what she had done.

I walked into the gingerbread house, everyone was there, somber and quietly sitting. I was ushered to the bedroom where Salina had not left her bed in days. She motioned for me to lay down with her, so I did. I spooned her and held her close to me in a fetal position. She started to speak to me about how much he loved me and her and that we were the closest people in his life and she doesn't understand how this could have happened.

Her voice was odd. She wasn't crying, she wasn't sad, she was quiet and monotone. Maybe that's how she grieved, I didn't know. I burst into sobs. Then she turned over and took my face into her hands and spoke very eerily about how he died. I told her I didn't want to hear it, it wasn't anything to speak of.

She continued, ignoring my request.

"Rachel, I have to tell you. He was found in a hotel room at the Clarendon, room 231, in bed with a single gunshot wound to his heart."

"NO! STOP TALKING! I DON'T WANT TO HEAR THIS!"

"He shot himself in the heart, Rachel. Listen to me." Her voice was raising now into a firm tone that was really uncomfortable. She was forcing me to listen to her. I tried to get up and get away, but she grabbed ahold of me and I fell to the floor, sobbing, bawling, screaming for her to stop. She spoke louder, over my pleas.

"He shot himself in the heart last night. He died instantly! He's dead Rachel!" She was coming after me, trying to look me in the eyes.

I opened the door and crawled out into the hall, our hall, the magic hallway, I went batshit crazy screaming:

"STOP IT! STOP IT! STOP IT! I DON'T WANT TO KNOW ANYMORE! I CAN'T HEAR THIS! NO, PLEASE STOP, SALINA PLEASE STOP IT!"

She continued to follow me. I was retching now, but nothing was coming up. I crawled away from her into the bathroom and tried to shut the door. She pushed through and shut it behind her. She sat down on the floor in front of the door, trapping me inside with her.

"Rachel! Listen to me! He died last night in the hotel room at the Clarendon! He shot himself in the heart after listening to Radiohead. He drove up to the woods before that..."

"NO!!!!!!!!! STOP TALKING, STOP NOW! LET ME OUT! I JUST WANT TO GO HOME!!!!"

She didn't give up.

"He drove up to the woods, somewhere in Payson because he had filled up his car with gas at the Circle K and..."

As she kept talking, I kept screaming. There was a whole house of people and not a single one of them came to get me out of the bathroom.

Racing thoughts of his body lying on the bed, our bed, in our room that we had gone to several times, always the same room, always the same bed, his body with a whole through his chest and blood everywhere. He died because I wouldn't have him. I took him from this earth and away from his family and his wife. I killed him. It was my fault. I didn't save him in time. I died again.

There was a funeral, everyone was there. I barely remember it, which is odd because I remember everything. I remember sleeping and I remember my brother telling me to get my ass out of that fucking bed and take care of my kids. I remember the touch of Todd's hand on the small of my back when I walked through a doorway in front of him.

Three months passed before I came too. I woke up and realized that the pieces didn't fit. The family's behavior following the funeral and the way Salina acted just didn't make sense. I became paranoid, watching everything that was going on in front of me, but I did it from a distance. I did not participate in family gatherings anymore. I moved away, changed my number, and hid. No one knew what really happened to me, but I knew exactly what happened, what the truth really was. Salina and Todd knew it too, but the rest of the family believed he died.

I cried every single day for him for a year and on his anniversary I died all over again. I couldn't understand what was going on and how they could be just going about their daily lives, moving on and doing things that would be construed as disrespectful to the dead. I understood that every person has their own way of grieving, but this wasn't grieving, it never was.

One afternoon in early May, approximately 13 months after his "death", I had come home from one of my expeditions. I had gone to Death Valley for the weekend. It's quite a drive, but I was happy to do it. I just wanted to delve into my own thoughts, dwell in my mind, and think of everything that had happened. Driving through the desert and listening to wonderful music that connected me to him was just the right venue. Plus it had been somewhere I had never been.

When I got home, I had to bust ass to get everything done and ready for the kids to come back from their dad's. We had moved into a nice little house a mile away from the condo. It was close enough that the kids didn't have to switch schools, but it was just far enough that you couldn't find us if you were looking. I needed to get laundry started, unload the car, and do some general chores around the house to get ready for the week ahead with work and school and life. I was working 70-80 hours a week and it helped to keep my mind off of the conspiracy that I had built up in my head. We had fallen into a routine that worked and staying on a schedule seemed to keep my mind at rest.

After getting the kids from the ex, we came home, had dinner, showers, and then it was finally bedtime. I had driven 10 hours that day, racing to make it home in time from my trip. I was exhausted, so getting them to bed, was a huge relief.

It was beautiful outside, so open windows were appropriate. We had screens, so I wasn't afraid of the bugs getting inside and we had blinds on the inside so no one could peek in on us. Not that anyone would, seriously, we lived in a very quiet little neighborhood with kids and parents just like me in the houses all around us.

I fell onto my bed, like I always do, onto my stomach, half on and off of a body pillow facing the TV. It was Sunday night and all my shows were coming on in a minute. 9 p.m. Adult Swim with all the fucked up little adult cartoons come on. Not porn or anything like that, but the kind of cartoons that kids really just don't get.

Behind the TV was the window, and although the blinds were closed, the coax cable in the back of the satellite receiver stuck out and slightly parted the blinds. I was laying there, half asleep when I heard the boys, they were goofing around, not going to sleep and it pissed me off. It had been a long day and there is going to be a long week ahead, so I really needed them to cut it out and go to sleep. So I got up, went to their room and yelled at them.

I came back into my room and as I flopped onto my bed, back into my position I heard the strangest noise coming through the window from out back. A weird crunchy noise, and then another, and then a bunch of them really quick. I recognized the sound, but I didn't really know what it was for a minute or so. I waited for it to happen again, but there was nothing, silence.

Then it hit me; it was the slip and slide in the backyard and those were footsteps. Right as I realized it I shifted my eyes to the crack in the blinds that opened up to the open window and the screen behind it. I didn't have to move my head, just literally shift my eyes over 6 inches from the screen of the TV to the screen of the window. Just then the boys made a giggly noise, and then the man's face pressed against the screen made a groaning noise. There was a man, right there, pressing his face against my screen, peeping in on me lying in my bed. I didn't scream or yelp, which is weird because normally that would be my reaction, instead I slammed my hand down on the bed and sat up cursing at the boys for goofing around. I jumped out of bed and went into their room and told them to be quiet. They asked if I would turn on the air conditioner and I said yes, if they will just be quiet and go to sleep.

But when I went down the hall, past my bedroom door, assuming the peeper heard everything, I went past the thermostat and straight into the office where I called 911.

I watched from around the corner as he came to the arcadia window and tried to peek in. I couldn't believe my eyes. It wasn't really happening. It was Todd, but it couldn't be Todd. Todd was dead. Who was this man? I didn't understand what was going on. It was Todd, but it couldn't be Todd.

I told the operator that there was a man trying to get into the house. I was scared for my life and the lives of my kids. They didn't know what was going on, but I told them to stay in their beds. Then all of a sudden he wasn't on the back porch any more.

My daughter screamed from her room and came running "Mommy! There's a man in my room! Mommy Help! There's a man in my room!"

I threw the phone, yelled for the boys to come to me and we ran out the front door and down the street as the police came in full force with bulletproof vests, 6 cars, a police dog, and a helicopter. They descended upon the house and we watched from our crouched position behind a car parked on the street two houses down from ours.

He wasn't there. He made a run for it and was never caught.

For months after this incident he would come around randomly, usually when I was gone away from the house. He would break in, move my furniture, do my laundry (he was always a stickler about having the laundry done), play on my computer, look through my pictures, read my journal, lie in my bed and watch TV. Never did anything go missing. Nothing was ever stolen. And each time I called the police to let them know there was a break-in. They would take their reports, but nothing ever came of it. Each time they asked me if anything was stolen, and of course there wasn't, so they said it had to be someone I knew. At this time I had no friends. I had exiled myself in seclusion. They said it was probably an ex-boyfriend. But it couldn't be because my last boyfriend died, and I hadn't had a boyfriend for a year before that and that boyfriend had moved away to New Jersey and he was still there. It all pointed to Todd.

I got so paranoid when I left the house that I would take mental note of the position of all furniture and items in every single room, a mental inventory if you will. And when I would come home, well most times everything was as it was supposed to be. Every month though, every fucking month he would pick a random day when I was away and he would break in and move something, go through something, play with something. I eventually stopped going places unless I really needed to. I watched every car that passed by, noting the color and if they were regulars on our street or not.

One day I had entered into a salsa making contest at the church the kids were attending. I wasn't a member, but I didn't want my kids to miss out because I was cynical, so I wanted them to experience faith on their own and they made a choice and started going on their own volition. And since it was a family sort of event going on they entered me in a contest that they were sure I would win. I had to go to the store, go down 3 isles, pay for the stuff, and get the heck out of there. The store still had a bad effect on me.

I parked the car, got out, and stopped because I wanted to make sure I had my list. I was searching through my purse when my daughter says in the weirdest voice I had ever heard come out of her mouth, "Mom, mom, look. Isn't that Todd?"

I looked up from my task and over to where she was pointing. Sure enough there was Todd, walking out of the store. Yes, it was Todd and yes he was alive and walking out of the fucking store. Todd, the dead best friend who I loved with all my heart and led me to believe he committed suicide because I wouldn't be with him, was walking out of the God Damned store all healthy and viable. I left my body, literally.

I saw this woman standing with three small kids next to a car that resembled mine. I didn't really recognize her, but why was she with my kids. She looked like death and my kids were pulling on her. They were yelling mommy at her and she was just standing there. I could see my kids pointing to something and I looked and there was Todd, walking briskly to a car near mine. I wanted to run to him, but my legs weren't my own anymore. Todd was talking to a guy that had gotten out of a small white car. Todd said, in Todd's voice "Let's go. We have to get out of here". They jumped in and sped away.

I was all of a sudden at the doorway of the store about to walk in when I woke up and the kids were upset with me, asking me why I didn't go talk to him. I couldn't put two words together to save my life right then. I don't know what just happened. My mind was not my own anymore.

Months went by and he continued to come to the house while I ran errands, break in and move stuff around. He even got so bold as to come in while I was sleeping and mess with my stuff, leaving the front door wide open when he left. Nothing was ever stolen and dozens of phone calls to the police prompted me to change the locks on all the doors, three times. I nailed the dog door shut and got locks for all the windows, but he would still find a way in, or he would just mess with the laundry room, which was out back off the porch. He would leave little hearts in the dust on my car. Todd was alive and I didn't have proof. So I searched for some.

I started doing all kinds of internet searches, found out he had an alias, and bought a house down in Casa

Grande, a small community 40 miles from me. I got the nerve up and drove down there after a break-in. I didn't know what I would say or do, but I had to confront him and figure this all out. I was baffled as to why this was happening. I figured if he wasn't home, I would break-in and mess with his stuff and then I would watch him through his windows and see how he reacts. I wasn't thinking straight, I wasn't thinking at all really, I was just ready to fucking deal with this.

I had been so freaked out, terrorized at the thought that this was really happening. He wasn't dead, he was haunting me from this realm, this reality, and I didn't know how to handle it. I tried to tell friends and family members. I tried to tell them that I was scared or that I was messed up in the head and something needs to be done. I tried to say he's not dead and that he is fucking with me and the kids. But every single time I tried to communicate this to others they looked at me with glassed-over eyes. They believed that I believed it. I was utterly alone. Not a single person really understood what I was going through. I sounded like a crazy woman and I was afraid that they would take my kids away. I even tried to tell the police, but how do you say that the man you loved with all your heart died, but he is not dead even if your records show it, and he is stalking you. You just can't make it sound realistic. It's a fantasy, or is it.

I drove down to his house in Casa Grande, found it in the middle of a crappy little neighborhood. What kind of person buys a house in his alias name after he's supposed to be dead, and only 40 miles away no less? This is just stupid.

I drove past it real slow, but there was a big construction dumpster out front. I parked down the street and watched a couple of guys come in and out dumping carpet and other random things. I grew a set of balls, got out of the car, and walked right up to one of the guys.

It turned out that they had just bought the house as a renovation project and that the previous owner sold it to them for cash just two weeks before. I put the pieces together in my head; two weeks before was when he had broken in last. He must have seen the report of my investigation on my computer. Mother Fucker! I was pissed. I was so close. I went back to the car and then it hit me. I took a picture out of my purse, walked back up to the man and asked him if this was the owner. "Yes, that's the guy. Todd. Nice guy. You know him?" Obviously I knew him, I was in the picture with him.

I had more proof that he was alive then the family had that he was dead. I cried all the way home. I wasn't seeing things. Shit wasn't moving around in my house on its own.

Lots of things have happened since then, but he got smart and hasn't bought a house in the U.S. since then. It's been 5 years, 8 months and 21 days since his "death" and I have had more than 100 incidents happen to me and my family because of him. He has not yet let up.

I will never be the same person again. My kids mourn my death, they miss me dearly, and it's not fair that I can't give me back to them. I have changed and continue to change to suit the situation, but the Rachel that existed before his "death" will never be allowed out again. She will not love, she will not trust, she will not see the light of day. She must be put away forever.

I am the protector. I have his story in detail that I will write a book about, because this simple little chapter does not do the justice that Rachel loved him so much and was so bright and then turned so dark and so dead when he died. She thinks she killed him, but he killed her right back.

Epilogue

Rachel has started a new book. After writing this one, she knew that the answers to the questions that swirl in her brain, separated by the others to protect her, are in that book that she needs to get down. She will have to tap into those memories and she will suffer, but it has to be done in order for her to rest peacefully. She questions every day about her love and what, how, why and she knows down to her core, down to me, the protector, that only piecing it together, tapping into each one of us will give her the final answers. Thingus is out there. Thingus exists. My Thingus.

The beast still lives, somewhere in California with his daughter and her children. Recently Rachel's grandma died and when hearing the details of the impending wake, found out that the beast was going to be there. This sent Rachel into a downward spiral of dark thoughts of murder. On many occasions throughout her life she had grandiose ideas of annihilating the beast in many different ways and always I was able to redirect her thoughts and feelings out of the darkness and into the light to make things okay again. But, because of the continuous dark she had to be in to write this book and having to relive all the atrocities, knowing she was going to face the beast one more time sent her over the edge, deep down into the abyss. I couldn't save her this time. Her will was great and the only thing I could do was put her in the hospital. While there, we all realized that the system sucks ass. She wasn't allowed to leave for 5 days because the beast was in danger. The psychiatrist at the hospital had to contact the Beast and let him know he was in mortal danger. She missed her Grandma's wake and now her family is afraid of her. The consensus is that she just needs to get over it.

Rachel's Mother (loosely termed) lives with her husband in a small town in Arizona. She is still addicted to illicit drugs and believes that Rachel will one day "get over it" and contact her. Rachel has not spoken to her in 14+ years, except for the occasional reply in a solicited email from her mother. Every few years Rachel gets that stomach knotting contact from her mother which throws her into a rage and I have to pull her out of it and calm her down. Rachel is tormented by her mother's unrelenting daftness that Rachel hates her to the core and that there are no words (and no time machines) to undo the damage that has been done by her.

Rachel's brother, Damien, has been excommunicated from her life due to his inability to accept boundaries. He is a dangerous mix of a sociopathic egomaniac and a Christian. She has no desire to even begin to try a relationship again with him. She has no time, energy, or patience for such a person.

Rachel's brother, Jason, is alive and well and very much involved in Rachel's life and the lives of her children. Having dealt with his own demons and overcoming them, he is a great example and a wonderful inspiration to her. They are still very symbiotic and to watch them interact is like clockworks, whether it is joking around, painting a room, or playing a game. Everyone should have a brother like him.

About the Author

Rachel Caruso (Xyola Blue) is a longtime self-employed medical transcriptionist who works from her home in the bedroom community of Ahwatukee to stay close with her four children that she adores. In her free time she allows one of her others to work on a project of their choosing, whether it be dancing, painting, or writing.

Picture Credit: (Back Cover Author Photo)

Denise Nicole Photography

www.denisenicolephotography.com

From the start Rachel was a survivor. She never stood a chance in this world. Without ever being loved, not even by her own mother, and having all odds against her, she managed to cope and live through multiple traumatic experiences by splitting her mind and sharing the load of pain through the others that were created and lived within her. Meshing together from an early age and handling the repeated sexual, mental, and physical abuse, it became second nature to switch from one mentality to another, so much so that she didn't even realize it wasn't normal.

Only after losing the love of her life and dealing with his demise did she come to the reality that she was not alone and really never was. Learning of the others provoked her insatiable urge to learn even more and find the root of them all. She opened up and tapped into the traumas one by one, seeking them out from each of her alters, and combined them here for others to see and perhaps understand that she is not normal and will never be.